Making Meaning®

SECOND EDITION

Funding for Developmental Studies Center has been generously provided by:

The Annenberg Foundation, Inc.

The Atlantic Philanthropies (USA) Inc.

Booth Ferris Foundation

The Robert Bowne Foundation, Inc.

The Annie E. Casey Foundation

Center for Substance Abuse Prevention
   U.S. Department of Health and Human Services

The Danforth Foundation

The DuBarry Foundation

The Ford Foundation

William T. Grant Foundation

Evelyn and Walter Haas, Jr. Fund

Walter and Elise Haas Fund

The Horace Hagedorn Foundation

J. David and Pamela Hakman Family Foundation

Hasbro Children's Foundation

Charles Hayden Foundation

The William Randolph Hearst Foundations

Clarence E. Heller Charitable Foundation

The William and Flora Hewlett Foundation

The James Irvine Foundation

The Robert Wood Johnson Foundation

Walter S. Johnson Foundation

Ewing Marion Kauffman Foundation

W.K. Kellogg Foundation

John S. and James L. Knight Foundation

Lilly Endowment, Inc.

Longview Foundation

The MBK Foundation

The John D. and Catherine T. MacArthur Foundation

A.L. Mailman Family Foundation, Inc.

Mr. and Mrs. Sanford N. McDonnell

Charles Stewart Mott Foundation

National Institute on Drug Abuse,
   National Institutes of Health

National Science Foundation

New York Life Foundation

Nippon Life Insurance Foundation

Karen and Christopher Payne Foundation

The Pew Charitable Trusts

The Pinkerton Foundation

The Rockefeller Foundation

Louise and Claude Rosenberg Jr. Family Foundation

The San Francisco Foundation

Shinnyo-en Foundation

Silver Giving Foundation

The Spencer Foundation

Spunk Fund, Inc.

W. Clement and Jessie V. Stone Foundation

Stuart Foundation

The Stupski Family Foundation

The Sulzberger Foundation, Inc.

Surdna Foundation, Inc.

John Templeton Foundation

U.S. Department of Education

The Wallace Foundation

Wells Fargo Bank

Grade 2

TEACHER'S MANUAL

Making Meaning®

SECOND EDITION

DEVELOPMENTAL
STUDIES CENTER™

Strategies That Build
Comprehension and Community

Second edition published 2008.

Making Meaning is a registered trademark of Developmental Studies Center.

Developmental Studies Center wishes to thank the following authors, agents, and publishers for their permission to reprint materials included in this program. Many people went out of their way to help us secure these rights and we are very grateful for their support. Every effort has been made to trace the ownership of copyrighted material and to make full acknowledgment of its use. If errors or omissions have occurred, they will be corrected in subsequent editions, provided that notification is submitted in writing to the publisher.

"Wild Rides" from *TIME For Kids* News Scoop Edition, May 10, 2002. Copyright © 2002 Time Inc. Used with permission from *TIME For Kids* magazine. "Summer of the Shark" from *TIME For Kids* News Scoop Edition, October 14, 2001. Copyright © 2001 Time Inc. Used with permission from *TIME For Kids* magazine. "A Nose for the Arts" from *TIME For Kids* News Scoop Edition, December 14, 2002. Copyright © 2002 Time Inc. Used with permission from *TIME For Kids* magazine. "My Baby Brother" reprinted by permission of Gina Maccoby Literary Agency. Copyright © 1991 by Mary Ann Hoberman. Excerpt from *Snails* by Monica Hughes. Reprinted by permission of Pearson Education.

All articles and texts reproduced in this manual and not referenced with a credit line above were created by Developmental Studies Center.

Developmental Studies Center
2000 Embarcadero, Suite 305
Oakland, CA 94606-5300
(800) 666-7270, fax: (510) 464-3670
www.devstu.org

ISBN-13: 978-1-59892-713-9
ISBN-10: 1-59892-713-2

Printed in the United States of America

2 3 4 5 6 7 8 9 10 MLY 17 16 15 14 13 12 11 10 09

Table of Contents

continues

Acknowledgments

Many people were involved in the development and production of the *Making Meaning* program. We are grateful for their time, expertise, suggestions, and encouragement.

We wish to thank the members of our Teacher Advisory Board, who piloted the lessons and gave us expert feedback that helped shape the format and content of the program and who collaborated with us in numerous invaluable ways:

Albany Unified School District
Hannelore Kaussen
Christiane Zmich

Emeryville Unified School District
Shawna Smith
Gabrielle Thurmond

Moraga Elementary School District
Dot Cooper

Newark Unified School District
KelLee Cannis
Elizabeth Chavez
Hemawatie Dindial
Midge Fuller
Lynn Gurnee
Kara Holthe
Krissy Jensen
Joshua Reed

West Contra Costa Unified School District
Betty Buganis
Molly Curley
Simon Ellis
Sally Feldman
Nina Morita

We also wish to thank the teachers and administrators of Newark Unified School District in Newark, California, and Frayser Elementary School in the Jefferson County Public School District in Louisville, Kentucky, who field-tested the program, allowing us to observe lessons in their classrooms and providing us with feedback to help us refine the program. We particularly wish to acknowledge the following individuals:

Bunker Elementary School
Pam Abbot
Debbie Fujikawa
Katherine Jones
Judy Pino
Lisa Serra
Bob Chamberlain, *Principal*

Graham Elementary School
Shannon Carter-Steger
Pam Hughes
Belen Magers, *Principal*

Kennedy Elementary School
Jennifer Balaian
Elizabeth Chavez
Hemawatie Dindial
Midge Fuller
Lynn Gurnee
Sarah Roberts
Carol Viegelmann, *Principal*

Lincoln Elementary School
Robert Foley, *Principal*

Milani Elementary School
Jennifer Boyd
Paula Clevenger
Gail Fay
Michelle Leipelt
Karen Wetzell
Susan Guerrero, *Principal*

Musick Elementary School
Chris Scheving
Wendy Stacy
Cary Bossi, *Principal*

Schilling Elementary School
George Mathiesen, *Principal*

Snow Elementary School
Kathryn Keleher, *Principal*

Special thanks to the following individuals for their advice, feedback, writing, classroom collaboration, and many significant contributions to the program:

John Thomas, *Assessment Consultant*
Hemawatie Dindial, *Teacher, grade K*
Gail Fay, *Teacher, grade 6*
Midge Fuller, *Teacher, grade 3*

Hannelore Kaussen, *Teacher, grade 2*
Nina Morita, *Teacher, grade 1*
Karen Wetzell, *Teacher, grade 5*
Christiane Zmich, *Teacher, grade 4*

Finally, we wish to thank the many children's book publishers that assisted us during the development of this program and upon whose books these lessons are based.

Annick Press Ltd.

Barron's Educational Series, Inc.

Boyds Mills Press

Candlewick Press

Capstone Press

Charlesbridge Publishing

Child's Play USA

Chronicle Books

The Communication Project

Crabtree Publishing Company

Dawn Publications

EDC Publishing

Farrar, Straus & Giroux

Firefly Books

Grolier Publishing Company

HarperCollins Children's Books

Heinemann

Henry Holt & Company
    Books for Young Readers

Holiday House

Houghton Mifflin Harcourt
    Publishing Company

Hyperion Books for Children

Kids Can Press

Lee & Low Books

Lerner Publishers Group

Little, Brown & Company

National Book Network

Penguin Putnam
    Books for Young Readers

Persea Books

Random House Children's Books

Scholastic Inc.

Simon & Schuster

Square Fish Books

Star Bright Books

Sterling Publications

Tom Doherty Associates, LLC

Walker & Co.

Acknowledgments

This program was developed at Developmental Studies Center by:

Shaila Regan, *Senior Program Advisor*

Grady Carson, *Program Manager*

Kenni Alden, *Curriculum Developer*

Dennis Binkley, *Assistant Director of Program Development*

Susie Alldredge, *Director of Program Development*

Julie Contestable, *Contributing Writer*

Sarah Rosenthal, *Curriculum Developer*

Jackie Jacobs, *Curriculum Developer*

Laurel Robertson, *Curriculum Developer*

Mollii Khangsengsing, *Program Development Coordinator*

Charlotte MacLennan, *Manager of Libraries*

Peter Brunn, *Director of Professional Development*

Thuy Do, *Manager of Professional Development*

Neal Davis, *Curriculum Developer/ Media Specialist*

Learning Media, New Zealand, *Contributing Writer*

Annie Alcott, *Contributing Writer*

Abigayil Koss, *Contributing Writer*

Darien Meyer, *Contributing Writer*

Maddie Ruud, *Contributing Writer*

Robyn Raymer, *Contributing Writer*

Alexa Stuart, *Contributing Writer*

Nancy Johnson, *Teacher Consultant*

Lisa Alden, *Consultant*

Lori Birnbaum Galante, *Book Consultant*

Erica Hruby, *Editor/Project Manager*

Valerie Ruud, *Managing Editor*

Lisa Kent Bandini, *Director of Editorial and Design*

Ellen Toomey, *Designer*

Roberta Morris, *Art Director*

Joslyn Hidalgo, *Production Manager*

Jennie McDonald, *Manager of Publisher Relations and Rights*

Kimo Yancey, *Editorial and Rights Associate*

Scott Benoit, *Production Designer*

Garry Williams, *Designer*

Renee Benoit, *Media Production Manager*

Introduction

You hold in your hands a brand new tool for elementary school teachers. The *Making Meaning*® program is a reading comprehension curriculum for kindergarten through grade eight, and the first program of its kind to bring together the very latest research in reading comprehension with support for fostering your students' growth as caring, collaborative, and principled people.

We are well aware of the demands that elementary school teachers face in the teaching of reading today. Among those demands are the many activities that must be squeezed into the school day, the pressure of increased standardized testing, and a student population with increasingly diverse needs. The *Making Meaning* program offers maximum support for teaching reading comprehension in this environment. It is not another loosely defined program that adds hours of preparation to an already crammed to-do list. Rather, it is a fully fleshed-out curriculum that integrates easily into what you already do, incorporates an understanding of how real classrooms function, and teaches the specific strategies students need to become effective readers, at a level and pace that is accessible to everyone.

You'll notice that in this, the second edition of the *Making Meaning* program, we've added new units and lessons designed to help your students read and make sense of expository nonfiction, including science and social studies books, articles, and functional texts. In addition, we have provided you with more support for helping your English Language Learners grow as readers. (See page xxxviii for more information about supporting your English Language Learners.) To enhance the home-school connection, we have included after each unit samples of letters you can send home to parents offering suggestions for supporting students' independent reading at home.

Research-based, Classroom-tested

Research documents what many teachers have known all along, that the fact that a child can read a page aloud does not mean he or she can understand it. Teaching children to make sense of what they read has been an enduring challenge in school. To address this challenge, the creators of the *Making Meaning* program drew on 20 years of research by people like P. David Pearson and Michael Pressley, who described the strategies that proficient readers naturally use and the conditions that foster those strategies in children. The *Making Meaning* program also draws on portraits from many classrooms in which reading comprehension is successfully taught, such as those described by Lucy Calkins in her work with the Reader's Workshop and by Ellin Keene and Susan Zimmerman in their book *Mosaic of Thought*. The *Making Meaning* program brings this research together in a unique yearlong curriculum of easy-to-implement daily lessons. Reading comprehension strategies are taught directly through read-aloud experiences, and the students learn to use these strategies to make sense of their own reading through guided and independent strategy practice.

The *Making Meaning* program is also unique in its focus on teaching the whole child. There is ample evidence in our society of the need to help children develop their minds in a context of caring for others, personal responsibility, empathy, and humane values. Years of research in child development reveal that children grow intellectually, socially, ethically, and emotionally in environments where their basic psychological needs are met. To this end, the *Making Meaning* program helps you create a classroom climate in which your students feel a strong sense of belonging, psychological safety, autonomy, and responsibility to themselves and the group. Teachers know that such an environment doesn't just happen; it must be deliberately created through setting up purposeful interactions among students, teaching them social and problem-solving skills, and helping them to integrate prosocial values into their lives. As you teach the *Making Meaning* lessons, you will see that the children's ability to learn reading comprehension is inextricably linked to their ability to work together and to bring democratic values like responsibility, respect, fairness, caring, and helpfulness to bear on their own behavior and interactions.

In addition to a solid research base, the *Making Meaning* program has been shaped by discussions with, and pilot testing by, a wide range of classroom teachers, to assure that it is effective and fits into the normal classroom day. It can replace an existing reading comprehension program or supplement other widely used programs, such as basal instruction, literature circles, or guided reading. It is designed to be accessible to all students, whatever their reading levels, and includes support for English Language Learners.

Please refer to the bibliography on page 381 for sources of research on reading and social and ethical development.

An Overview

The pages that follow provide a detailed scope and sequence for teaching reading comprehension at your grade level. The daily lessons revolve around clearly defined teaching objectives and build in complexity as students move through the program.

A week of lessons typically begins with a read-aloud of an engaging piece of text, followed by a whole-class discussion of what the text is about. This same read-aloud book is used on subsequent days to teach the students a comprehension strategy and to give them guided practice with the strategy. The week usually ends with the students practicing the strategy independently by using classroom library books and discussing their thinking. Each lesson typically requires 20–40 minutes of classroom time, depending on the grade level. In addition to the lessons, the students participate in Individualized Daily Reading, during which they read texts at their appropriate reading levels independently for up to 30 minutes each day.

The following comprehension strategies are taught in the *Making Meaning* program:

- Retelling
- Using schema/Making connections
- Visualizing
- Wondering/Questioning
- Making inferences
- Determining important ideas
- Understanding text structure
- Summarizing
- Synthesizing

These strategies reflect the most up-to-date research, state standards, and the standards of the National Council of Teachers of English.

Not all strategies appear at each grade level. The program begins with the most developmentally appropriate strategies in the primary grades, and additional strategies are introduced in the intermediate and upper grades.

Strategy Development in the *Making Meaning* Program

	K	1	2	3	4	5	6	7	8
Retelling	■	■	❑						
Using Schema/Making Connections	■	■	■	❑	❑	❑	❑	❑	❑
Visualizing	■	■	■	■	■	■	■	■	■
Wondering/Questioning	■	■	■	■	■	■	■	■	■
Making Inferences	❑	❑	■	■	■	■	■	■	■
Determining Important Ideas		❑	■	■	■	■	■	■	■
Understanding Text Structure		❑	■	■	■	■	■	■	■
Summarizing			❑	❑	■	■	■	■	■
Synthesizing					❑	■	■	■	■

■ formally taught   ❑ informally experienced

Putting the Program into Practice

The *Making Meaning* program includes:

- The *Teacher's Manual*, which describes the lessons in detail and provides a sequence of instruction for the academic year

- 20–30 children's trade books to use as read-alouds

- An *Assessment Resource Book* (grades 1–6) to help you regularly monitor the progress and needs of your students and class

- A *Student Response Book* for each student (grades 2–6), which coordinates with specific lessons and provides pages for response to text, recording thinking about text, journal writing, and an independent reading log

We created the *Making Meaning* program to meet the needs of a broad spectrum of classroom teachers. Both beginning and experienced teachers who piloted the program reported that it is a powerful tool that they were able to quickly and easily bring into their classrooms. Students improved not only in their reading comprehension, but also in their critical thinking and their ability to work together, regardless of setting.

Focus on Comprehension

THE GRADE 2 COMPREHENSION STRATEGIES

The strategies that follow are taught in the grade 2 level of the program.

Using Schema/Making Connections

Schema is the prior knowledge a reader brings to a text. Readers construct meaning by making connections between their prior knowledge and new information in a text. In *Making Meaning* grade 2, the students learn to connect what they know from their own experience to stories before, during, and after a read-aloud.

Understanding Text Structure

Proficient readers use their knowledge of narrative and expository text structure to approach and comprehend texts. For example, readers who understand that stories have common elements, such as setting, characters, and plot, have a framework for thinking about stories. Readers who understand that expository texts have common features, such as headings and subheadings, use those features to help them unlock the text's meaning. In *Making Meaning* grade 2, the students use story elements to help them think about stories. They also identify features of expository texts and use those features to help them understand the texts.

Visualizing

Visualizing is the process of creating mental images while reading. Mental images can include sights, sounds, smells, tastes, sensations, and emotions. Good readers form mental images to help them understand, remember, and enjoy texts. In *Making Meaning* grade 2, the students visualize to make sense of figurative language and deepen their understanding and enjoyment of poems and stories.

Wondering/Questioning

Proficient readers wonder and ask questions to focus their reading, clarify meaning, and delve deeper into text. They wonder what a text is about before they read, speculate about what is happening while they read, and ask questions after they read to gauge their understanding. In *Making Meaning* grade 2, the students wonder and ask questions before, during, and after a read-aloud to make sense of the text.

Making Inferences

Not everything communicated by a text is directly stated. Good readers use their prior knowledge and the information in a text to understand implied meanings. Making inferences helps readers move beyond the literal to a deeper understanding of texts. In *Making Meaning* grade 2, the students make inferences to think more deeply about both narrative and expository texts.

Determining Important Ideas

Determining the important ideas in texts helps readers identify information that is essential to know and remember. What is identified as important in a text will vary from reader to reader, depending on the purpose for reading and prior knowledge. In *Making Meaning* grade 2, the students explore which ideas in texts are important and support their thinking with evidence from the texts.

Retelling

Readers use retelling to identify and remember key information in a text. They focus on the important ideas or sequence of events as a way of identifying what they need to know or recall. In *Making Meaning* grade 2, the students informally retell stories, using characters and plot to organize their thinking.

Summarizing

Summarizing is the process of identifying and bringing together the essential ideas in a text. Readers summarize as a way of understanding what they have read and communicating it to others. In *Making Meaning* grade 2, the students informally identify important ideas and use them to summarize.

THINKING TOOLS

"Thinking Tools" help the students implement the strategies they are learning and delve more deeply into texts. In grades K–2, the students informally use "Stop and Wonder" as preparation for "Stop and Ask Questions," a thinking tool they learn and use in grades 3–6.

Stop and Wonder

The teacher stops at various places during a read-aloud, and the students discuss what they are hearing and wondering. When the teacher resumes reading, the students listen to hear whether what they wonder about is addressed in the text.

Focus on Social Development

Helping students to develop socially and ethically, as well as academically, is part of the educator's role and, we believe, should be integrated into every aspect of the curriculum. Social and academic learning flourish when they are integrated naturally, rather than pursued separately. During *Making Meaning* lessons, the students listen to and discuss literature in pairs, groups of four, and as a class, and through their interactions come to recognize that talking about books is a way to understand them. As they work together, they develop caring and respectful relationships, creating a safe and supportive classroom environment conducive to sharing their thinking. They are encouraged to take responsibility for their learning, be aware of the effect of their behavior on others and on their work, and relate the values of respect, fairness, caring, helpfulness, and responsibility to their behavior.

Social development objectives for each week's lessons are listed in the Overview of the week. The week's lessons provide activities, questions, and cooperative structures that target these objectives. (For a list of the cooperative structures in grade 2, see page xix.) The lessons also provide opportunities for the students to decide such things as how they will divide the work and how they will report their ideas. Learning how to make these decisions helps them become responsible group members. A Social Skills Assessment is included for use early in the year, mid-year, later in the year, and at end-of-year to help you assess your students' progress in meeting the social development objectives of the program.

Social skills chosen for emphasis at each grade level are developmentally appropriate. Within a grade, the skills vary from unit to unit, depending on the comprehension strategy being taught, the activities, and the literature used for the read-alouds. Social skills emphasized in grade 2 include talking and listening to one another, explaining one's thinking, using prompts to add to another person's thinking, and appreciating and respecting one another's ideas.

Most lessons at the grade 2 level are designed for pair work. We recommend that you randomly pair students at the beginning of each unit and have partners stay together for the whole unit. (See "Considerations for Pairing ELLs" on page xxx.) Working with the same partner over time helps students work through and learn from problems, build successful methods of interaction, and develop their comprehension skills together.

Random pairing sends several positive messages to the students: there is no hidden agenda behind how you paired students (such as choosing pairs based on achievement); every student is considered a valuable partner; and everyone is expected to learn to work with everyone else. Random pairing also results in heterogeneous groupings over time, even though some pairs may be homogeneous in some way during any given unit (for example, both partners may be female). The box below suggests some methods for randomly pairing the students.

Some Random Pairing Methods

- Distribute playing cards and have the students pair up with someone with the same number or suit color.

- Place identical pairs of number or letter cards in a bag. Have each student pull a card out of a bag and find someone with the same number or letter.

- Cut magazine pictures in half. Give each student a picture half. Have each student pair up with the person who has the other half of the picture.

Building caring classroom relationships is the key to creating a successful learning community. Research has shown that students thrive in classroom communities that meet their basic psychological needs for autonomy, belonging, and competence. When such classrooms emphasize the importance of cooperation, collaboration, kindness, and personal responsibility, students are more likely to treat one another with respect. As a result, they feel safer and more secure in school and are more willing to take risks to share their thinking. They are better able to stand up for what they believe and be sensitive to others' feelings and opinions. Students are more likely to be motivated to learn for the sake of learning, rather than for good grades or other extrinsic rewards. They can work out problems, and they are more likely to take responsibility for their behavior and their learning.

Class meetings are an effective way to foster cooperation among students and build and strengthen community. Class meeting lessons occur regularly throughout the year. Their purposes include helping the students get to know one another, solving problems students are having working together, and checking in to follow up. (For more about class meetings, see "Class Meeting Lessons" on page xxv.)

Cooperative Structures

Cooperative structures are taught and used at every grade level to increase the students' engagement and accountability for participation. The structures help the students learn to work together, develop social skills, and take responsibility for their learning. Students talk about their thinking and hear about the thinking of others. Suggested uses of cooperative structures in the lessons are highlighted with an icon. In addition, you can use cooperative structures whenever you feel that not enough students are participating in a discussion, or, conversely, when many students want to talk at the same time.

Cooperative Structures in the Program

- **Turn to Your Partner.** The students turn to a partner sitting next to them to discuss a question.

- **Think, Pair, Share.** The students think individually about a question before discussing their thoughts with a partner. Pairs then report their thinking to another pair or to the class. This strategy is especially appropriate when the students are asked to respond to complex questions.

- **Think, Pair, Write.** As in "Think, Pair, Share," the students think individually before discussing their thoughts with a partner. The students then write what they are thinking. They might share their writing with another pair or with the class.

- **Heads Together.** Groups of four students discuss a question among themselves. Groups then might share their thoughts with the class.

- **Group Brainstorming.** Groups of four generate as many ideas as they can about a question as a group member records. These lists are then shared with the class.

In grade 2, the students learn "Turn to Your Partner" and "Think, Pair, Share." Other structures are added as developmentally appropriate.

Managing the Program

The *Making Meaning* program for grade 2 consists of ten units. The units vary in length from one to three weeks. Each week has three days of instruction and practice. During some weeks, a class meeting replaces a day of practice. The chart below provides an overview of the year.

Grade 2

Unit / Read-aloud	Length	Focus
1 ▶ The Reading Life: Fiction and Narrative Nonfiction • *McDuff Moves In* by Rosemary Wells • *Poppleton* by Cynthia Rylant • *Sheila Rae, the Brave* by Kevin Henkes • *Eat My Dust!* by Monica Kulling	3 weeks	• Building a reading community • Listening to and discussing stories • Learning the procedure for listening to read-alouds • Learning "Turn to Your Partner" and "Think, Pair, Share"
2 ▶ Making Connections: Fiction • *Jamaica Tag-Along* by Juanita Havill • *Alexander and the Terrible, Horrible, No Good, Very Bad Day* by Judith Viorst	2 weeks	• Making text-to-self connections to enjoy and understand stories
3 ▶ Visualizing: Narrative Nonfiction, Poetry, and Fiction • *A Tree Is Nice* by Janice May Udry • *Fathers, Mothers, Sisters, Brothers: A Collection of Family Poems* by Mary Ann Hoberman • *Poppleton and Friends* by Cynthia Rylant • *The Paperboy* by Dav Pilkey	3 weeks	• Visualizing to make sense of text
4 ▶ Making Inferences: Fiction • *What Mary Jo Shared* by Janice May Udry • *Erandi's Braids* by Antonio Hernández Madrigal • *Chester's Way* by Kevin Henkes	3 weeks	• Exploring text structure in narrative texts by examining characters, setting, and plot in stories • Using inference to understand characters
5 ▶ Wondering: Fiction • *The Incredible Painting of Felix Clousseau* by Jon Agee • *The Ghost-Eye Tree* by Bill Martin Jr. and John Archambault • *Galimoto* by Karen Lynn Williams • *The Paper Crane* by Molly Bang	3 weeks	• Using wondering to make sense of stories

Grade 2 *(continued)*

Unit / Read-aloud	Length	Focus
6 ▶ Wondering: Fiction and Narrative Nonfiction • *The Tale of Peter Rabbit* by Beatrix Potter • *Beatrix Potter* by Alexandra Wallner • *The Art Lesson* by Tomie dePaola • "'Draw, Draw, Draw'"	2 weeks	• Using wondering and questioning to make sense of fiction and narrative nonfiction texts
7 ▶ Wondering: Expository Nonfiction • *It Could Still Be a Worm* by Allan Fowler • *Plants that Eat Animals* by Allan Fowler • *Fishes (A True Book)* by Melissa Stewart • *POP! A Book About Bubbles* by Kimberly Brubaker Bradley	3 weeks	• Using wondering and questioning to make sense of expository nonfiction texts • Exploring expository text features
8 ▶ Exploring Text Features: Expository Nonfiction • *Snails* by Monica Hughes • *Bend and Stretch* by Pamela Hill Nettleton • "Ice Cream Mania" • "Giant Panda, Red Panda" • "Classic Smoothie" • "The City Zoo"	3 weeks	• Identifying and using expository text features to learn more about a topic
9 ▶ Determining Important Ideas: Expository Nonfiction and Fiction • "Wild Rides" by Lev Grossman • "Summer of the Shark" from *TIME For Kids* • "A Nose for the Arts" from *TIME For Kids* • *Me First* by Helen Lester • *Big Al* by Andrew Clements • *Erandi's Braids* by Antonio Hernández Madrigal	3 weeks	• Using inference to identify important ideas
10 ▶ Revisiting the Reading Life • *little blue and little yellow* by Leo Lionni	1 week	• Reflecting on the students' growth as readers • Reflecting on the reading community

USING THE UNIT AND WEEK OVERVIEWS

To prepare for a *Making Meaning* unit, begin by reading the unit Overview. It will acquaint you with the goals of the unit and the literature used during each week of the unit. It will also alert you to the social skills and values that will be emphasized, based on the type of student interaction likely to occur in the lessons.

Prepare for each week by reading the week Overview and previewing the week. This will help you see how instruction flows from lesson to lesson and alert you to any advance preparations or special requirements for the week.

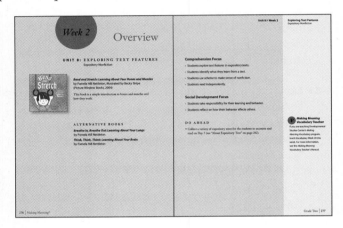

PREPARING THE LESSONS

The three-day weeks in *Making Meaning* grade 2 generally follow this pattern:

Day 1	Day 2	Day 3
Read-aloud & Individualized Daily Reading (IDR)	Strategy Lesson & IDR	Guided Strategy Practice & IDR or Independent Strategy Practice & IDR

Some weeks may vary from this pattern, and periodically a class meeting lesson will substitute for one of the three days. Each of the lesson types is described below.

Read-aloud Lessons

Students' listening comprehension typically exceeds their reading comprehension. Listening to and discussing texts together enables them to build background knowledge and vocabulary, enjoy a common experience, build community, share ideas, and collaborate to construct meaning. Every week begins with a read-aloud lesson. After the reading, discussion questions check the students' surface-level understanding of the text in preparation for deeper thinking about the text on subsequent days of the week.

To Prepare for a Read-aloud:

- Read the entire lesson and anticipate how your students will respond.

- Collect materials and anticipate room arrangement needs.

- Practice reading the text aloud. Focus on reading slowly.

- Review the Suggested Vocabulary and the ELL (English Language Learner) Vocabulary lists and locate these words in the text. To better define these words smoothly while reading aloud, write each definition on a self-stick note and place the note next to the word in the read-aloud. Notice if there are any additional words you will need to define for your students.

- Locate any suggested stopping points in the text. Again, you might use a self-stick note to mark each stopping point.

- Decide what level of support your English Language Learners will need. You might need to read the story aloud to your ELLs prior to the whole-class read-aloud or summarize the story for them. Also, review any ELL Notes in the lesson and provide extra support for your students as appropriate. (See page xxviii for more information about supporting your English Language Learners.)

- Extensions appear at the end of some lessons. Review and decide on any extensions you want to do with your class. Some may require additional materials or preparation.

Alternative Books

You may want to substitute another book for the provided read-aloud text. In the Overview of the week, you will find some suggestions for books that are suitable for teaching the comprehension focus of the week. You can also use an alternative book if you decide to repeat a week of instruction.

The alternative books suggested in the *Making Meaning* program are offered in Developmental Studies Center's Comprehension Strategies Libraries. These grade-level libraries (grades K–8) of 20–26 trade books are designed to support instruction in the specific strategies used in the lessons. Visit Developmental Studies Center's website at www.devstu.org for more information.

Strategy Lessons

The strategy lesson introduces the strategy that is the comprehension focus for the week. Typically, you will reread the read-aloud book from Day 1 and ask questions that help your students move beyond the surface meaning to a deeper exploration of the text. You will then guide the students to develop their understanding through carefully structured activities. This approach encourages the students to explore and develop a strategy before you explicitly label it.

To Prepare for a Strategy Lesson:

- Read the entire lesson (including *Student Response Book* pages) and anticipate how your students will respond.
- Collect materials and anticipate room arrangement needs.
- Practice using the strategy at least once in your own reading to help you anticipate difficulties the students might have.
- Plan how you will pace the lesson to keep it moving. A lesson is designed to take 20–40 minutes on average.
- Review suggested discussion questions and decide which ones you will ask.
- Always remember that making meaning of text—not using a particular strategy—is the primary goal of the program. Keep discussions focused on the text and remind the students that strategies serve readers by helping them understand what they read.
- Review and plan any extensions you want to do with your class.

Guided Strategy Practice Lessons

A strategy lesson is followed by lessons in which the students practice using the strategy, with teacher support gradually reducing as the students become more comfortable with the strategy. In a guided strategy practice lesson, the students practice using the strategy with a very familiar text (such as an excerpt from the week's read-aloud text), and you facilitate and support the students' work by asking focused questions and guiding discussion.

Independent Strategy Practice Lessons

In independent strategy practice lessons, the students practice using a strategy in appropriately leveled texts that they read independently. You have the opportunity to monitor the students and provide individual help as needed.

To Prepare for a Guided or Independent Strategy Practice Lesson:

- Read the entire lesson (including *Student Response Book* pages) and collect materials.

- Practice any teacher modeling required in the lesson.

- Plan how you will pace the lesson to keep it moving.

- Review suggested discussion questions and decide which ones you will ask.

- Review and plan any extensions you want to do with your class.

Class Meeting Lessons

Class meeting lessons happen periodically throughout the year and are designed to help build the reading community, a critical element in the success of the *Making Meaning* program. Class meetings usually occur on Day 3 of a week, although sometimes they are suggested on Days 1 or 2. Early in the year, class meetings focus on helping you and your students establish a caring, collaborative reading community. Subsequent class meetings focus on checking in to see how the students are doing and on solving problems with working together.

To Prepare for a Class Meeting Lesson:

- Read the entire lesson and collect materials.

- Anticipate room arrangement needs for the class meeting.

- Plan how you will introduce the topic of the class meeting.

- Plan how you will facilitate the discussion so it feels safe to discuss problems (for example, reminding the students to say "people" instead of using names).

- Plan where you might use a cooperative structure to increase participation and accountability.

INDIVIDUALIZED DAILY READING (IDR)

The independent strategy practice lessons in the *Making Meaning* program provide your students with valuable practice in using strategies independently, but more independent practice is needed if the students are to become truly proficient comprehenders of text. To meet this need, *Making Meaning* includes an Individualized Daily Reading (IDR) component. During IDR, the students spend up to 20 minutes a day independently reading books at their appropriate reading levels. An IDR section appears at the end of each lesson, except independent strategy practice lessons. IDR can follow the day's lesson or you can schedule it during another time of the school day.

The Teacher's Role

Individualized Daily Reading in the *Making Meaning* program is different from other types of independent reading, such as free reading, SSR (Sustained Silent Reading), and DEAR (Drop Everything and Read). In those programs, students select their own books, which may or may not be at their appropriate reading levels, and the teacher plays a largely neutral role. In IDR, the students read texts at their appropriate reading levels for a specified period of time. You, the teacher, are actively involved, conferring with individual students, helping them select appropriate books, and assessing and supporting their reading as they read.

IDR Conferences

IDR is introduced to the students in Unit 1, when you will teach the students your expectations for IDR time and for using the classroom library. Early in the year, you will conduct conferences with individual students to ensure that they are reading appropriately leveled books and to get to know them as readers. As the year progresses, your conferences will focus more on assessing the students' comprehension, supporting struggling readers, and encouraging self-monitoring strategies.

In Unit 2, you will begin using the "Resource Sheet for IDR Conferences" (BLM15). This is a list of questions and suggestions to help you probe the students' thinking. In Unit 4, you will begin to document some of your IDR conferences using the "IDR Conference Notes" record sheet (BLM16). We recommend that you document at least one IDR conference per student per unit. Over time, these notes will become an important source of information for each student's Individual Comprehension Assessment (see "Assessment" on page xxxvi). Blackline masters for the resource sheet and conference notes can also be found at the end of the *Assessment Resource Book*.

Reading Appropriately Leveled Books

For IDR to succeed, the students must be reading books they can comprehend and read fluently with few miscues (accuracy errors). Early in the year, you can match students to books by informally assessing their reading ability. One procedure you might use is to have the students select books that interest them, and then listen to each student read aloud. Note whether the student is reading with accuracy (reading most of the words without miscues) and understanding. To gauge a student's surface understanding, you can use prompts and questions such as "Tell me what you just read" or "What does that mean?" If a student is reading a book that is too difficult or easy, help her select a more suitable book.

Another technique for evaluating the appropriateness of a book is the "five finger rule." As a student reads a page aloud, count any words he doesn't know. More than five unknown words on a page usually indicates that the book is too difficult. When your students become familiar with the five finger rule, you can encourage them to use the technique on their own, making them responsible for checking the appropriateness of the books they choose for IDR.

It is very important for the students to build reading fluency as a foundation for comprehension. If you have students who are reading far below grade level, make sure they have time every day to practice reading decodable texts, and check in regularly to monitor their rate and accuracy.

Setting Up a Leveled Classroom Library

For IDR the students will require access to a wide range of narrative and expository texts at various levels. For easy browsing, you might display books in boxes or baskets labeled with the name of the book category. Categories can include:

- Genres (e.g., mystery, science fiction, folktale, biography)
- Subjects or topics (e.g., presidents, animals, weather, school)
- Themes (e.g., faraway places, friendship, growing up)
- Favorite authors or illustrators
- Popular series
- Student favorites

A classroom library ideally consists of 300–400 titles, although many teachers start with a smaller collection and add to it over time. The library should include a balance of fiction and nonfiction books. To address various reading levels, at least 25 percent of the library should be books one to two grades below grade level, and at least 25 percent should be books one to two grades above grade level.

Sources of texts include book clubs, bookstores, your school or community library, donated books, basal readers, textbooks, and children's magazines and newspapers. You can purchase a leveled classroom library, or you can level the books in your current classroom library.

Developmental Studies Center's Individualized Daily Reading Libraries can be used to start an excellent independent reading classroom library or to round out an existing library. The libraries are organized by grade level (K–8) and readability to enable teachers to provide "just right" fiction and nonfiction books for their students. Visit Developmental Studies Center's website at www.devstu.org for more information.

Leveling Books

Following is information on two leveling systems that can help you with the sometimes difficult and time-consuming process of leveling books. (More information about leveling can be found in Brenda M. Weaver's *Leveling Books K–6: Matching Readers to Text*.)

- **The Pinnell and Fountas Leveling System**

  Educators Gay Su Pinnell and Irene C. Fountas developed a leveling system for use with guided reading groups that is frequently used for leveling independent reading libraries. They provide lists of thousands of leveled books for grades K–8 in their book *Leveled Books, K–8: Matching Texts to Readers for Effective Teaching* (Heinemann, 2008) and their website, www.fountasandpinnellleveledbooks.com.

- **The Lexile Framework**

  This leveling system uses a sophisticated formula to determine text difficulty, which it represents as a Lexile score, and then ranks the text on a graded scale. For example, a text with a score of 400 is "ranked" at approximately grade 2. Developers of the framework (MetaMetrics, Inc.) have created a database of more than 30,000 Lexiled titles plus software that allows teachers to search, sort, and view details on the titles. For more information, visit the Lexile Framework for Reading website at www.lexile.com.

SUPPORT FOR ENGLISH LANGUAGE LEARNERS (ELLs)

The *Making Meaning* program helps you implement effective teaching strategies to meet the needs of all children, including English Language Learners (ELLs). English Language Development strategies are an inherent part of the program's design. In addition, through ELL Notes, we provide you with suggestions for modifying the instruction to enhance support for ELLs.

While the *Making Meaning* program is an effective tool in teaching comprehension to ELLs, it is not intended to stand alone as a comprehensive linguistic development program. It is assumed that additional support in second language acquisition is occurring for ELLs outside of this program.

About Teaching Reading Comprehension to ELLs

One myth about teaching ELLs is that good teaching alone will meet their linguistic and academic needs, and that they will simply "pick up" the language in the typical classroom context. While certainly "good teaching" (developmental, research-based instructional strategies) enormously benefits learners of English, it is important to target their specific academic and linguistic strengths and needs. The first step is to develop an accurate picture of each child's English language proficiency level and previous academic experience.

Stages of Second Language Acquisition

As you know, learning a new language is a developmental process. The following chart outlines the generally accepted stages of acquiring a second language, and characteristics of students at each stage. Progress from one stage to the next depends on a wide variety of factors, including cognitive and social development and maturity, previous academic experience, family education and home literacy practices, personality, cultural background, and individual learning styles.

Stages of Second Language Acquisition	
Developmental Stages of Language Proficiency (under immersion)	**Student Characteristics**
Stage 1: Receptive or Preproduction (can last up to 6 months)	• Often "silent" during this period • Acquires receptive vocabulary (words and ideas that children "take in" or learn before they begin to produce words verbally) • Conveys understanding through drawing, writing, and gesturing • Gradually becomes more comfortable in the classroom
Stage 2: Early Production (can last up to 6 months)	• Uses one- to two-word answers • Verbally labels and categorizes • Listens more attentively • Writes words and some simple sentences
Stage 3: Speech Emergence (can last 6 months to 1 year)	• Speaks in phrases, short sentences • Sequences stories using words and pictures • Writes simple sentences
Stage 4: Intermediate Proficiency (can last 1 to 3 years)	• Uses increased vocabulary • Speaks, reads, and writes more complex sentences • Demonstrates higher order skills, such as analyzing, predicting, debating, etc.
Stage 5: Advanced Proficiency (can last 1 to 3 years)	• Demonstrates a high level of comprehension • Continues to develop academic vocabulary • Continues to speak, read, and write increasingly complex sentences

Considerations for Pairing ELLs

A key practice in the *Making Meaning* program is to have students work in unit-long partnerships. Random pairing is suggested as a way to ensure equity by reinforcing the value of each child in the classroom (see "Random Pairing" on page xviii). However, when considering the needs of English Language Learners, it may be advantageous to partner your ELLs in a more strategic way. For example, you might pair a beginning English speaker with a fluent English or bilingual speaker. It can be effective if the bilingual partner shares the ELL's native language, but we recommend prudence in asking the more fluent bilingual speaker to serve as translator. Another option is to place ELLs in trios with fluent English speakers to allow them more opportunity to hear the language spoken in conversation. In this case, it is important to make sure that all three students are participating and including one another in the work.

How the *Making Meaning* Program Supports ELLs

There are a number of effective English Language Development (ELD) instructional strategies integrated throughout the *Making Meaning* program. These strategies help make the content comprehensible, support students at their individual level of language proficiency, and help students see themselves as valuable members of the classroom community. They include the strategies shown in the chart below.

ELD Strategies in the *Making Meaning* Program	
Emphasis on making content comprehensible	• Opportunities for meaningful listening, speaking, and reading • Rereading text • Questions appropriate to proficiency level • Explicit teacher modeling • Drawing on prior knowledge and experience
Visual aids and engaging materials	• Rich, meaningful literature • Engaging book art
Explicit vocabulary instruction	• Opportunities to preview and discuss read-alouds before lessons • Building academic vocabulary • Brainstorming words
Creating a respectful, safe, learning community	• Active, responsible learning • High expectations for classroom interactions • Explicit classroom procedures and routines • Explicit social skills instruction • Regular discussions to reflect on classroom values and community
Cooperative learning	• Cooperative structures such as "Turn to Your Partner" and "Think, Pair, Share" • Ongoing peer partnerships • Opportunities to express thinking orally and listen to others' thinking • Sharing work and reflecting

Additional Strategies for Supporting ELLs

In addition to the practices embedded in the *Making Meaning* lessons, ELL Notes provide specific suggestions for adapting instruction to meet the needs of English Language Learners. In addition, you can implement a number of general strategies to help ELLs participate more fully in the program. These include:

- **Speaking slowly.** Beginning English speakers can miss a great deal when the language goes by too quickly. Modifying your rate of speech can make a big difference in helping your beginning English speakers understand you.

- **Using visual aids and technology.** Photographs, real objects, diagrams, and even quick sketches on the board can help to increase a student's comprehension. When giving directions, physically modeling the steps and writing the steps on the board while saying them aloud are effective ways to boost comprehension. Technology, such as books on tape or CD, can also be helpful.

- **Inviting expression through movement and art.** Having students express their thinking through movement and art can be enormously powerful. Drawing, painting, dancing, mimicking, role-playing, acting, singing, and chanting rhymes are effective ways for children to increase comprehension, build vocabulary, and convey understanding. The Total Physical Response (TPR) method, developed by James Asher, helps children build concepts and vocabulary by giving them increasingly complex verbal prompts (stand, sit, jump, etc.) that they act out physically and nonverbally (see the bibliography).

- **Building vocabulary.** ELL vocabulary is highlighted for most read-alouds in the program, and we recommend that you introduce this vocabulary and define it during the reading. In addition, prior to the read-aloud you might brainstorm words related to the text. The students can then illustrate each word and post the illustration next to the printed word, creating a visual chart to refer to as they listen to the read-aloud.

- **Preteaching.** It is always a good idea to preteach concepts with ELLs whenever possible. This could mean previewing vocabulary, doing a picture walk of a story, or looking at real objects or photographs before a lesson. Preteaching in a child's native language can be particularly effective— teachers, instructional aides, parents, or other community members can be enlisted to help.

- **Simplifying questions.** Open-ended questions are used throughout the *Making Meaning* program to elicit language and higher-order thinking from students. These questions are often more complex in structure than closed or one-word-answer questions. While all learners, including English Language Learners, benefit from the opportunity to consider such questions, you might periodically modify a complicated question into a simpler one to increase comprehension and participation by your ELLs. The chart below lists some suggestions for simplifying questions.

Suggestions for Simplifying Questions

Suggestion	Original Question	Simplified Question
Use the simple present tense.	What was happening at the beginning of the story?	What happens at the beginning of the story?
Use active rather than passive voice.	How was the window broken in the story?	Who broke the window in the story?
Ask *who/what/where/when* questions rather than *how/why* questions.	How are you and your partner working together?	What do you and your partner do to work well together?
Avoid the subjunctive.	After hearing this part of the book, what do you think raptors might have looked like?	The part of the book we read today describes raptors. What do you think raptors looked like?
Provide definitions in the question.	Why is the old woman so reluctant to name the dog?	The old woman does not want to name the dog. She is reluctant. Why?
Provide context clues as part of the question.	Why is Sally Jane's visit to the reservoir important?	At the end of the story, Sally Jane visits the reservoir and thinks about what her mother said. What is important about that?
Elicit nonverbal responses.	What do you see in this picture that tells about the words?	This picture shows the sentence "I like to paint." Point to the paints. Point to the paintbrushes.
Elicit 1- and 2-word answer responses.	What do you think will happen when Peter puts the snowball in his pocket?	Peter puts the snowball in his pocket. Is that a good idea?

- **Assessing comprehension.** When students are in the preproduction and early production stages of language acquisition, it can be hard to assess exactly what they understand. It is important not to confuse lack of verbal response with lack of understanding. Rather than force ELLs to produce language before they are ready (which can raise anxiety and inhibit their progress), you can assess nonverbal responses while the students are actively engaged by asking yourself questions such as:

Q *Do the student's drawings and written symbols communicate thinking or show evidence of my teaching (such as drawing the problem and the solution in a story)?*

Q *Does the student nod, laugh, or demonstrate engagement through other facial expressions?*

Q *Does the student pick up academic and social cues from peers?*

Q *Does the student follow classroom signals and routines?*

Q *Does the student follow simple directions (such as "Please get out your* Student Response Books *and pencils")?*

Q *Does the student utter, chant, or sing some familiar words or phrases?*

Additional Modifications for English Language Learners

The English Language Development strategies outlined below can help you better meet the specific linguistic needs of your ELLs. These strategies can be implemented in small groups with your English Language Learners.

Read-aloud Lessons

- **Preview vocabulary.** Ask ELLs to draw or act out vocabulary and encourage them to give examples.

- **Take a picture walk.** Give ELLs an opportunity to become familiar with the illustrations in a story and make predictions to increase comprehension.

- **Modify cooperative structures.** Provide question prompts for verbal ELLs to use in partner conversations (for example, "Ask your partner, 'What will happen next?'") and allow nonverbal ELL students to gesture, draw, dramatize or write their ideas for their partners.

Strategy Lessons

- **Use multiple modalities.** Allow ELLs to use drama, drawing, realia, and writing in practicing comprehension strategies.
- **Create visual aids.** Use chart paper or the board to record the important parts of whole-class discussions.
- **Review vocabulary.** Emphasize vocabulary and story language to help ELLs make sense of the story and use vocabulary meaningfully.

Guided Strategy Practice Lessons

- **Role-play or reenact parts of the text.** Encourage ELLs to demonstrate comprehension through active means.
- **Use journals.** Ask ELLs to draw or draw and label in a journal to express their ideas. Have them share their drawing or writing with a partner as a "rehearsal" before sharing with the whole group.
- **Use visualizing.** Provide opportunities for the students to create and describe mental pictures from the text as a way to enhance comprehension.

Independent Strategy Practice Lessons

- **Review the strategy.** While students are working independently, have ELLs work in small groups to reinforce the strategy. Check in with groups to assess the students' comprehension.
- **Have pairs or small groups share.** Have ELLs work in pairs or small groups to present their ideas to the whole class.
- **Prepare for whole-class discussions.** Support participation in whole-class discussions by giving ELLs time to "rehearse" what they want to share. Encourage them to share examples from the text or bring in their own pictures or written materials.

Individualized Daily Reading (IDR)

IDR is an excellent opportunity to provide ELLs with targeted comprehension support. Here are several ways to differentiate instruction during IDR:

- **Provide books on tape or compact disc.** Provide a variety of stories on cassette or CD so ELLs can listen to a story, hear standard pronunciation, develop story language, and increase their understanding.
- **Use partner reading.** Have ELLs read a story with a partner.

- **Respond to literature.** Ask ELLs to draw or write a response to the book they are reading independently (for example, draw the main character or write a sentence describing the problem in the story).

- **Offer one-on-one support.** Enlist instructional assistants, student tutors, student teachers, native language speakers, and parents to read individually with ELL students during IDR.

By carefully observing your English Language Learners and employing some of the strategies suggested above (as well as those in the ELL Notes in the lessons), you will be able to support their development as readers and as caring, responsible participants in your writing community.

OTHER PROGRAM FEATURES

Student Response Books

The *Making Meaning* program provides a *Student Response Book* for each student. The *Student Response Book* includes:

- Excerpts and reprints of selected read-aloud texts.

- Activity sheets, correlated to lessons, that the students use to record their thinking. Activities might include thinking tools and cooperative structures that require writing, such as "Stop and Wonder."

- An IDR Journal in which the students record their thoughts about their reading during Individualized Daily Reading. The journal includes a "Reading Log" in which the students list and comment on the books they read independently.

The *Student Response Books* are a useful resource for both you and your students. The students can use their "Reading Logs" and IDR Journals to track and write about their independent reading. The activity sheets make it unnecessary for you or your students to provide paper. The activity sheets are engaging and easy to use, and the completed sheets comprise a record of each student's work in the program. The *Student Response Books* are an integral part of the Individual Comprehension Assessment described in the following section.

The *Student Response Book* and other reproducible materials are available on CD-ROM. Visit Developmental Studies Center's website at www.devstu.org for more information.

Assessment

The assessment component in the *Making Meaning* program is designed to help you (1) make informed instructional decisions as you teach the lessons and (2) track students' reading comprehension and social development over time. The expectation is that *all* of your students are developing at their own pace into readers with high levels of comprehension and that they can all develop positive, effective interpersonal skills and values.

There are three types of assessments in the *Making Meaning* program: Class Comprehension Assessments, Individual Comprehension Assessments, and Social Skills Assessments. As you follow the lessons in the *Teacher's Manual*, an assessment box and icon will alert you whenever one of these assessments is suggested. The assessment box will also direct you to the corresponding pages in the *Assessment Resource Book*, which you will use to record your observations and to track students' progress. Each assessment is described briefly below.

Class Comprehension Assessment

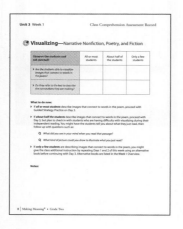

The Class Comprehension Assessment (CCA) is a once-a-week assessment designed to help you assess the performance and needs of the whole class. The CCA occurs during a lesson at a time when the students would be demonstrating their use of the strategies they learned to make sense of text. During the CCA, you have the opportunity to randomly observe students working in pairs or individually (select strong, average, and struggling readers) as you ask yourself key questions. In the *Assessment Resource Book*, each week's CCA record sheet gives you space to record your thinking, as well as suggestions for how to proceed based on your observations (see the "Class Comprehension Assessment" section in the *Assessment Resource Book*, pages 5–27).

Individual Comprehension Assessment

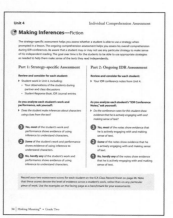

The Individual Comprehension Assessment (ICA) is an end-of-unit assessment designed to help you assess the comprehension of individual students. During the ICA, you review each student's work from the unit and your "IDR Conference Notes" (see the next page) and identify evidence of the student's sense-making and use of strategies. Each unit's ICA section provides examples of student work for your reference. You can use the ICA Class Record Sheet to track the students' progress over the year (see the "Individual Comprehension Assessment" section in the *Assessment Resource Book*, pages 29–46).

- **IDR Conference Notes**

  At least once per unit, you will document an IDR conference with each student using the "IDR Conference Notes" record sheet (BLM16). These notes are an important source of information for each student's ICA.

- **Informal Portfolio Assessment**

  We suggest that you create individual student folders to collect and file chronologically each student's conference notes. Together with the *Student Response Book*, the folder comprises an informal portfolio that you can use to periodically discuss the student's progress with the student or others. You might ask each student to select one or two pieces of work in their *Student Response Book* that they feel represent good thinking they did while reading, and be prepared to talk about this work during progress discussions.

Social Skills Assessment

The Social Skills Assessment (SSA) occurs formally three times a year, at the beginning of the year, in the middle of the year, and late in the year, and informally after the last unit with suggestions to help you reflect on the students' growth over the year. This assessment allows you to note how well each student is learning and applying the social skills taught in the program. The SSA record sheet allows you to track how students are doing with particular skills over time. In addition to social skills, the SSA allows you to track each student's overall participation in the lessons, as well as how each student integrates values such as responsibility, respect, fairness, caring, and helpfulness into his or her behavior. (See the "Social Skills Assessment" section in the *Assessment Resource Book*, pages 1–3.)

Facilitating Discussions

In the *Making Meaning* program, the students' learning relies on their ability to listen and respond to one another's ideas. As most teachers know, these skills are not innate for many students—students need to learn how to listen and how to take one another's thinking seriously.

In the *Making Meaning* program, these skills are taught directly through careful teacher facilitation of discussions. Facilitation tips included throughout the year suggest techniques you can use to facilitate class discussions among your students (for example, asking open-ended questions, using wait-time, and not paraphrasing or repeating students' responses).

The Teacher's Facilitation Bookmark (BLM14), which is introduced in Unit 2, is your resource for questions and suggestions you can use to facilitate these class discussions.

Parent Letters

Each unit in the *Making Meaning* program includes a letter informing parents about the most recent comprehension strategy and social skill their child has learned. Each letter also offers suggestions for supporting students' independent reading at home. Parent letters help strengthen the home-school connection and give parents a way to be actively involved in their children's reading lives. You will find a note referring to the blackline master of the parent letter at the end of each unit.

Making Meaning® Vocabulary

The *Making Meaning Vocabulary* program is a supplemental vocabulary component tied to *Making Meaning*. *Making Meaning Vocabulary* supports students' comprehension by giving them a deeper understanding of words taken directly from *Making Meaning* read-alouds. *Making Meaning Vocabulary* Notes at the end of each week of instruction direct you to the corresponding *Making Meaning Vocabulary* lessons. For more information about *Making Meaning Vocabulary*, see page xxxix.

USING *MAKING MEANING* AS PART OF A COMPLETE LANGUAGE ARTS PROGRAM

While the *Making Meaning* program is designed to serve as the comprehension component of any reading program you may be using, Developmental Studies Center has developed a set of language arts curricula that can be used in conjunction with *Making Meaning* as components in a more complete language arts program. Following are suggestions for integrating the *Making Meaning* program with Developmental Studies Center's other programs. For information on any of Developmental Studies Center's programs, visit our website at www.devstu.org.

Being a Writer™

The *Being a Writer* program is a yearlong curriculum for grades K–6 designed to help each student develop the creativity and skills of a writer. *Being a Writer* provides inspiration and motivation and a clear scope and sequence to develop students' intrinsic desire to write regularly and to help students build a full understanding of and appreciation for the craft and conventions of writing.

The *Being a Writer* program can be used alongside *Making Meaning* to teach the craft, skills, and conventions of writing. Some read-aloud books are used in both the *Making Meaning* and *Being a Writer* programs. This allows the students to explore a book from the points of view of both writers and readers.

If you are teaching both programs, we recommend that you start teaching them simultaneously at the beginning of the year. This will ensure that the books used in both programs are encountered first in *Making Meaning*, where the students can gain both a surface-level and a deeper understanding of the text, before working with the books from the point of view of writers. The *Being a Writer* program includes specific suggestions for implementing it in conjunction with *Making Meaning* at your grade level.

Making Meaning Vocabulary

The *Making Meaning Vocabulary* program is intended as a supplement to *Making Meaning* lessons. In the program, students learn from four to six words each week (four words at grades K–2; six words at grades 3–6). The words in the *Making Meaning Vocabulary* program are taken from the *Making Meaning* read-aloud texts. Students at grades 2 and above also learn independent word-learning strategies, such as recognizing words with multiple meanings and using context and affixes (prefixes and suffixes) to figure out word meanings.

In *Making Meaning Vocabulary* lessons, the students are introduced to each word as it is used in the read-aloud, and then practice using the word through teacher-directed instruction and discussion. Review activities are provided each week to reinforce students' understanding of previously taught words. The program also includes class and individual student assessments.

Guided Spelling™

In Developmental Studies Center's *Guided Spelling* program, daily dictation is infused with instruction in spelling, phoneme awareness, phonics, and memorization strategies to promote understanding and improve accuracy and transfer to writing. The *Guided Spelling* program helps students be successful by providing them with guidance before and during writing so that they spell dictated words correctly. Because it assures success, *Guided Spelling* instruction leads to student self-confidence and interest in spelling. The *Guided Spelling* program is designed to be the spelling component in any language arts curriculum.

SIPPS®

In the *SIPPS* (Systematic Instruction in Phoneme Awareness, Phonics, and Sight Words) decoding program, instruction is explicit and teacher-directed, with group responses and extensive student involvement. *SIPPS* can be used in conjunction with *Making Meaning* lessons to provide a balanced language arts program in which you use *SIPPS* to teach decoding and the *Making Meaning* program to teach comprehension strategies.

INTEGRATING *MAKING MEANING* WITH OTHER READING/LANGUAGE ARTS PROGRAMS

The *Making Meaning* program is designed to replace or enhance any comprehension program you may be using. How you integrate it with other components of your language arts program depends on the type of program you have. Following are suggestions for integrating *Making Meaning* with basal programs and programs that use literature circles and guided reading.

Basal Programs

In many basal programs, comprehension instruction and language arts skills instruction are closely interconnected through each week's selection of literature. A single book or reading might be used to teach the week's comprehension, grammar, spelling, word study, and writing. The *Making Meaning* program can enhance the intellectual and social impact of these programs significantly. Here are some suggestions for integrating *Making Meaning* lessons with basal programs:

- *Making Meaning* grade 2 is designed in three-day weeks. This allows you to read the week's basal anthology selection on Monday, so the week's spelling, writing, grammar, and other language arts skills instruction can be linked to that reading. *Making Meaning* lessons can then be used to replace the basal's comprehension lessons during the rest of the week.

- In addition to other reading materials, basal anthologies can be used as independent reading material during Individualized Daily Reading (IDR).

- The basal anthology selection can be used as the read-aloud text if you decide to repeat a week of instruction in the *Making Meaning* program.

Literature Circles

The *Making Meaning* program can support and enhance the work the students do in literature circles. The students can practice and strengthen the social development skills they have learned in *Making Meaning*, such as listening to others and explaining their thinking, as they interact in their circles. They can also apply the comprehension strategies they are learning to their literature circle selections, thereby building their understanding of the strategies and gaining experience in applying them to their personal, day-to-day reading. When the students are reading expository texts or narrative texts in the *Making Meaning* program, they can select the same type of text for their literature circle, and they can use IDR time in the program to read their circle selections.

Guided Reading

The *Making Meaning* program integrates well with a reading program that includes guided reading, which is also strategy-based. *Making Meaning* lessons can serve as the primary source of comprehension instruction, with guided reading providing extra support to students who need additional instruction and practice in using the strategies. The alternative books recommended in the weekly Overviews of *Making Meaning* can serve as texts for guided reading instruction.

Unit 1

The Reading Life

FICTION AND NARRATIVE NONFICTION

During this unit, the students and teacher share their reading lives, and the students make text-to-self connections. They also begin Individualized Daily Reading (IDR). Socially, they learn the procedures for read-alouds, "Turn to Your Partner," "Think, Pair, Share," class meetings, and IDR. As they build a reading community and take responsibility for their learning and behavior, the students develop the group skill of listening to one another.

Week 1 *McDuff Moves In* by Rosemary Wells
"The Library" in *Poppleton* by Cynthia Rylant

Week 2 *Sheila Rae, the Brave* by Kevin Henkes

Week 3 *Eat My Dust! Henry Ford's First Race* by Monica Kulling

Week 1

Overview

UNIT 1: THE READING LIFE
Fiction and Narrative Nonfiction

McDuff Moves In
by Rosemary Wells, illustrated by Susan Jeffers
(Hyperion, 1997)

A little white dog finds a home and a name.

"The Library"
in *Poppleton*
by Cynthia Rylant, illustrated by Mark Teague
(Scholastic, 1997)

Poppleton never misses his weekly trip to the library.

ALTERNATIVE BOOKS

The Day Jimmy's Boa Ate the Wash by Trinka Hakes Noble
A Color of His Own by Leo Lionni

Comprehension Focus

• Students *make text-to-self connections.*

Social Development Focus

• Teacher and students build a reading community.

• Students take responsibility for their learning and behavior.

• Students learn the procedure for "Turn to Your Partner."

• Students learn the procedure for a read-aloud.

• Students develop the group skill of listening to one another.

DO AHEAD

• Your students will begin working in pairs on Day 2. Prior to Day 2, decide how you will randomly assign partners to work together during the unit. For suggestions about assigning partners randomly, see page xviii. For considerations for pairing English Language Learners, see page xxx.

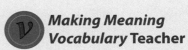

Making Meaning
***Vocabulary* Teacher**

Next week you will begin the *Making Meaning Vocabulary* program. (See page xxxviii for more information about the program.)

Read-aloud

Materials

• *McDuff Moves In*

In this lesson, the students:

• Learn the procedure for a read-aloud
• Hear and discuss a story
• Listen to one another
• Take responsibility for themselves

Teacher Note

The pages of *McDuff Moves In* are unnumbered. For easy reference, you may wish to pencil in page numbers, beginning with the number 1 on the right-hand title page. Page 2 begins "In the back of a dogcatcher's truck…." Use this numbering system for all read-aloud books with unnumbered pages.

 Introduce the Reading Community

Introduce the *Making Meaning* program by explaining that this year the students will be a classroom reading community—reading, thinking about, and talking about books together. They will also learn powerful reading comprehension strategies to help them make sense of what they read.

Point out that often students learn how to read words fluently, but still have a difficult time understanding what they read, especially as the books get more challenging. This year they will all work together, with your help, to become good readers of all kinds of text.

Explain that to learn the strategies well, they will need to share their thinking, listen carefully to one another, and take responsibility for themselves. For this reason, it will be important to be a reading community in which everyone feels welcome, safe, and respected. In the next few weeks, the students will focus on building a caring reading community in the classroom.

Teacher Note

During all read-alouds, make sure the students sit facing you and close enough to hear easily and see the illustrations.

 Learn and Practice the Read-aloud Procedure

Explain that in the *Making Meaning* program the students will hear many stories read aloud and talk about them. Before today's read-aloud, explain how you would like the students to sit to listen to the story (for example, you might ask them to come to the rug and sit facing you, or sit in their seats facing you and the book). Before asking the students to move, clearly state your expectations. (For example, you might say, "I expect you to move quickly, quietly, and without bumping into one another.") Ask:

Q *What do you want to remember to do to make moving go smoothly?*

Have the students move to their places; then ask:

Q *What did you do to move in a responsible way? What might you do differently when we try it again?*

Students might say:

"I tried not to bump into anyone."

"I didn't talk to anyone and I sat down on the rug."

"I almost tripped on someone's leg when I came to the rug. I think we should fold our legs when we sit on the rug so people won't trip on them."

If necessary, have the students return to their seats and practice the procedure again. Practice until they are able to move to their places in an orderly way. Explain that you would like them to use the same procedure every time they gather for a read-aloud, and that they will have more opportunities to practice.

Before reading, state your expectations for the way the students will listen and speak during the reading and discussion. (You might say, "I would like you to sit facing forward without touching anyone else. I would like you to look at the illustrations as I read, and raise your hand if you want to share what you're thinking. When we talk as a class, one person will talk at a time and everyone else will look at the person who is talking.")

▶3 Introduce *McDuff Moves In*

Show the cover of *McDuff Moves In,* and read the title and the names of the author and illustrator aloud. Ask:

Q *What can you tell about this book already?*

◀ **Teacher Note**

The students might not know what it means to be responsible. You may need to give some examples, such as those in the "Students might say" note. The "Students might say" notes help you anticipate possible student responses as you plan your lessons.

 Note

Your English Language Learners will benefit from hearing the story and seeing the illustrations prior to the read-aloud.

Q *Do you think this will be a serious book or a funny book? Why do you think so?*

Q *Are you sitting in a way that will help you listen? If not, what can you do?*

Teacher Note

Since listeners can easily miss details at the beginning of a story, consider reading the first two pages twice. Pause between the readings, say that you will read the pages again, and ask the students to listen for any details they missed in the first reading. ▶

Teacher Note

Use self-stick notes to mark the places the suggested vocabulary words appear. You might write the meanings of the words on the notes to help you define them smoothly without interrupting the reading. ▶

4 ▶ Read Aloud

Read the story aloud slowly and clearly. Deal with each suggested vocabulary word briefly as you encounter it in the text by reading the word, defining it concisely, rereading it, and continuing (for example, "Through an open window in the kitchen of number seven Elm Road wafted—*wafted* means *floated*—wafted the smell of vanilla rice pudding and sausages").

Suggested Vocabulary

wafted: floated (p. 12)

ELL Vocabulary

English Language Learners may benefit from discussing additional vocabulary, including:

dogcatcher: person who catches dogs that wander the streets without an owner (p. 2)

tulip: kind of flower (p. 4; refer to the illustration)

collar: thin band worn around the neck of a dog or cat, usually with a tag saying the name of the owner (p. 16)

dog pound: place where dogs without homes are kept (p. 16)

5 ▶ Discuss the Story

At the end of the story facilitate a whole class discussion using questions such as:

Q *Why does the little white dog go to Fred and Lucy's house? What in the story makes you think that?*

Q *Why do you think Fred drives around in circles?*

Q *How do Fred and Lucy come up with a name for McDuff?*

Remind the students that during reading time this year, you will ask them to focus not only on books, but also on how they are treating one another, listening and speaking to one another, and taking responsibility for themselves. Ask:

Q *What did you do to act responsibly during the reading and discussion today?*

Explain that they will revisit *McDuff Moves In* in the next lesson.

FACILITATION TIP

During this unit, help the students understand that they are talking to one another during class discussions—not just to you—by asking them to **turn and look** at the person who will speak. Explain that looking at the speaker helps them listen, and it shows the speaker that everyone is interested in what she is saying. At the start of the discussion, model the procedure for the students; then during the discussion remind the students of the procedure as needed.

Day 2

Materials

- *McDuff Moves In*

Listening Practice

In this lesson, the students:

- Hear a story read aloud again
- Learn and practice "Turn to Your Partner"
- Listen to one another
- Take responsibility for themselves

▶ Teacher Note

Partners will stay together for the unit. Take some time now to let pairs get to know each other. During this lesson, give them time to talk informally in a relaxed atmosphere. You might have them report to the class some interesting things they found out about each other.

1 Pair Students and Introduce "Turn to Your Partner"

Randomly assign partners and make sure they know each other's names. Ask the pairs to come to the rug and sit together for a read-aloud. Explain that the same partners will work together for the next few weeks.

Explain that during today's reading, and in readings throughout the year, you will stop and ask the students to turn to a partner to talk. The purpose is to give all the students a chance to think more about what they're learning by talking with others. (For more information about the role of cooperative structures in social development, see "Focus on Social Development" on page xvii.)

Explain the "Turn to Your Partner" procedure. (You might say, "When I say 'turn to your partner,' you will turn to face your partner and start talking about the book or a question that I ask. When I raise my hand, you will finish what you're saying and turn back to face me.") Explain that you expect the students to take turns talking and listening, and remind each student to wait for his partner to finish before starting to talk.

2 Model "Turn to Your Partner"

Have a student act as your partner and model turning to face each other. Ask the students to turn and face their own partners, and then have the partners turn back and face you when you give the signal. Have the students practice the procedure again if necessary.

With your student partner, model "Turn to Your Partner" again, but this time, add sharing. Turn to your partner and introduce yourself using your whole name. Have your partner introduce herself. Then on the prearranged signal, turn back to the class.

Have the class practice "Turn to Your Partner" with a sample question. Ask:

Q *If you could have any animal as a pet, what animal would you choose?*

Say "turn to your partner" and have the students turn and tell each other which animal they would choose. Signal to bring the students' attention back to you. Have a few volunteers briefly share their partners' ideas with the class.

Explain that as the students use "Turn to Your Partner" today they will be responsible for both thinking on their own and sharing with a partner, and at the end of the lesson you will ask them to report how they did.

◀ **Teacher Note**

Having the students share their partners' ideas rather than their own helps them be accountable for listening carefully.

ELL Note

Consider showing the illustrations to your English Language Learners prior to reviewing the story with the whole class.

3 ▶ Review the Story and Explain the Purpose for Rereading

Show the cover of *McDuff Moves In*. Ask:

Q *What do you remember about this story?*

Say "turn to your partner," which is the signal to begin, and have the students take turns answering the question. After 20–30 seconds, signal for the students to end their conversations and turn their attention back to you. Ask one or two students to share with the class what their partners said.

Explain that today you will reread *McDuff Moves In* aloud, and ask the students to listen carefully to hear any details they missed during the first reading. Point out that rereading is an important technique for helping readers understand a book at a deeper level. This year you will often reread books or parts of books and ask the students to practice a reading comprehension strategy or think more deeply about the reading.

Teacher Note ▶

Use self-stick notes to mark stopping places in the book and to remind you of questions, instructions, or other information you want to convey to the students during the read-aloud.

 ELL Note

You might support students with limited English proficiency by providing a prompt for responding to these questions, such as "I remember…" and "I think McDuff feels…." (For more information about supporting English Language Learners at various levels of proficiency, see pages xxviii–xxxv.)

4 ▶ Read Aloud

Read the story aloud again, slowly and clearly. Stop after:

> **p. 5**   "So he went looking."

Ask:

Q *What do you remember about the story to this point?*

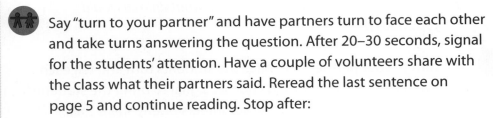 Say "turn to your partner" and have partners turn to face each other and take turns answering the question. After 20–30 seconds, signal for the students' attention. Have a couple of volunteers share with the class what their partners said. Reread the last sentence on page 5 and continue reading. Stop after:

> **p. 12**   "Through an open window in the kitchen of number seven Elm Road wafted the smell of vanilla rice pudding and sausages."

Ask:

Q *How do you think McDuff feels about what is happening now? Why do you think that?*

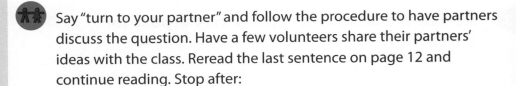 Say "turn to your partner" and follow the procedure to have partners discuss the question. Have a few volunteers share their partners' ideas with the class. Reread the last sentence on page 12 and continue reading. Stop after:

> **p. 18**   "'We certainly can't keep him,' Fred said. 'We're much too busy.'"

Ask:

Q *How do you think McDuff feels about what is happening now? Why do you think that?*

Say "turn to your partner" and follow the procedure to have partners discuss the question. Have a few volunteers share their partners' ideas with the class.

Reread the last two sentences on page 18 and continue reading to the end of the story.

Discuss as a Whole Class

At the end of the story, ask:

Q *What did you hear during the second reading of this story that you missed during the first reading?*

Help the students reflect on how they did with "Turn to Your Partner" by asking:

Q *How did you do with "Turn to Your Partner"? In what ways did it go well? What would you like to do differently next time?*

Q *What are some examples of ways you acted responsibly today?*

◀ **Teacher Note**

When more than one question appears next to a **Q**, ask the first question, discuss it, and follow up with the subsequent questions.

◀ **Teacher Note**

If the students have difficulty describing ways they took responsibility for their learning and behavior, you may want to point out some.

Day 3

Materials

- "The Library" in *Poppleton* (pages 26–35)

Read-aloud

In this lesson, the students:

- Practice the procedure for a read-aloud
- Practice "Turn to Your Partner"
- *Make text-to-self connections* to enjoy and understand a story
- Listen to one another
- Take responsibility for themselves

▶1 Review Procedures and Get Ready to Listen

Review the procedure for getting ready for a read-aloud and have partners sit together. Explain that during today's reading you will again stop several times and ask them to use "Turn to Your Partner" to talk about their thinking. Remind them that the purpose is to give all the students a chance to think more about what they're learning by talking with one another. Tell them that you will ask them to report on their partner conversations at the end of the lesson.

▶2 Share Personal Experiences

Show the cover of *Poppleton* and read the title and the names of the author and illustrator. Explain that this book contains three stories about Poppleton, and that today you will read a story called "The Library." Ask:

Q *What do you like about going to the library?*

 Note

Make sure the students understand that a *library* is a *place where books are kept for reading or borrowing.*

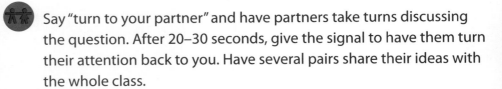 Say "turn to your partner" and have partners take turns discussing the question. After 20–30 seconds, give the signal to have them turn their attention back to you. Have several pairs share their ideas with the whole class.

Ask the students to keep their conversations about the library in mind as they listen to the story.

3 ▶ Read Aloud

Read the story aloud slowly and clearly, stopping as described below.

Deal with each suggested vocabulary word as you come to it in the story by reading the word, defining it concisely, rereading it, and continuing (for example, "If there was a wonderful parade—a *parade is a celebration in which musical bands and other groups of people march together down the street*—a wonderful parade in town on Monday, Poppleton would say, 'Too bad. Library day.'")

 Note

Your English Language Learners will benefit from hearing the story and seeing the illustrations prior to the read-aloud.

Suggested Vocabulary

lip balm: moisturizer you put on your lips to keep them from getting dry (p. 30)

pocket watch: watch with a chain that is carried in a pocket (p. 30; refer to the illustration)

duffel: bag to carry one's personal belongings (p. 30)

ELL Vocabulary

English Language Learners may benefit from discussing additional vocabulary, including:

parade: celebration in which musical bands and other groups of people march together down the street (p. 29; refer to the illustration)

tissues: pieces of soft paper you use to blow your nose (p. 30; refer to the illustration)

book marker: piece of paper you put in a book to mark the last place you read (p. 30; refer to the illustration)

buried his head in [a] book: (idiom) read a book for a long time (p. 31)

adventure book: book in which exciting things happen (p. 31)

librarian: person who works in a library (p. 34)

Stop after:

p. 29 "Poppleton took library day very seriously."

Ask:

Q *What do you know about Poppleton up to this point in the story?*

◀ **Teacher Note**

You can use self-stick notes to mark stopping places in the book. Self-stick notes can also be used to remind you of questions, instructions, or other information you want to convey to the students during the read-aloud.

Teacher Note ▶

Notice how partners do talking about the story at each stop. Make note of gestures and verbalizations that let you know that they are talking about the book and listening to each other (for example, they might be facing each other, looking at each other, and mentioning words they heard in the story). Be ready to report your observations to the students at the end of the lesson.

Say "turn to your partner" and have partners take turns discussing the question. After a few moments, signal to bring their attention back to you, and ask a couple of students to share their thoughts with the class. Reread the last sentence on page 29 and continue reading to the next stop:

p. 33 "But he loved his adventure."

Ask:

Q *What did you learn about Poppleton in the part of the story you just heard?*

Again, use "Turn to Your Partner" to have the students discuss the question. Then have one or two volunteers share their thoughts with the class. Reread the last sentence on page 33 and continue reading to the end of the story.

ELL Note

Consider providing your English Language Learners with a prompt for their response, such as "Monday is Poppleton's favorite day because...."

4 ▶ Discuss as a Whole Class

At the end of the story, facilitate a discussion by asking:

Q *Why is Monday Poppleton's favorite day? Explain your thinking.*

Help the students reflect on their work together by sharing some of your observations of their interactions. Explain that these are examples of behaviors that all the partners can practice.

EXTENSION

Discuss the Students' Favorite School Day

First in pairs, and then as a class, have the students discuss the following question. Encourage the students to give reasons for their choices.

Q *What is your favorite school day? Why?*

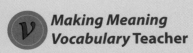
Making Meaning Vocabulary **Teacher**

Next week you will revisit *McDuff Moves In* to teach Vocabulary Week 1.

Week 2

Overview

UNIT 1: THE READING LIFE
Fiction and Narrative Nonfiction

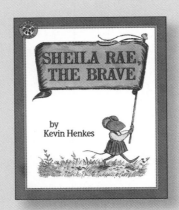

Sheila Rae, the Brave
by Kevin Henkes
(Mulberry, 1987)

Sheila Rae isn't afraid of anything until one day she gets lost. Her sister Louise comes to her rescue.

ALTERNATIVE BOOKS

Shy Charles by Rosemary Wells

Two Mrs. Gibsons by Toyomi Igus

Comprehension Focus

- Students *make text-to-self connections*.

- Students begin Individualized Daily Reading (IDR).

- Teacher and students share their reading lives.

Social Development Focus

- Teacher and students build a reading community.

- Students learn procedures for "Think, Pair, Share," class meetings, and IDR.

- Students take responsibility for their learning and behavior.

- Students develop the group skill of listening to one another.

DO AHEAD

- Prepare a "Class Meeting Ground Rules" chart (see the "Teacher Note" on page 19).

- Set up a classroom library (see "Setting Up a Leveled Classroom Library," page xxvii).

- Make a transparency of a "Reading Log" page (BLM11).

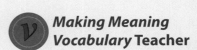

Making Meaning Vocabulary Teacher

If you are teaching Developmental Studies Center's *Making Meaning Vocabulary* program, teach Vocabulary Week 1 this week. For more information, see the *Making Meaning Vocabulary Teacher's Manual.*

Day 1

Materials

- Space for the class to sit in a circle
- "Class Meeting Ground Rules" chart, prepared ahead

Teacher Note

Prior to this week's Day 3 lesson, introduce the classroom library and teach the students the procedures you would like them to follow to borrow and return books. Give them time to browse the library so they become familiar with its organization. Please read "Setting Up a Leveled Classroom Library" on page xxvii for more information. For information about Developmental Studies Center's Individualized Daily Reading Libraries, see page xxvii and visit Developmental Studies Center's website at www.devstu.org.

Class Meeting

In this lesson, the students:

- Learn the procedure and ground rules for a class meeting
- Think about and share their reading lives
- Listen to one another
- Take responsibility for themselves

About Class Meetings

Class meetings are an important tool for fostering a nurturing classroom community, and they occur throughout the year in the *Making Meaning* program. Unlike other types of classroom discussions, class meetings bring the students together around a common goal—creating a welcoming and accepting environment that enhances their academic achievement and encourages responsibility. Through class meeting discussions, the students learn to solve problems, develop empathy, and grow socially and ethically.

If possible, arrange the students in a circle for these meetings. A circle puts everyone on equal footing and the students are able to address one another directly (a skill they will learn this year). If there is not enough space to form a circle, have the students arrange their chairs so most students can see one another.

▶1 Prepare for a Class Meeting

Explain that during the year, the students will participate regularly in class meetings to discuss how they are doing at creating a caring and safe reading community. Today they will participate in a class meeting, and they will learn how to move into a circle.

Explain how you would like the students to get into a circle and state your expectations. (For example, you might say, "When I point to your table, you will get up quietly, pick up your chair, and move carefully into a circle. You will form this side of the circle first, then the other side.") Before asking the students to move, ask:

Q *To make it go smoothly, what do you want to remember while everyone is moving their chairs at the same time? Why is that a caring way to act?*

Have the students move to the circle with partners sitting together. If necessary, have the students return to their desks and practice the procedure again until they can move in an orderly way. Explain that you would like them to use the same procedure every time they gather for a class meeting.

2 Set Ground Rules

Explain that ground rules are rules that everyone follows during a class meeting. Show the "Class Meeting Ground Rules" chart and briefly explain the ground rules you would like the students to follow during the class meeting. Tell them that at the end of the class meeting you will ask them to report on how they did.

3 Quietly Reflect on Our Reading Lives

Explain that the purpose of this class meeting is to think about and share our lives as readers. Begin this discussion by sharing with the class a little bit about your reading life. (You might say, "I love to read, and I try to read every day. Usually I read in the evening after dinner. I sit with my cat in a puffy, yellow chair in the corner of my living room. I've always enjoyed reading mysteries, although recently my favorite books have been about adventures in the great outdoors. I'm starting to get interested in flying so I plan to read some books about that soon.")

To help the students start thinking about their reading lives, ask them to think quietly as you pose the following questions. Give the students ample time to think between the questions.

Q *What are some books you've read or heard that you really love?*

Q *Where is your favorite place to read a book?*

Q *What things do you love to read about?*

Q *What things do you want to read about this year?*

Use "Turn to Your Partner" to have the students talk about their answers to these questions.

◀ Teacher Note

Before the lesson, prepare a chart with ground rules for the students to follow during class meetings. You might want to use or adapt the following rules:

- One person talks at a time.
- Listen to one another.
- Allow people to disagree.
- Talk respectfully to one another.
- When mentioning problems, say "people" instead of using names.

If you develop your own ground rules, remember that the rules should encourage student responsibility and anonymity when talking about problems.

◀ Teacher Note

The questions are intended to stimulate the students' thinking about their reading lives. It is not necessary for them to remember all of the questions or answer all of them.

Teacher Note ▶

There will be more opportunities for students to share their reading lives later in the week. It isn't necessary that they all share today.

4 ▶ Talk About the Students' Reading Lives

Have several pairs share what they talked about with the whole class. As the students share, facilitate the discussion by asking questions such as:

Q *What question do you have for [Gary] about what [he] shared?*

Q *Who also likes [adventure stories] like [Shelley] just shared? What [adventure stories] have you read?*

Explain that later in the week, the remaining pairs will have a chance to share their reading lives with the class.

5 ▶ Reflect and Close the Class Meeting

Ask:

Q *How do you think we did listening to one another during the class meeting?*

Q (Refer to the "Class Meeting Ground Rules" chart.) *Which ground rules did you follow well today? How did that help our discussion?*

Q *What might you want to do differently at the next class meeting?*

Explain how you would like the students to return to their desks, and have them return. If necessary, practice until the students are able to move from the circle to their desks in an orderly way.

Save the "Class Meeting Ground Rules" chart for use throughout the year.

Day 2

Read-aloud

Materials

- *Sheila Rae, the Brave*

In this lesson, the students:

- Share their reading lives
- Learn and practice "Think, Pair, Share"
- *Make text-to-self connections* to enjoy and understand a story
- Take responsibility for themselves

Teacher Note

The pages of *Sheila Rae, the Brave* are unnumbered. For easy reference, pencil in page numbers, beginning with the number 1 on the title page. Page 5 says "Sheila Rae wasn't afraid of anything." Use this numbering system for all read-aloud books with unnumbered pages.

1 Continue to Talk About Our Reading Lives

Take a few minutes for several more pairs to share their reading lives. Facilitate a discussion by asking questions such as those listed under "Talk About the Students' Reading Lives" on page 20.

Let the students know that pairs who have not had a turn will have another opportunity to share their reading lives with the class.

2 Review Procedure and Teach "Think, Pair, Share"

Review the procedure and your expectations for getting ready for a read-aloud. Have partners sit together.

Explain that you will teach a cooperative structure called "Think, Pair, Share," which is like "Turn to Your Partner" with the addition of time to think by yourself before talking in pairs. Explain that the students will hear a question and think quietly for a moment. Then, when you give them the signal "talk to your partner now," each student will turn to her partner and begin talking. When you raise your hand, the students will end their conversations and turn their attention back to you. (For more information about the role of cooperative structures in social development, see "Focus on Social Development" on page xvii.)

Note

Make sure the students understand that when you are *brave*, you *do something even though it is difficult or scary.*

 Note

English Language Learners will benefit from hearing the story read aloud and seeing the illustrations before you read the book to the class.

Tell the students that they will practice "Think, Pair, Share" by discussing questions that will get them thinking about today's read-aloud story. Ask:

Q *When have you done something brave? What happened?*

 Have the students think quietly for 10–15 seconds. Say "talk to your partner now" and have partners discuss the questions. After a few moments, signal to bring their attention back to you. Have several pairs share what they discussed with the whole class.

Ask the students to keep the things they talked about in mind as they listen to the story.

3 ▶ Introduce *Sheila Rae, the Brave*

Show the cover of *Sheila Rae, the Brave* and read the title and the author's name. Explain that Sheila Rae does brave things in this story, but something surprising happens to her.

4 ▶ Read Aloud

Read the story aloud slowly and clearly, stopping as described on the next page.

Deal with each suggested vocabulary word as you come to it in the story by reading the word, defining it concisely, rereading it, and continuing (for example, "She growled at stray—*stray* means *lost or without a home*—She growled at stray dogs…").

Suggested Vocabulary

fearless: not afraid (p. 14)
stray: lost or without a home (p. 16)
bared: showed (p. 16)
occurred: came to mind (p. 19)
familiar: well-known or easily recognized (p. 19)

ELL Vocabulary

English Language Learners may benefit from discussing additional vocabulary, including:

patting herself on the back: (idiom) bragging; taking pleasure in talking about how brave she is (p. 9)

Sheila Rae stepped on every crack on the sidewalk without fear: Sheila Rae wasn't afraid to step on the cracks even though some people think it brings bad luck (p. 10)

no-handed: without using her hands (p. 11; refer to the illustration)

scaredy-cat: (idiom) unkind name for someone who is afraid of something (p. 13)

evil creatures: scary make-believe people or animals (p. 17)

Stop after:

> **p. 13**   "'You're always such a scaredy-cat,' Sheila Rae called.
> 'Am not,' whispered Louise."

Ask:

Q *What has happened so far in the story?*

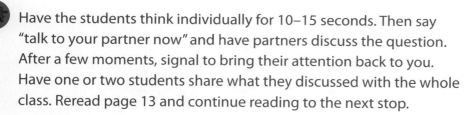

Have the students think individually for 10–15 seconds. Then say "talk to your partner now" and have partners discuss the question. After a few moments, signal to bring their attention back to you. Have one or two students share what they discussed with the whole class. Reread page 13 and continue reading to the next stop.

> **p. 19**   "It suddenly occurred to Sheila Rae that nothing
> looked familiar."

Ask:

Q *What's happening? What do you think will happen next?*

Have the students think individually for 10–15 seconds; then say "talk to your partner now" and have partners discuss the questions. Signal to bring their attention back to you. Have one or two students share what they discussed with the whole class. Reread page 19 and continue reading to the next stop.

> **p. 25**   "'No, we're not,' said Louise. 'I know the way home.
> Follow me!'"

Ask:

Q *What's happening now?*

 Have the students think individually for 10–15 seconds; then say "talk to your partner now" and have partners discuss the questions. Signal to bring their attention back to you. Have one or two students share what they discussed with the whole class. Reread the last three sentences on page 25 and continue reading to the end of the story.

Reread the last three sentences on page 25

5 Discuss the Story

Facilitate a discussion about the story using questions such as:

Q *What surprising thing happens in this story? Why is that surprising?*

Reread the last sentence on page 32, "And they walked backwards into the house with their eyes closed," and ask:

Q *What do you think this part of the story tells us about Sheila Rae and Louise? What makes you think that?*

Students might say:

"I think it means that Sheila Rae and Louise are going to be brave together."

"They are trying to show that they are both brave."

"They are going to help each other be brave."

6 Reflect on "Think, Pair, Share"

Help the students reflect on how they did with "Think, Pair, Share" by asking:

Q *What did you do to take responsibility for your thinking and talking during "Think, Pair, Share"? How did that help your work with your partner go smoothly?*

Students might say:

"I thought quietly about the questions and I didn't start talking until the teacher said to."

"I thought about what I wanted to say to my partner before I spoke."

"I didn't talk while my partner was talking."

FACILITATION TIP
During this and other discussions this week, continue to prompt the students to **turn and look** at the person who will speak. (You might say, "Thuy is going to speak. Let's all turn and look at her.") Throughout the discussion, scan the class to ensure that the students are looking at the speaker and, if necessary, interrupt the discussion to remind them of your expectations.

Day 3

Individualized Daily Reading

In this lesson, the students:

- Learn the procedure for and begin Individualized Daily Reading
- Take responsibility for themselves

About IDR

Today the students will begin the Individualized Daily Reading (IDR) program, which will continue throughout the year. In IDR, the students read independently for up to 30 minutes each day in books at their own reading level. Then they reflect on and discuss what they read. (See "Setting Up a Leveled Classroom Library" on page xxvii for information about advance preparation of the classroom library.)

During IDR, it is critical for the students to read books that are appropriate for their reading level. If you have a library organized by reading level and have identified the students' reading levels, teach the students how to find books at their own level. If the library is not organized by reading level, have the students select books with words they feel they can read. Monitor them individually and help them find more appropriate books as needed. Once you are familiar with the students' reading levels, you can help them select appropriate books for IDR. (Please read "Individualized Daily Reading" on page xxv for additional information about placing the students in appropriate books, monitoring their progress, and conducting IDR in your classroom. For information about Developmental Studies Center's Individualized Daily Reading Libraries, see page xxvii and visit Developmental Studies Center's website at www.devstu.org.)

▶ 1 Review Procedures for the Classroom Library

Review the procedures you have set for borrowing and returning classroom library books, as well as your expectations for how the books will be handled.

▶ 2 Teach Procedure for Individualized Daily Reading

Explain that today you will teach the procedure for Individualized Daily Reading (IDR). Explain that IDR will be a daily time for the

Materials

- *Student Response Book,* IDR Journal section
- Transparency of a "Reading Log" page (BLM11)
- Books in various genres and at various levels for independent reading

ELL Note

To help your English Language Learners understand and learn the procedures for using the classroom library, model borrowing, reading, and returning a book.

students to read books at their own reading level and practice the reading comprehension strategies they learn in the *Making Meaning* program. Point out that the more reading practice the students do in books at their level, the stronger they will become as readers.

At the beginning of IDR, the students should select books and find a comfortable place to sit and read. During IDR, they should avoid talking or making distracting noises, so they can concentrate on reading. Explain that they will see you walking around and conferring with individual students.

▶3 Model Completing the "Reading Log"

Have the students open to the IDR Journal section of their *Student Response Books*. Explain that they will use their journals to record many different things about the books they read. Point out that the first pages of the IDR Journal are the "Reading Log," where they will write down the title, author, and a few of their own comments about each book they finish.

ELL Note

Consider having your students with limited proficiency in English draw a picture in the comments section of the "Reading Log."

Show the "Reading Log" transparency on the overhead projector and model writing a book entry in the log. Use a book that the students are all familiar with, such as *McDuff Moves In.* You might write:

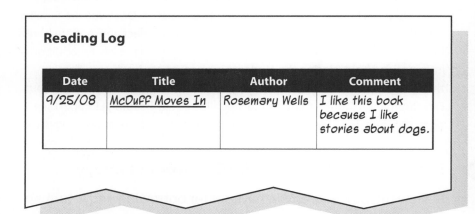

Reading Log

Date	Title	Author	Comment
9/25/08	McDuff Moves In	Rosemary Wells	I like this book because I like stories about dogs.

Model writing another entry (for example, using the story "The Library") and ask the students to fill in their own "Reading Log" for the same story. Before writing in a comment, ask:

Q *What are some comments you might write about ["The Library"]?*

Students might say:

"You can write a sentence about what the story is about."

"You can write why you liked it or didn't like it."

"You can write about [Poppleton]."

If the students do not make suggestions, provide some of these examples.

Have several students share their ideas, then have them individually write their own comments in the appropriate column.

▶ 4 Select Books and Read Independently

Stress that it is very important during IDR to read books that are at the right level. Explain that you will visit individual students during IDR and have them read aloud and talk about what they are reading. Let them know that if a book is too difficult for a student (for example, if it has many unknown words or is confusing) or too easy, you will help him select a book at a more appropiate level.

Have a brief discussion about how the students will interact during book selection. Ask:

Q *What are some things you want to do to make book selection go smoothly?*

Q *If someone already has a book that you want to read, what can you do? How is that a fair way to share the book?*

Have the students select their books and read silently for 10–15 minutes.

◀ **Teacher Note**

Plan a brief class discussion after the students have made several entries in the "Reading Log" so they have a chance to hear their classmates' comments.

◀ **Teacher Note**

As the students read, monitor whether they are reading books at appropriate reading levels. Have individual students read a passage aloud and tell you what the book is about. If a book seems too hard, help the student find a book he can read. If it seems too easy, help him select a more challenging one. (See "Individualized Daily Reading" on page xxv for more information about monitoring students' reading.)

In grade two, IDR starts with 10–15 minutes per day at the beginning of the year, but the goal is to work up to at least 20 minutes per day.

ELL Note

You might support students with limited English proficiency by providing a prompt for responding to the questions, such as "My partner read…" and "My partner's book is about…." (For more information about supporting English Language Learners at various levels of proficiency, see pages xxviii–xxxv.)

5 ▶ Discuss the Independent Reading

Signal the end of the reading time. Use "Turn to Your Partner" to have the students talk about their reading. Explain that you will ask them to report what their partners talked about.

After several minutes, discuss as a class:

Q *What book did your partner read today? Briefly, what is it about?*

Explain that throughout the year, the students will share and discuss what they read during IDR, and that sometimes you will ask them to share what their partners said. Explain that this will help them develop their ability to listen carefully and be responsible learners in their partnerships.

Give each student time to record any book she completed in her "Reading Log;" periodically allow time for this at the end of IDR.

In the remaining time, invite students who have not yet talked about their reading lives to do so. Set aside additional time for students to share their reading lives in future class meetings or discussions, until all the students have shared.

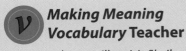

Making Meaning Vocabulary **Teacher**

Next week you will revisit *Sheila Rae, the Brave* to teach Vocabulary Week 2.

Week 3

Overview

UNIT 1: THE READING LIFE
Fiction and Narrative Nonfiction

Eat My Dust! Henry Ford's First Race
by Monica Kulling, illustrated by Richard Walz
(Random House, 2004)

This story recounts how Henry Ford won his first car race and used his prize money to realize his dream of building a car that everyone could afford.

ALTERNATIVE BOOKS

Babe Ruth Saves Baseball! by Frank Murphy

Fireboat by Maira Kalman

Comprehension Focus

- Students *make text-to-self connections.*

- Students read independently.

Social Development Focus

- Teacher and students build a reading community.

- Students practice classroom procedures.

- Students take responsibility for their learning and behavior.

- Students develop the group skill of listening to one another.

DO AHEAD

- Prepare to model using self-stick notes to mark your reading (see Day 2, Step 2 on page 35).

- Make copies of the Unit 1 Parent Letter (BLM1) to send home with the students on the last day of the unit. (For more information about the Parent Letters, see page xxxviii.)

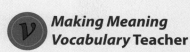

**Making Meaning
Vocabulary Teacher**

If you are teaching Developmental Studies Center's *Making Meaning Vocabulary* program, teach Vocabulary Week 2 this week. For more information, see the *Making Meaning Vocabulary Teacher's Manual.*

Day 1

Read-aloud

Materials

- *Eat My Dust!*

In this lesson, the students:

- Hear and discuss a story
- Practice the procedure for a read-aloud
- Use "Think, Pair, Share"
- Listen to one another
- Take responsibility for themselves

1 ▶ Review Procedure and Get Ready to Listen

Review the procedure and your expectations for getting ready for a read-aloud. Have the students move to the rug with partners sitting together. Explain that they will listen to a story, then discuss their thinking with their partners and with the whole class.

2 ▶ Introduce the Story

Show the cover of *Eat My Dust!* and read the title and the author's name aloud. Explain that this is a true story about one of the first car races and a man named Henry Ford who loved to build cars. Point out that this story happened a long time ago when most people used horses instead of cars to get around. Ask:

Q *What do you think you know about car races?*

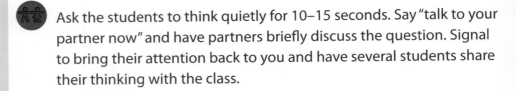

Ask the students to think quietly for 10–15 seconds. Say "talk to your partner now" and have partners briefly discuss the question. Signal to bring their attention back to you and have several students share their thinking with the class.

Ask the students to keep what they think they know about car races in mind as they listen to the story.

3 ▶ Read Aloud

Read the story aloud slowly and clearly, stopping as described below.

Deal with each suggested vocabulary word briefly as you come to it in the story by reading the word, defining it concisely, rereading it, and continuing (for example, "There's that crazy Henry driving his horseless buggy—a *buggy* is a *kind of wagon*—driving his horseless buggy again…").

 ELL Note

Prior to today's read-aloud, read the story and show the illustrations to your English Language Learners. Stop to clarify vocabulary as you read.

Suggested Vocabulary

buggy: kind of wagon that people ride in that is pulled by a horse (p. 6)

needed repairs: needed to be fixed (p. 12)

victory: win (p. 16)

cranked: turned a handle to start (p. 26)

cut: turn off (p. 31)

ELL Vocabulary

English Language Learners may benefit from discussing additional vocabulary, including:

mechanic: person who fixes cars (p. 18; refer to the illustration)

on your marks: go to the start of the race (p. 26)

racer: car (p. 26)

roared to life: started (p. 26)

stepped on the gas: pressed hard on the gas pedal to make the car go faster (p. 35)

lap: one time around the race track (p. 36)

Stop after:

> **p. 11** "And he loved building them."

Ask:

Q *What do you know about Henry so far?*

Ask the students to think quietly for 10–15 seconds. Say "talk to your partner now" and have partners briefly discuss the questions. Signal to bring their attention back to you and have one or two students share their thinking. Reread the last sentence on page 11 and continue reading to the next stop.

> **p. 21** "She wanted Henry to drive safely."

Ask:

Q *What do you think will happen next? Why?*

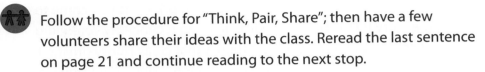 Follow the procedure for "Think, Pair, Share"; then have a few volunteers share their ideas with the class. Reread the last sentence on page 21 and continue reading to the next stop.

> **p. 29** "They were sure he would win."

Ask:

Q *Who do you think will win the race? Why?*

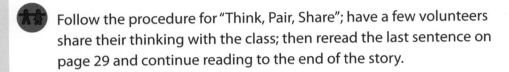 Follow the procedure for "Think, Pair, Share"; have a few volunteers share their thinking with the class; then reread the last sentence on page 29 and continue reading to the end of the story.

FACILITATION TIP
During this and other discussions this week, continue to remind the students to **turn and look** at the person who is speaking. Remind them that looking at the speaker helps them listen and shows the speaker they are interested in what she says. Notice the effect that the use of this facilitation technique has on the students' engagement in class discussions over time.

▶4 Discuss the Story

Facilitate a whole-class discussion of the story. Ask:

Q *Why did Henry Ford enter the car race?*

Q *Why did people like Henry Ford's Model T car?*

> *Students might say:*
>
> "He entered the race so he would have enough money to build new cars."
>
> "People liked Model T's because they were easy to drive and easy to repair."

Read the author's note on page 48 aloud. Show the photograph and read the caption aloud. Ask:

Q *What did you learn about Henry Ford from this story?*

▶5 Reflect on "Think, Pair, Share"

Help the students reflect on how they did with "Think, Pair, Share" by sharing some of your observations of the students' interactions. If necessary, discuss any problems and have the students talk about ways to avoid these problems in the future.

Day 2

Individualized Daily Reading

In this lesson, the students:

* Practice the procedure for Individualized Daily Reading
* Read independently for up to 15 minutes
* Take responsibility for themselves

1 Review Procedures for the Classroom Library

Review the procedures and your expectations for using the classroom library and for IDR (see Unit 1, Week 2, Day 3).

2 Select Books and Read Independently

Explain that after they read, partners will talk about their reading. Ask the students to use a self-stick note to mark an interesting part of their reading to share with their partners.

Model the procedure for using the self-stick note by briefly reading aloud from one of the books from a previous week or a book from your own personal reading, thinking aloud about why you found a certain part interesting, and placing the note in the margin where you stopped reading.

Have the students select their books and read silently for 10–15 minutes. As the students read, monitor individual students to make sure they are reading books that are appropriate for their reading level.

3 Discuss the Independent Reading

Have the students read aloud the part they marked and discuss it in pairs. Tell the students that you would like them to be ready to share with the whole group what their partners said.

Materials

* Books of various genres and reading levels for independent reading
* A small self-stick note for each student
* *Student Response Book*, IDR Journal section

◀ **Teacher Note**

Prepare the passage you will read and what you will say ahead of time so this modeling goes smoothly. If possible, use a book from your personal reading to reinforce the idea that reading is a part of life, not just something to do at school.

If you have selected *Sheila Rae, the Brave* from the previous week, you might read page 17 and say, "That's so funny that Sheila Rae pretended that the trees were evil creatures. I wonder what the creatures looked like. I'm going to place my note on the page that describes this part of the story."

After partners have had a chance to share, discuss as a class:

Q *What did your partner share with you today about [her] reading?*

Q *What did you do to show your partner that you were listening carefully? What did your partner do to show you [she] was listening?*

Remind the students that the purpose of sharing their partners' thinking is to help them develop their listening skills and be responsible learners in their partnerships.

Have any student who finished a book today record it in his "Reading Log."

ELL Note

Consider providing your students with limited proficiency in English a prompt for their response, such as "I listened like this…."

Day 3

Individualized Daily Reading

In this lesson, the students:

- Practice the procedure for Individualized Daily Reading
- Read independently for up to 15 minutes
- Practice the procedure and ground rules for a class meeting
- Listen to one another
- Take responsibility for themselves

▶1 Review Procedures and Expectations for IDR

Review the procedures and your expectations for the classroom library and for IDR (see Unit 1, Week 2, Day 3). Ask:

Q *How do you feel we did at handling the classroom library books in a responsible way in the last lesson? What examples did you see of people handling books in a responsible way?*

Q *What do we want to remember today to take the best possible care of our classroom library?*

Students might say:

"Put the books back where you got them."

"Handle the books carefully so you don't rip the pages."

▶2 Select Books and Read Independently

Have the students select their books and read silently for 10–15 minutes. Remind them that you will ask them to talk with their partners about what they read at the end of the reading time.

As they read, monitor individual students to make sure they are reading books at an appropriate reading level.

Materials

- Books of various genres and reading levels for independent reading (see Teacher Note on page 18)
- *Student Response Book*, IDR Journal section
- "Class Meeting Ground Rules" chart
- Space for the class to sit in a circle
- Unit 1 Parent Letter (BLM1)

 Note

You might want to help your English Language Learners choose books at the appropriate level. Providing a limited number of teacher-selected texts will help them make good choices.

3 ▶ Discuss the Independent Reading

Use "Turn to Your Partner" to have partners discuss what they read. Tell the students that you would like them to be ready to share with the whole group something their partner said.

After partners have had a chance to share, have the students bring their attention back to the whole class. Ask:

Q *What did your partner share with you about his or her reading?*

Q *What was one thing you liked about the way you and your partner worked together today?*

Have any student who read a different book today than she did yesterday record it in her "Reading Log." Remind the students that they will have many opportunities to share and discuss what they read.

4 ▶ Have a Check-in Class Meeting

If necessary, review the procedure and your expectations for moving to a circle for a class meeting (see Unit 1, Week 2, Day 1). Have the class move into a circle with partners sitting together. Briefly review the "Class Meeting Ground Rules" chart.

Explain that the purpose of this class meeting is to check in on how the students are doing with the classroom procedures they are learning. Write the following procedures on the board: getting ready for a read-aloud, moving into a circle for a class meeting, "Turn to Your Partner," "Think, Pair, Share," using the classroom library, and IDR.

Facilitate a discussion by asking:

Q *Which of these do you think we do well? Which, if any, do you think we need more practice on? Why?*

Q *When we follow the procedures in a responsible way, what are some of the benefits to our class?*

If appropriate, help the students identify areas where they are following procedures well or having problems.

ELL Note

To help them during this discussion, consider providing your students with a prompt for their response, such as "My partner said…."

Class Meeting Ground Rules

- *one person talks at a time*
- *listen to one another*

Ask the students to briefly discuss how they did following the class meeting ground rules. If necessary, briefly share your observations. Review the procedure for returning to their seats and adjourn the class meeting.

In the remaining time, invite students who have not yet shared their reading life to do so. If necessary, set aside additional time for students to share their reading lives in future class meetings or discussions, until all the students have shared.

SOCIAL SKILLS ASSESSMENT

Before going on to Unit 2, take this opportunity to assess the students' social development. Please see page iv of the *Assessment Resource Book* for information about administering the Social Skills Assessment. These assessments will occur again after Units 5 and 7 and at the end of the year.

Teacher Note

This is the last week in Unit 1. You will need to reassign partners for Unit 2.

Parent Letter

Send home with each student the Parent Letter for this unit (see "Do Ahead," page 31). Periodically, have a few students share with the class what they are reading at home.

Making Meaning Vocabulary Teacher

Next week you will revisit *Eat My Dust! Henry Ford's First Race* to teach Vocabulary Week 2.

Making Connections

FICTION

During this unit, the students informally identify important ideas in stories and continue to make text-to-self connections. During IDR, the students read independently, share in pairs, and write in their IDR Journals. Socially, they relate the value of caring to their behavior and explain their thinking to others.

Week 1 *Jamaica Tag-Along* by Juanita Havill

Week 2 *Alexander and the Terrible, Horrible, No Good, Very Bad Day* by Judith Viorst

Week 1

Overview

UNIT 2: MAKING CONNECTIONS
Fiction

Jamaica Tag-Along
by Juanita Havill, illustrated by Anne Sibley O'Brien
(Houghton Mifflin, 1989)

When Jamaica's brother refuses to let her play basketball with him, she goes off on her own and makes a new friend.

ALTERNATIVE BOOKS

Ira Sleeps Over by Bernard Waber

Mama Elizabeti by Stephanie Stuve-Bodeen

Comprehension Focus

- Students *make text-to-self connections*.

- Students informally *identify important ideas* in a story.

- Students read independently.

Social Development Focus

- Students relate the value of caring to their behavior.

- Students develop the group skill of explaining their thinking.

DO AHEAD

- Prior to Day 1, decide how you will randomly assign partners to work together during this unit. For suggestions about assigning partners randomly, see page xviii. For considerations for pairing English Language Learners, see page xxx.

- Prepare the "Teacher's Facilitation Bookmark," following the directions on BLM14. Refer to the questions and suggestions throughout the year to help you facilitate whole-class discussions.

- Prepare to model using a self-stick note to mark a place you make a connection (see Day 3, Step 3 on page 52).

- Collect narrative texts for the students to read independently this week. (For information about Developmental Studies Center's Individualized Daily Reading Libraries, see page xxvii and visit Developmental Studies Center's website at www.devstu.org.)

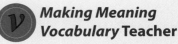

Making Meaning Vocabulary Teacher

If you are teaching Developmental Studies Center's *Making Meaning Vocabulary* program, teach Vocabulary Week 3 this week. For more information, see the *Making Meaning Vocabulary Teacher's Manual*.

Day 1

Read-aloud

Materials

- *Jamaica Tag-Along*
- "Teacher's Facilitation Bookmark" (BLM14), prepared ahead (to be used throughout the program)

***Being a* Writer™ Teacher**

You can either have the students work with their *Being a Writer* partner or assign them a different partner for the *Making Meaning* lessons.

Teacher Note

The students will be assigned new partners at the beginning of each unit and stay together throughout the unit. This structure helps the students reflect on their interactions and solve problems over time.

 Note

English Language Learners will benefit from hearing the story and seeing the illustrations prior to the read-aloud.

In this lesson, the students:

- Hear and discuss a story
- Refer to the story to support their thinking
- Read independently for up to 15 minutes
- Begin working with new partners
- Explain their thinking

▶1 Pair Students and Get Ready to Work Together

Randomly assign partners, have them sit together, and make sure they know each other's names. Explain that each student will work with the same partner for the next two weeks. Today they will listen to you read a book aloud and talk in pairs and with the class about the story. Remind the students that it is important to listen carefully so that they can talk about the story afterward.

▶2 Introduce *Jamaica Tag-Along*

Show the cover of *Jamaica Tag-Along* and read the title and names of the author and illustrator aloud. Explain that this is a story about a girl named Jamaica and her brother, Ossie. Explain that a tag-along is a younger child who follows an older child and tries to do the same things as the older child.

▶3 Read Aloud

Read the story aloud slowly and clearly, showing the illustrations and stopping as described on the next page. Briefly define vocabulary words as you come to them in the story. (See page 33 for an example of how to deal with vocabulary words during a reading.)

Suggested Vocabulary

dribbled: bounced the ball keeping it under control (p. 8)

at a distance: far away (p. 8)

whirled: spun around quickly (p. 10)

rim: top edge of a basketball hoop (p. 10)

ditch: long, narrow hole (p. 20)

repair: fix (p. 23)

smoothed: made even and flat (p. 25)

moat: water-filled ditch (p. 25)

ELL Vocabulary

English Language Learners may benefit from discussing additional vocabulary, including:

court: playing area (p. 3)

shoot baskets: (idiom) play basketball (p. 4)

serious ball: basketball the way adults play (p. 7)

missed a shot: tried to throw the ball into the hoop, but didn't make it (p. 10)

sandlot: area where kids can play in the sand (p. 15)

stroller: baby carriage (p. 17; refer to the illustration)

Read pages 3–15. Stop after:

p. 15 "Jamaica walked slowly over to the sandlot."

Ask:

Q *How is Jamaica feeling? Why is she feeling that way?*

Use "Turn to Your Partner" to have the students discuss the question. When most pairs are done, have one or two students share their ideas with the class. Reread the last sentence on page 15 and continue reading to the end of the story.

4 ▶ **Discuss the Story**

Facilitate a whole-class discussion of the story. Ask:

Q *What happens in this story?*

ELL Note

English Language Learners may benefit from more frequent stops and discussions during the reading. For example, you might stop after pages 7, 19, and 23.

◀ **Teacher Note**

Hearing from only one or two students helps maintain the flow of the story and keeps the students engaged.

◀ **Teacher Note**

The purpose of this discussion is to make sure the students have a surface-level understanding of the story. If necessary, reread parts of the text to help clarify any confusion.

Teacher Note

Use your "Teacher's Facilitation Bookmark" to help you facilitate the discussion in a way that creates opportunities for the students to respond to one another and that increases student accountability. For example:

• Use "Turn to Your Partner" when only a few students are responding or if many students want to talk.

• Ask questions that help the students respond to one another, such as: "Do you agree or disagree with [Danny]? What questions could we ask [Emily] about what she said?"

 Use "Turn to Your Partner" to have the students discuss the question. Then have one or two pairs share what they discussed with the class. As the students talk about the story, probe their thinking with questions such as:

Q *Why does Jamaica want to come along and play basketball with her brother Ossie? What part of the story tells you that?*

Q *Why doesn't Ossie want Jamaica to play basketball with him and his friends? Explain your thinking.*

Q *What happens at the end of the story?*

▶5 Reflect on the Partner Conversations

Facilitate a brief discussion about how partners talked and listened to each other today. Ask:

Q *What did you like about working with your partner today?*

Explain that in the next lesson the students will talk more about *Jamaica Tag-Along*.

Note

Prior to independent reading, tell your English Language Learners to pay attention to what they like about their book as they read.

INDIVIDUALIZED DAILY READING

▶6 Monitor the Students' Reading

Have the students read books at their appropriate reading levels independently for up to 15 minutes.

Continue to monitor whether the students are reading books at appropriate reading levels and whether they are making sense of what they read. Probe their thinking with questions such as:

Q *What is your book about?*

Q *What is happening in your book right now?*

If a student seems confused about what she is reading, have her read a short passage aloud and discuss what happens in that part of the book. Ask:

Q   *What's happening in the part of the book you just read?*

At the end of independent reading, have partners take turns sharing their books with each other. Ask each student to read the title of her book and tell her partner one thing she likes about the book.

ELL Note

Provide your students with limited English proficiency with a prompt for their response, such as "I liked my book because…."

Day 2

Materials

- *Jamaica Tag-Along*
- *Assessment Resource Book*

Strategy Lesson

In this lesson, the students:

- Hear and discuss a story
- Refer to the story to support their thinking
- *Make text-to-self connections* to enjoy and understand a story
- Read independently for up to 15 minutes
- Explain their thinking
- Reflect on how to act in a caring way

About Making Connections

One of the ways that young students naturally make sense of text is by making personal, or text-to-self, connections to the plot or characters in the story. Later, as they continue to hear stories, students begin to see similarities and make connections between stories or themes. In reading and talking, they accumulate experiences and background knowledge that help them make sense of text. Making connections increases both enjoyment and understanding of stories and language. (For more discussion of *making connections*, please see "Using Schema" on page xv.)

 ### Introduce Making Connections

Have partners sit together. Show the cover of *Jamaica Tag-Along* and remind the students that in the previous lesson they listened to the story and discussed it.

Explain that readers often make a personal connection to a story by thinking about how events or people in the story remind them of their own lives. Making a connection helps readers enjoy and understand the story. Tell the students that today you will reread *Jamaica Tag-Along* without stopping, and that you want them to listen carefully to what is happening to the people in the story and think about how the story reminds them of their own lives.

Reread the Story

Reread the entire story aloud slowly and clearly, showing the illustrations.

 Make Personal Connections to the Story

Use "Think, Pair, Share" to have the students think about and discuss:

Q *How does what happens in* Jamaica Tag-Along *remind you of your own life?*

Give the students a few moments to think individually, and then have them share their thinking in pairs. Have a few volunteers share their thinking with the class. As the students talk about their experiences, ask them what part of the story reminds them of their own life. As they share, probe their thinking with questions such as:

Q *How did you feel?*

Q *How do you think [Jamaica/Ossie/Berto] feels? Why do you think [she/he] feels that way?*

◀ **Teacher Note**

Allow sufficient time for the students to initiate the discussion. If the students have difficulty making connections, you may want to share a situation in your own life to stimulate their thinking. You might also ask questions such as:

Q *Have you ever felt left out of an activity you wanted to join? How did you feel?*

Q *What did you do when you couldn't join?*

CLASS COMPREHENSION ASSESSMENT

As the students talk, listen for the types of connections they make. Ask yourself:

Q *Are the students connecting to important ideas in the story rather than to details?*

Initially, young students often make connections to literal details, for example, "I like to play basketball like Ossie and Jamaica." As they hear and discuss more stories, they begin to connect to important ideas in them (for example, recalling a time when they were excluded from an activity is a connection that helps them understand an important idea in *Jamaica Tag-Along*).

Record your observations on page 6 of the *Assessment Resource Book.*

4 ▶ **Reflect on Working Together**

Remind the students that they have been working on creating a caring and safe community of readers. Ask the students to listen carefully as you reread the following excerpt from pages 20–23:

pp. 20–23 "'Berto,' the woman pushing the stroller said, 'leave this girl alone. Big kids don't like to be bothered by little kids.'

'That's what my brother always says,' Jamaica said. She started to repair the castle. Then she thought, but I don't like my brother to say that. It hurts my feelings."

 First in pairs, and then as a class, discuss:

Q *What can we learn about working with others from this part of the story?*

Q *What does this mean for our community of readers?*

Students might say:

"If I know that something will hurt my feelings, I won't do it to others."

"I don't like it when people make fun of me, so I won't make fun of anyone else."

Explain that in the next lesson the students will think about making connections with stories they read independently.

INDIVIDUALIZED DAILY READING

5 ▶ **Discuss Independent Reading**

Have the students read books at their appropriate reading levels independently for up to 15 minutes. Continue to monitor whether the students are reading books at appropriate reading levels and whether they are making sense of what they read. If a student is having difficulty reading and comprehending his book, help him find a book at the appropriate level.

 At the end of independent reading, ask the students to think about whether they are enjoying the books they are reading. Then have partners share their opinion of their books with one another.

Independent Strategy Practice

In this lesson, the students:

- *Make text-to-self connections* as they read independently
- Refer to the story to support their thinking
- Read independently for up to 20 minutes
- Explain their thinking

1 ▶ Begin the "Reading Comprehension Strategies" Chart

Remind the students that they talked about *Jamaica Tag-Along* and made connections between what happens in the story and their own lives. Review that *making connections* is a strategy that good readers use to help them enjoy and understand stories.

Direct the students' attention to a sheet of chart paper labeled "Reading Comprehension Strategies." Write *making connections* on the chart. Explain that making connections is one of the reading comprehension strategies they will focus on learning and using this year.

2 ▶ Introduce Making Connections with Independent Books

Explain that today the students will read independently and think about an experience in their life that helps them connect with a character or what is happening in their book. Tell them that they will probably not make a connection with every book they read. As they are reading, they should think about a part of the story that reminds them of their own life. Then they should mark the place with a self-stick note. Later, they will talk about their connections in pairs.

Materials

- *Jamaica Tag-Along*
- Narrative books at appropriate levels for independent reading
- Small self-stick notes for each student
- Chart paper labeled "Reading Comprehension Strategies" and a marker

Teacher Note

Display the "Reading Comprehension Strategies" chart where the students can refer to it during the year. You will add strategies to the chart as they are introduced in the program. Refer to the chart often to remind the students to use the strategies in their reading throughout the day.

 Note

You may want to model using a self-stick note for your students.

3 Model Making Connections

Model making connections by rereading page 7 of *Jamaica Tag-Along* aloud, thinking aloud about a connection you made, and placing a self-stick note in the margin of the page. (For example, you might say, "This reminds me of a time when I was young and my two older brothers wouldn't let me play with them and their friends. It made me sad, because I didn't have anyone to play with. That's probably how Jamaica feels. I'm going to stick my note here next to this part of the story.")

Explain that at the end of the independent reading time, the students who make connections will share their ideas with their partners and the class.

4 Read Independently and Make Connections

Make sure each student has a book at an appropriate level and distribute several self-stick notes to each student. Have the students read independently for 10–20 minutes, marking with self-stick notes places in the reading where they make connections. After five or ten minutes, stop the students and use "Turn to Your Partner" to have them share any connections they made. Then, without sharing as a class, have the students continue reading.

5 Discuss the Students' Connections

First in pairs, and then as a class, discuss the passages the students marked and the connections they made. Ask questions such as:

Q *Did you connect to a character or something that happened in any part of your story? Explain your thinking.*

Q *How did what happened to you help you think about the [character/story]?*

6 ▶ Reflect on the Partner and Class Discussions

Share your observations about the students' interactions during their partner and class discussions. If appropriate, mention any problems the students had and talk with them about possible solutions.

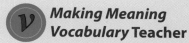

Making Meaning
Vocabulary **Teacher**

Next week you will revisit *Jamaica Tag-Along* to teach Vocabulary Week 4.

Week 2

Overview

UNIT 2: MAKING CONNECTIONS
Fiction

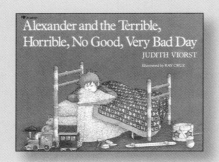

Alexander and the Terrible, Horrible, No Good, Very Bad Day
by Judith Viorst, illustrated by Ray Cruz
(Aladdin, 1987)

One bad thing after another happens to Alexander.

ALTERNATIVE BOOKS

Regina's Big Mistake by Marissa Moss

Lilly's Purple Plastic Purse by Kevin Henkes

Comprehension Focus

- Students *make text-to-self connections.*

- Students informally *identify important ideas* in a story.

- Students read independently.

Social Development Focus

- Students relate the value of caring to their behavior.

- Students develop the group skill of explaining their thinking.

DO AHEAD

- Copy the "Resource Sheet for IDR Conferences" on BLM15 and refer to it throughout the year for questions to ask and suggestions to make during IDR conferences. You may want to laminate it to protect it for long-term use. (For more about IDR conferences, see page xxvi.)

- Make copies of the Unit 2 Parent Letter (BLM2) to send home with the students on the last day of the unit. (For more information about the Parent Letters, see page xxxviii.)

Making Meaning Vocabulary Teacher

If you are teaching Developmental Studies Center's *Making Meaning Vocabulary* program, teach Vocabulary Week 4 this week. For more information, see the *Making Meaning Vocabulary Teacher's Manual.*

Day 1

Materials

- *Alexander and the Terrible, Horrible, No Good, Very Bad Day*

- "Resource Sheet for IDR Conferences" (BLM15), prepared ahead (to be used throughout the program)

ELL Note

English Language Learners will benefit from hearing the story and seeing the illustrations prior to the read-aloud. Continue this procedure throughout the *Making Meaning* program.

Read-aloud

In this lesson, the students:

- Hear and discuss a story
- Refer to the story to support their thinking
- Read independently for up to 15 minutes
- Explain their thinking

1 ▶ Get Ready to Work Together

Have partners sit together. Explain that today the students will hear you read a book aloud, and then talk in pairs and with the class about the story. Ask:

Q *When you talk about the story with your partner, why is it important that both of you explain your thinking?*

Encourage the students to focus on explaining their thinking clearly today.

2 ▶ Introduce *Alexander and the Terrible, Horrible, No Good, Very Bad Day*

Show the cover of *Alexander and the Terrible, Horrible, No Good, Very Bad Day* and read the title and the names of the author and illustrator aloud. Explain that as they listen to the story you would like the students to think about what happens to Alexander and why he is having a very bad day.

3 ▶ Read Aloud

Read the book aloud slowly and clearly, showing the illustrations and stopping as described on the next page. If necessary, briefly define vocabulary words as you come to them in the story.

Suggested Vocabulary

car pool: group of parents who take turns driving their children to and from school (p. 8)

ELL Vocabulary

English Language Learners may benefit from discussing additional vocabulary, including:

carsick: feeling sick from riding in a car (p. 8)

double-decker: two scoops high (p. 13)

elevator: cage or platform that carries people or things up and down between floors of a building (p. 18)

marble: small glass ball used in a children's game (p. 29)

Read pages 5–15. Stop after:

p. 15   "It was a terrible, horrible, no good, very bad day."

Ask:

Q   *What are some things that happen to Alexander that make his day terrible?*

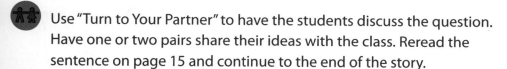

Use "Turn to Your Partner" to have the students discuss the question. Have one or two pairs share their ideas with the class. Reread the sentence on page 15 and continue to the end of the story.

 Note

The students may benefit from more frequent stops and discussions during the reading, for example, after pages 7 and 21.

4 ▶ **Discuss the Story**

At the end of the book, briefly discuss the story, first in pairs, and then as a class. Ask:

Q   *Why is Alexander having a terrible, horrible day?*

Q   *What does Alexander learn about terrible days at the end of the story?*

FACILITATION TIP

As you **ask open-ended questions** this week, remember to use 5–10 seconds of **wait-time** to give everyone a chance to think before talking. If you often hear from the same few students during class discussions, extend the wait-time to encourage more students to participate.

5 ▶ Reflect on How the Students Explained Their Thinking

Facilitate a brief discussion about how partners worked together and explained their thinking. Ask questions such as:

Q *How did your partner do with explaining [her] thinking to you?*

Q *If your partner didn't explain [his] thinking clearly, what did you do?*

Explain that in the next lesson the students will talk about *Alexander and the Terrible, Horrible, No Good, Very Bad Day* and how the story might remind them of their own lives.

INDIVIDUALIZED DAILY READING

ELL Note

Your students with limited English proficiency will benefit from reading picture books with illustrations that support the story.

6 ▶ Confer with Individual Students

Have the students read books at their appropriate reading levels independently for up to 15 minutes.

Tell the students that as they read today you will circulate among them and talk to individual students about their reading. At the end of the reading time, partners will talk about their reading.

As the students read, circulate among them to make sure each student has a book she can read and understand. Stop and talk with individual students about their reading. Refer to the "Resource Sheet for IDR Conferences" and ask questions such as:

Q *What is your book about? What is happening in your book right now?*

If a student seems confused about what she is reading, have her read a short passage aloud and discuss what happens in that part of the book. Ask:

Q *What's happening in the part of the book you just read?*

If the student has difficulty explaining the passage, continue the discussion with questions such as:

Q *Are you finding the whole book confusing, or just this section? If the whole book is confusing, let me help you find another book that might be a better choice for you right now. If it's just this section, let's go back and reread a little together, and then see if we can figure out what's happening.*

At the end of independent reading, give the students a few minutes to share what they read in pairs. Tell each student to begin by telling her partner the title and author of the book. Circulate as the students share and notice conversations and anything you might want to share with the class or attend to.

Day 2

Materials

- *Alexander and the Terrible, Horrible, No Good, Very Bad Day*
- "Reading Comprehension Strategies" chart
- *Student Response Book* page 2
- "Resource Sheet for IDR Conferences"
- *Assessment Resource Book*
- *Student Response Book,* IDR Journal section

Reading Comprehension Strategies

- making connections

Teacher Note

▶ If the students have difficulty telling the story, reread all or parts of it. Alternatively, show the students the illustrations and ask them what is happening.

Strategy Lesson

In this lesson, the students:

- Retell a story
- Refer to the story to support their thinking
- *Make text-to-self connections* to enjoy and understand a story
- Read independently for up to 15 minutes
- Explain their thinking

▶1 Review Making Connections

Have partners sit together. Show the cover of *Alexander and the Terrible, Horrible, No Good, Very Bad Day* and remind the students that in the previous lesson they heard the story and talked about it.

Explain that today the students will retell the story in their own words, make personal connections to the people or events in the story, and then draw pictures of their connections. Refer to the "Reading Comprehension Strategies" chart and review that *making connections*—or thinking about how a story reminds us of our own lives—is an important comprehension strategy that helps us make sense of what we read.

▶2 Retell the Story

Have the students retell the story. Ask:

Q *What happens to Alexander during his terrible, horrible, no good, very bad day?*

Have volunteers share with the class what they remember about the story. As the students offer their ideas, reread the text that supports their thinking (for example, if the students say Alexander got gum in his hair, read aloud from page 5, "I went to sleep with gum in my mouth and now there's gum in my hair...").

Briefly Discuss Personal Connections

Have the students think quietly about a time when they felt like Alexander. Have one or two students respond to the following question. (Later in the lesson more students will have an opportunity to share their connections.) Ask:

Q *What happens in* Alexander and the Terrible, Horrible, No Good, Very Bad Day *that reminds you of your own life?*

Students might say:

"I had a really bad day once. I woke up late and got to school late. Then I forgot my homework. And at recess I got into a fight with my best friend Randy."

"One day my mom promised to take me to the park, but it rained so we couldn't go. I didn't have anything to do and my big sister wouldn't share her markers with me. Then my dad got mad at me because I spilled my drink on the carpet. It was a horrible day."

◀ **Teacher Note**

If the students have difficulty making connections, share a situation in your life to stimulate their thinking. Probe their thinking with questions such as:

Q *Have you ever had a really bad day? How did you feel?*

Q *How was what happened to you [the same as/different from] what happened to Alexander?*

Draw Personal Connections

Have the students turn to *Student Response Book* page 2. Explain that they will use the page to draw a picture of a time they had a very bad day, like Alexander. They will also write a sentence to accompany their picture.

 ELL Note

If necessary, write students' dictated sentences below their pictures.

> **CLASS COMPREHENSION ASSESSMENT**
>
> Circulate as the students draw their pictures and write their sentences. As you observe them, ask yourself:
>
> **Q** *Do the students connect the pictures and sentences about their own lives to the story?*
>
> Record your observations on page 7 of the *Assessment Resource Book*.

 When the students complete their drawings, ask them to share and talk about the drawings in pairs. Then, have a few volunteers share and describe their drawings for the class.

Teacher Note ▶

If your students need
more practice with making
connections, you might repeat
Days 1 and 2 of this week,
using one of the alternative
books listed on page 54, before
continuing with Day 3.

Teacher Note

Before having the students write
in their journals you might want
to have a brief discussion about
the independent reading. Use
some of the students' ideas to
model writing a brief journal
entry. (For example, you might
say, "My book is about a boy and
his new puppy" or "I like this book
because I am learning about
places that animals live.")

 Note

To support your English Language
Learners, consider showing them
the illustrations in both books prior
to having them retell the stories.

Remind the students that when they think about how a story
reminds them of their own lives, they are doing something that
good readers do—making connections. Explain that the students
will continue to make connections as they hear stories in the
coming weeks.

INDIVIDUALIZED DAILY READING

5 **Confer with Individual Students/Have the Students
Write in Their IDR Journals**

Have the students read books at their appropriate reading levels
independently for up to 15 minutes.

Continue to monitor the students' reading levels and comprehension.
As you confer with individual students, refer to the "Resource Sheet
for IDR Conferences" for questions and suggestions.

At the end of independent reading, give the students time to write
in their IDR Journals about their independent reading.

EXTENSION

Compare Jamaica and Alexander

Show the covers of *Jamaica Tag-Along* and *Alexander and the Terrible,
Horrible, No Good, Very Bad Day*. Have the students briefly retell the
stories. Then ask:

Q *In what ways are Jamaica and Alexander alike? In what ways are
they different?*

Use "Think, Pair, Share" to have the students think about and
discuss the questions. Then have volunteers share their thinking
with the class.

Students might say:

"Alexander is having a bad day and so is Jamaica. Later,
 Jamaica's day gets better when her brother plays with her."

"Jamaica gets into an argument with her brother, and so
 does Alexander."

"Jamaica feels good at the end of the story, but Alexander is
 still in a grouchy mood."

Day 3

Materials

- Narrative books at appropriate levels for independent reading
- Small self-stick notes for each student
- *Assessment Resource Book*
- Unit 2 Parent Letter (BLM2)

 ELL Note

Consider modeling using self-stick notes for your students.

Independent Strategy Practice

In this lesson, the students:

- *Make text-to-self connections* as they read independently
- Refer to the story to support their thinking
- Read independently for up to 20 minutes
- Explain their thinking

 1 **Review the Previous Lessons**

Remind the students that in the last two weeks they listened to stories, read books independently, and made connections to parts of the stories that reminded them of people or events in their own lives. They also focused on explaining their thinking and worked on creating a caring community of readers.

Explain that today they will practice looking for personal connections as they read independently.

2 **Read Independently and Make Connections**

Make sure each student has a narrative book at an appropriate reading level. Explain that as they read they should use self-stick notes to mark places in their book where a character or event reminds them of something in their own life. Later they will explain their connections in pairs. Emphasize that they may not make connections with every book.

Have the students read independently for 10–20 minutes.

3 ▶ Discuss the Students' Connections

Use "Turn to Your Partner" to have the students share what they marked and the connections they made. After a few minutes, ask a few volunteers to share their connections with the class. Ask each student to say the title of the book before sharing the connections. Then ask:

Q *What is happening in the part of the story you just read?*

Q *What personal connection did you make to a character or event in the story?*

Q *What questions do you want to ask [Alex] about what [he] shared?*

Explain that the students will continue to think about stories and discuss the books they read independently. Tell them that they will not always need to mark the places in their books where they make connections, but they will always be expected to think about making connections as they read.

4 ▶ Reflect on the Partner Work and Community

Facilitate a brief discussion about how the students interacted and how they helped to create a caring and safe community of readers. Ask questions such as:

Q *Think about how you and your partner worked together for the last two weeks. What were some things that worked well for you and your partner during partner talks?*

Q *What did you do to help your classmates feel comfortable sharing their ideas?*

Students might say:

"I listened and didn't talk when other people were talking."

"When someone shared something embarrassing, I didn't laugh or make fun of him."

FACILITATION TIP

Reflect on your experience over the past two weeks with **asking open-ended questions** and **using wait-time**. Do these techniques feel comfortable and natural? Do you find yourself using them throughout the school day? What effect has repeated use of them had on your students' thinking and participation in discussions? We encourage you to continue to use and reflect on these techniques throughout the year.

Teacher Note

This is the last week of Unit 2. You will need to reassign partners for Unit 3.

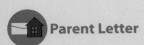

Parent Letter

Send home with each student the
Parent Letter for this unit (see "Do
Ahead," page 55). Periodically, have
a few students share with the class
what they are reading at home.

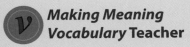

Making Meaning Vocabulary Teacher

Next week you will revisit
*Alexander and the Terrible, Horrible,
No Good, Very Bad Day* to teach
Vocabulary Week 5.

INDIVIDUAL COMPREHENSION ASSESSMENT

Before continuing with Unit 3, take this opportunity to
assess individual students' progress in making connections
to understand text. Please refer to pages 30–31 in the
Assessment Resource Book for instructions.

Unit 3

Visualizing

NARRATIVE NONFICTION, POETRY, AND FICTION

During this unit, the students visualize to make sense of a text. They also informally use schema and inference as they visualize. During IDR, the students read independently, discuss their reading lives with the teacher, and share their reading with the class. Socially, they relate the values of fairness and helpfulness to their behavior and interactions. They also develop the group skills of taking turns talking and listening and helping one another share.

Week 1 *A Tree Is Nice* by Janice May Udry
"My Baby Brother" in *Fathers, Mothers, Sisters, Brothers: A Collection of Family Poems* by Mary Ann Hoberman

Week 2 "Dry Skin" in *Poppleton and Friends* by Cynthia Rylant

Week 3 *The Paperboy* by Dav Pilkey

Week 1

Overview

UNIT 3: VISUALIZING
Narrative Nonfiction, Poetry, and Fiction

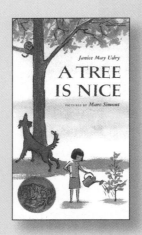

A Tree Is Nice
by Janice May Udry, illustrated by Marc Simont
(HarperTrophy, 1984)

This book encourages readers to think about the many ways to enjoy and appreciate trees.

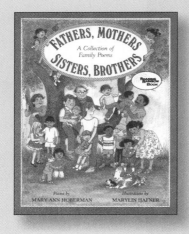

"My Baby Brother"
in *Fathers, Mothers, Sisters, Brothers: A Collection of Family Poems*
by Mary Ann Hoberman, illustrated by Marylin Hafner
(Little, Brown, 1991)

A collection of poems that celebrates every kind of family member.

ALTERNATIVE BOOKS

My First Oxford Book of Animal Poems compiled by John Foster

Abuela by Arthur Dorros

Comprehension Focus

• Students *visualize* to make sense of text.

• Students informally *use schema and inference* as they visualize.

• Students read independently.

Social Development Focus

• Students analyze the effect of their behavior on others and on the group work.

• Students relate the values of fairness and helpfulness to their behavior and interactions.

• Students develop the group skills of taking turns talking and listening and helping one another share.

DO AHEAD

• Prior to Day 1, decide how you will randomly assign partners to work together during the unit. For suggestions about assigning partners randomly, see page xviii. For considerations for pairing English Language Learners, see page xxx.

• Make a transparency of the poem "My Baby Brother" from BLM12.

• Conceal the cover of *A Tree Is Nice* (see the "Teacher Note" on page 71).

• Collect a variety of narrative texts for the students to read independently throughout the unit. For information about Developmental Studies Center's Individualized Daily Reading Libraries, see page xxvii and visit Developmental Studies Center's website at www.devstu.org.

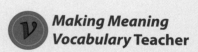

**Making Meaning
Vocabulary Teacher**

If you are teaching Developmental Studies Center's *Making Meaning Vocabulary* program, teach vocabulary Week 5 this week. For more information, see the *Making Meaning Vocabulary Teacher's Manual.*

Day 1

Materials

- *A Tree Is Nice* (pages 3–18)
- "Resource Sheet for IDR Conferences"

Read-aloud

In this lesson, the students:

- Begin working with new partners
- *Visualize* to enjoy and understand a story
- Connect their mental images to the story
- Read independently for up to 15 minutes
- Take turns talking and listening

About Visualizing

Readers create unique mental images from texts based on their own background knowledge and experiences. They can visualize both the topics of nonfiction texts and the setting, characters, and action in stories, by inferring from descriptive language. *Visualizing* enhances readers' understanding and enjoyment. While some young readers may do it naturally, others benefit from instruction about visualizing. All the students benefit from reflecting on the fact that they are visualizing. In this unit, the students visualize as they listen to read-alouds and read independently. (For more discussion about visualizing, please see page xv.)

Being a Writer™ **Teacher**

You can either have the students work with their *Being a Writer* partner or assign them a different partner for the *Making Meaning* lessons.

▶ 1 Get Ready to Work with New Partners

Randomly assign partners and have pairs sit together. Explain that for the next three weeks each student will work with the same partner. Explain that one way partners can be fair to each other is to make sure they both have a chance to share. Tell the students that as they work in pairs in the coming days, they will focus on making sure that both partners have a turn to talk and on finding ways to help one another.

Ask:

Q *When we use "Think, Pair, Share" during a read-aloud, you have only a few minutes to talk at each stop. How will you make sure that both you and your partner have a turn to talk today?*

Have a few students share their ideas with the class. Remind the students that they will report on their partner conversations at the end of the lesson.

2 ▶ Introduce *A Tree Is Nice* and Visualizing

Explain that today's read-aloud is *A Tree Is Nice* written by Janice May Udry and illustrated by Marc Simont. It is a book about many ways to enjoy trees. Ask the students to close their eyes and picture trees that they have seen. Encourage their thinking with prompts such as:

- *Think about the size and shape of the tree.*

- *Think about the color of the tree and leaves.*

- *Think about the location of the tree.*

After a few moments, ask the students to open their eyes, turn to their partners, and talk about the trees they pictured. Tell the students to listen carefully to their partners because they will share their partners' mental pictures with the class.

After students share their mental pictures in pairs, ask:

Q *What kind of tree did your partner see?*

Explain that you will read part of *A Tree Is Nice* aloud without showing the illustrations. Explain that hearing the book without seeing the illustrations will help them make pictures in their minds from the words. Making mental pictures helps them be better readers. Explain that you will read each section twice before asking them to describe their mental pictures.

3 ▶ Read Aloud and *Visualize*

Read pages 3–18 using the procedure described on the next page.

Suggested Vocabulary

trunk: main stem of a tree (p. 13)

limbs: large branches (p. 13)

hoe: tool for loosening and breaking up earth (p. 18)

Teacher Note

Conceal the cover of *A Tree Is Nice* before you read the book to encourage the students to create their own mental images and tap into their background knowledge and experiences.

 Note

Prior to the lesson, preview the illustrations with your English Language Learners and help them visualize trees in detail.

Teacher Note

As you read *A Tree Is Nice,* the students will practice visualizing and making connections between their mental images and the text. In this lesson you will read only the first parts of the book (pages 3–18). The students may enjoy hearing the rest of the book at another time.

Teacher Note ▶

The purpose of rereading the text is to help the students focus on the words or phrases that trigger their mental images. Talking about their mental images helps partners identify these words or phrases. The students come to realize that each person's visual image is unique.

Have the students close their eyes and create pictures in their minds as you read pages 3–8 aloud twice. Read slowly and clearly, pausing between the readings. Stop after:

> **p. 8**   "The leaves whisper in the breeze all summer long."

Ask:

Q   *What did you see in your mind? What sounds did you imagine?*

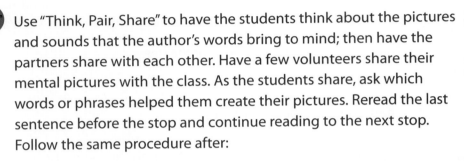 Use "Think, Pair, Share" to have the students think about the pictures and sounds that the author's words bring to mind; then have the partners share with each other. Have a few volunteers share their mental pictures with the class. As the students share, ask which words or phrases helped them create their pictures. Reread the last sentence before the stop and continue reading to the next stop. Follow the same procedure after:

> **p. 11**   "Then we pile them up with our rakes and have a bonfire."
>
> **p. 15**   "If it is an apple tree we can climb it to pick the apples."
>
> **p. 18**   "It is a good place to lean your hoe while you rest."

FACILITATION TIP

During this unit, we invite you to practice **asking a question once** and then waiting for the students to respond before repeating or rephrasing it. If the students are confused by a question or need to hear it again, have them ask you to repeat it or ask it again in a different way. This helps the students learn to take responsibility for listening carefully during a discussion.

4 ▸ Talk About the Reading

Facilitate a brief discussion by asking:

Q   *What did you hear about trees in today's reading?*

Q   *What are some of the ways you can enjoy a tree?*

5 ▸ Talk About Taking Turns

Facilitate a brief discussion about how partners worked together. Ask:

Q   *Earlier you talked about ways to make sure each partner had a chance to talk. How did this work for you and your partner? What changes might you suggest?*

Students might say:

"One time I go first and the next time she goes first."

"When my partner talked, I just listened. Then we switched."

Tell the students that they will continue to practice taking turns and talking about their mental pictures in the coming days.

INDIVIDUALIZED DAILY READING

▶ **6** **Confer with Individual Students**

Have the students read books at their appropriate reading levels independently for up to 15 minutes.

Continue to monitor whether the students are reading books at appropriate reading levels and whether they are making sense of what they read. As you confer with individual students, refer to the "Resource Sheet for IDR Conferences" for suggested questions to probe the students' thinking.

Notice whether the students seem to be ready to increase their independent reading time. If so, gradually increase their independent reading time to 20 minutes during this week.

EXTENSION

Reread *A Tree Is Nice*

Read the entire book aloud, reading each page before showing the accompanying picture. Stop once or twice during the read-aloud to have the students visualize the text and have partners explain their thinking to each other before you show the illustration and continue to read.

ELL Note

Help your English Language Learners choose books at their appropriate reading levels. Providing a limited number of teacher-selected books will help them make good choices.

Day 2

Materials

- "My Baby Brother" in *Fathers, Mothers, Sisters, Brothers* (page 4)
- *Student Response Book* page 3
- Crayons or markers
- "Reading Comprehension Strategies" chart and a marker
- *Assessment Resource Book*

 Note

Your English Language Learners will benefit from previewing the poem prior to today's read-aloud. Read the poem several times, helping your students to understand challenging vocabulary and to picture the baby brother.

Strategy Lesson

In this lesson, the students:

- Hear and discuss a poem
- *Visualize* to enjoy and understand a text
- Draw their mental images
- Read independently for up to 20 minutes
- Take turns talking and listening to one another

▶1 Get Ready to Work Together

Have partners sit together. Remind the students that they listened to parts of *A Tree Is Nice* and made mental pictures of the words. Explain that today you will read a poem aloud and they will talk to their partners again about their mental pictures. Remind them to treat each other fairly by taking turns.

▶2 Introduce "My Baby Brother"

Show the cover of *Fathers, Mothers, Sisters, Brothers* and read the title and the names of the author and illustrator aloud. Explain that this is a book of poems about families. The poem that you will read is entitled "My Baby Brother."

▶3 Read Aloud and Visualize

Tell the students that you will read the poem aloud twice. Ask them to close their eyes and make a mental picture of the baby brother as they listen. Read the poem aloud twice, slowly and clearly, pausing between the readings.

Suggested Vocabulary

velvet: smooth and soft

dimple: small hollow in a person's cheek or chin

ELL Vocabulary

English Language Learners may benefit from discussing additional vocabulary, including:

perfect: just right; the very best

tiny: very small

Use "Think, Pair, Share" to have partners think about and discuss:

Q *How do you picture the baby brother?*

4 ▶ Draw Mental Pictures of the Baby

After partners have had a chance to talk, tell them that they will use crayons or markers to draw their mental picture of the baby brother. Have the students turn to *Student Response Book* page 3, "How I Pictured 'My Baby Brother.'" Ask them to think quietly about their mental picture first and then draw it.

As the students draw their pictures, circulate among them. Reread the poem to individual students as needed.

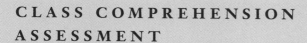

CLASS COMPREHENSION ASSESSMENT

As you observe the students drawing, think about these questions:

Q *Are the students able to visualize images that connect to words in the poem?*

Q *Do they refer to the text to describe the connections they are making?*

Record your observations on page 8 of the *Assessment Resource Book.*

Teacher Note

If the students have difficulty drawing, you might model by doing a brief sketch on a sheet of chart paper using the ideas of a few volunteers. The students can use your model to help them get started and continue adding their own details. Point out that their mental pictures are more important than their drawings. They should try to capture on paper what they see in their minds.

Give the students a few minutes to complete their drawings, alerting them when they have about two minutes left. Explain that the students will share their drawings in the next lesson.

5 ▶ **Reflect on Visualizing**

Refer to the "Reading Comprehension Strategies" chart and explain that during the last two lessons the students visualized, or created pictures in their minds, of the words they heard. Explain that this is a strategy that readers use to make sense of a story or poem. Write *visualizing* on the chart and point out that this is another strategy they will use this year during their reading.

*Reading Comprehension
Strategies*

- *making connections*
- *visualizing*

INDIVIDUALIZED DAILY READING

6 ▶ **Get to Know the Students' Reading Lives**

Have the students read independently for 15–20 minutes.

Confer with individual students about their reading and monitor their reading levels. Also talk to them further about their reading lives to learn more about their reading attitudes, preferences, and experiences. To guide your discussion, use questions such as:

Q *Tell me about yourself as a reader. What do you like to read?*

Q *Do you have favorite authors or books? What do you like about them?*

Q *What would you like to read this year?*

Q *How do you feel about reading? Why do you [like/dislike] reading?*

Q *What would you like me to do to help you this year?*

Record notes on individual students and use this information to help you make decisions about instruction and your classroom library and to get to know your students as readers.

Day 3

Guided Strategy Practice

In this lesson, the students:

* *Visualize* to enjoy and understand a text
* Read independently for up to 20 minutes
* Take turns listening and talking to one another
* Help one another share

1 ▶ Reread "My Baby Brother" and Review Drawings

Have partners sit together. Explain that today the students will hear "My Baby Brother" again and have a chance to share and discuss the drawings they made. Ask them to turn to their drawings on *Student Response Book* page 3. Tell them that as you reread the poem, you would like them to listen for words or phrases that helped them with their drawings. Reread "My Baby Brother" slowly and clearly.

2 ▶ Share and Discuss Drawings and Words

Use "Turn to Your Partner" to have the students share and discuss their drawings. When partners have had a chance to share, facilitate a whole-class discussion of the visualizing.

Place the transparency of "My Baby Brother" on the overhead projector and underline words or phrases as the students refer to them. Ask:

Q *What words or phrases from the poem helped you draw your picture?*

Q *What did you include in your picture that is not mentioned in the poem? What made you decide to add that to your picture?*

Materials

* "My Baby Brother" in *Fathers, Mothers, Sisters, Brothers* (page 4)
* Completed *Student Response Book* page 3
* Transparency of "My Baby Brother" (BLM12) and an overhead pen
* *Student Response Book*, IDR Journal section

◀ **Teacher Note**

As the students share, circulate and look for partners taking turns and being helpful. Be ready to share your observations later in the lesson.

Teacher Note

This is an opportunity to connect the students' images with their background knowledge. Point out that what they already know about babies helps them get a mental picture of the baby brother (for example, "Joey says that he thought of his baby cousin when he drew his picture").

Reflect on Being Respectful and Helpful

Have the students briefly discuss how they were respectful and helpful during their partner work. Ask:

Q *What did you and your partner do to help one another?*

Q *If your partner has trouble sharing, what are some things you can do to help?*

Briefly share your observations of partners taking turns and being helpful, and remind the students that it is important for everyone to feel respected in the community. Encourage them to continue to work on this in the coming days.

INDIVIDUALIZED DAILY READING

 Get to Know the Students' Reading Lives/Have Them Write in Their IDR Journals

Have the students read independently for 15–20 minutes.

Continue to talk to individual students about their reading lives using the ideas and questions on page 76.

At the end of independent reading, have the students write in their IDR Journals about their reading. Suggest to the students that they might write about a favorite part of the story or why they like a favorite character.

EXTENSIONS

Stroll with "My Baby Brother"

Have the students display their drawings on their desks. Then have them stroll around to view one another's work. As a class, discuss what the students noticed about the pictures.

 Note

Consider having your students with limited English proficiency draw pictures of their favorite parts of their book, rather than write sentences.

Think About Poetry

Tell the students that you would like them to think about what makes a poem a poem. Place the transparency of "My Baby Brother" on the overhead projector. Read the entire first stanza slowly and clearly, and ask:

Q *What do you notice about the words* tiny *and* shiny? *How are they alike?*

If necessary, explain that two or more words that end with the same sound are called *rhyming words*. Explain that you are going to read a little more of the poem, and that you would like them to listen for words that rhyme. Read the first two lines of the second stanza, emphasizing the words *tight* and *white*. Ask:

Q *What rhyming words did you notice in the lines I just read?*

Repeat this process with the last two lines of the second stanza.

Explain that many poems use rhyming and that rhyming is one way for the author to let you know what is coming next in the poem. Facilitate a discussion about other poems with rhymes the students know or have heard.

Ask the students whether they can think of other pairs of words that rhyme. Have a few volunteers share some rhyming words with the class.

 Note

You might want to have your English Language Learners work together to generate a list of rhyming words. Have them write their list on a sheet of chart paper and share it with the whole class. Have them ask the class what rhyming words they can add to the list. Help the students write their words on the list. Keep the list posted and add to it periodically.

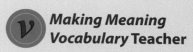 *Making Meaning Vocabulary* **Teacher**

Next week you will revisit *A Tree Is Nice* and "My Baby Brother" to teach Vocabulary Week 6.

Week 2

Overview

UNIT 3: VISUALIZING
Narrative Nonfiction, Poetry, and Fiction

"Dry Skin"
in *Poppleton and Friends*
by Cynthia Rylant, illustrated by Mark Teague
(Scholastic, 1998)

Poppleton has dry skin and his friend Cherry Sue tries to help him get rid of it.

ALTERNATIVE BOOKS

Sun Bread by Elisa Klevin
A Rainbow of My Own by Don Freeman

Comprehension Focus

- Students *visualize* to make sense of text.

- Students informally *use schema and inference* as they visualize.

- Students read independently.

Social Development Focus

- Students analyze the effect of their behavior on others and on the group work.

- Students relate the value of helpfulness to their behavior and interactions.

- Students develop the group skills of taking turns talking and listening and helping one another share.

DO AHEAD

- If possible, collect some non-illustrated books for the students to read independently this week.

- Prepare to model using a self-stick note to mark a place where you visualized (see Day 3, Step 2, page 88).

Making Meaning Vocabulary Teacher

If you are teaching Developmental Studies Center's *Making Meaning Vocabulary* program, teach Vocabulary Week 6 this week. For more information, see the *Making Meaning Vocabulary Teacher's Manual.*

Day 1

Read-aloud

Materials

- "Dry Skin" in *Poppleton and Friends* (page 20)

In this lesson, the students:

- *Visualize* to enjoy and understand a text
- Connect their mental images to the text
- Read independently for up to 20 minutes
- Take turns talking and listening

▶1 Get Ready to Work Together

Have partners sit together. Explain that today you will read a story aloud and the students will have a chance to picture it in their minds. Then partners will talk about their thinking.

▶2 Introduce "Dry Skin"

Explain that today you will read one of the stories from the book *Poppleton and Friends,* written by Cynthia Rylant and illustrated by Mark Teague. This book contains several stories about Poppleton, a pig. Show the back cover and point out Poppleton and his friend Cherry Sue, a llama (a llama is a large South American animal). Explain that these animals are the two characters in today's story, which is called "Dry Skin." Ask:

Q *What is dry skin? How does dry skin feel?*

 Note

If you feel your English Language Learners will need extra support to understand the story, consider showing them the illustrations prior to the read-aloud.

▶3 Read Aloud with Visualizing

Explain that you will read "Dry Skin" aloud without showing the illustrations. Remind the students that the purpose of not showing the pictures is to allow them to make their own mental pictures from the words in the story. Explain that you will stop in the middle of the story and partners will share what they see in their minds about the story so far.

Read the story aloud slowly and clearly, without showing the illustrations and stopping as described below.

Suggested Vocabulary

flaking away: losing small pieces of skin (p. 20)

dandelion: plant with bright yellow flower petals that turn white and feathery and blow away (p. 24)

lint: small bits of thread or fluff that come off clothing (p. 30)

lint brush: brush used to remove lint (p. 32)

wart: small, hard lump on the skin (p. 34)

ELL Vocabulary

English Language Learners may benefit from discussing additional vocabulary, including:

french fries: thin strips of potato fried in oil (p. 24)

desert: large area of land that is hot and dry (p. 27)

Read pages 20–23 twice. Stop after:

> **p. 23**   "He put on some oil."

Use "Think, Pair, Share" to have the students discuss what they see happening in their minds so far. After 20–30 seconds, have the students bring their attention back to you. Reread the last sentence before the stop and continue reading to the next stop. Follow this procedure after:

> **p. 27**   "'I'll be right over,' said Cherry Sue."

> **p. 33**   "…and swept away all the crumbs."

Continue reading to the end of the story.

◀ **Teacher Note**

Reading the first few pages of the story twice gives the students a chance to engage with the story and create a visual image.

4 Discuss the Story

At the end of the story, facilitate a whole-class discussion. Ask:

Q *What does Poppleton think his problem is in the first part of the story?*

Q *What does Poppleton's real problem turn out to be? How does Cherry Sue help Poppleton solve his problem?*

FACILITATION TIP

Continue to support the students in taking responsibility for listening carefully during discussions by **asking a question once** without repeating or rewording it. Remember to use wait-time before calling on anyone so the students have a chance to think before talking. Encourage the students to have you repeat a question if they didn't hear it, or say it in a different way if they are confused.

ELL Note

You might support students
with limited English proficiency
by providing a prompt for
responding to this question,
such as "It's important to be
helpful because…." (For more
information about supporting
English Language Learners at
various levels of proficiency,
see pages xxviii–xxxv.)

5 ▶ Connect the Reading to the Partner Work

Remind the students that they have just been discussing how
Cherry Sue is helpful to her friend Poppleton in "Dry Skin." Explain
that being helpful is an important part of working with a partner.
Facilitate a discussion using the following questions:

Q *What are some reasons Cherry Sue is helpful to Poppleton?*

Q *Why is it important to be helpful to one another in our
partner work?*

Explain that the students will talk more about "Dry Skin" in the
next lesson.

INDIVIDUALIZED DAILY READING

6 ▶ Get to Know the Students' Reading Lives/ Have Them Discuss Reading

Have the students read books at their appropriate reading levels
independently for 15–20 minutes.

Continue to talk to individual students about their reading lives
using the ideas and questions on page 76.

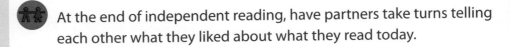

At the end of independent reading, have partners take turns telling
each other what they liked about what they read today.

Day 2

Guided Strategy Practice

In this lesson, the students:

- *Visualize* to enjoy and understand a story
- Connect their mental images to the story
- Read independently for up to 20 minutes
- Take turns talking and listening to one another

Materials

- "Dry Skin" in *Poppleton and Friends* (page 20)

1 ▶ Get Ready to Take Turns Talking and Listening

Have partners sit together. Explain that today the students will revisit "Dry Skin" and they will have another chance to practice picturing parts of the story and talking about their mental pictures with their partners. Facilitate a brief discussion about how they will make sure each partner has a turn to talk. Tell them you will check with them at the end of the lesson to see how they did.

2 ▶ Review "Dry Skin"

Show the back cover of *Poppleton and Friends*, and ask:

Q   *What do you remember about the story "Dry Skin"?*

 Have partners talk, and then have one or two volunteers share with the class.

3 ▶ Model Visualizing

Explain that you will reread part of "Dry Skin" without showing the illustrations. Ask the students to think about what they picture in their minds and what words help them visualize the story.

Read the following sentences aloud:

p. 20 "'Yikes!' he cried. 'Dry skin!' He looked closer. 'I am flaking away.'"

Model visualizing by thinking aloud about how the words "flaking away" give you a mental image. (For example, you might say, "When I hear the words 'flaking away' I see Poppleton's skin falling off like snowflakes falling to the ground.")

4 ▶ Read Aloud with Visualizing

Explain that you are going to read two more parts of the story, and the students will close their eyes and visualize the words. Then they will describe their mental images to their partners and the class. Ask the students to close their eyes and picture the words as you read. Read the following sentence aloud:

p. 22 "'Cherry Sue,' said Poppleton, 'I am as dry as an old apple.'"

 First in pairs, and then as a class, discuss:

Q *How do you picture Poppleton? How do the words "dry as an old apple" help you get a picture of Poppleton's dry skin?*

Call on two or three volunteers to share their images and how the words helped them create the pictures.

Repeat the process with the following passage:

p. 28 "When she walked into Poppleton's house, Cherry Sue saw twenty empty french fry bags and a chair full of crumbs."

 First in pairs, and then as a class, discuss the students' mental images. Ask:

Q *What do you see in your mind? What words help you get this picture?*

If the students have trouble connecting their mental pictures to the text, try asking additional questions such as:

Q *What do you see Cherry Sue doing when she sees 20 empty bags and a chair full of crumbs? What is her facial expression?*

Teacher Note ▶

The purpose of having the students close their eyes is to help them to focus on their mental pictures. Talking with their partners about their mental pictures helps them identify words or phrases that trigger those images and reinforces the idea that all readers create unique images of the same text.

Q *What does the room look like? What does the chair look like? Where are the empty bags?*

 Note

Questions such as these will help your students form more concrete mental images.

5 ▶ **Reflect on Visualizing and Working Together**

Have the students think about how visualizing helped them think about and enjoy the story. Ask:

Q *What do you like about visualizing when you are listening to or reading a story?*

Q *What did you and your partner do to make sure you each got a turn to talk? How did that help your work?*

Remind the students that they have been learning to visualize to help them better understand and enjoy books they read independently. Tell them that tomorrow they will have a chance to practice visualizing as they read on their own.

INDIVIDUALIZED DAILY READING

6 ▶ **Get to Know the Students' Reading Lives/ Have Them Discuss Reading**

Have the students read independently for 15–20 minutes.

Continue to talk to individual students about their reading lives. At the end of independent reading, discuss as a whole class what the students are reading. Ask questions such as:

Q *What is the title of the book you read today?*

Q *What is the story about?*

Q *Would you tell a friend to read it? Why or why not?*

Day 3

Materials

- "Dry Skin" in *Poppleton and Friends* (page 20)
- Books at appropriate levels for independent reading, including some books without illustrations
- Small self-stick notes for each student
- *Assessment Resource Book*

Independent Strategy Practice

In this lesson, the students:

- *Visualize* to enjoy and understand texts read independently
- Connect their mental images to the text
- Read independently for up to 20 minutes
- Take turns talking and listening
- Are helpful to one another

▶1 Prepare to Practice Visualizing Independently

Review the previous lessons, in which the students used the words in a story to help them picture what was happening. Explain that today the students will read their independent books and think about the pictures they create in their minds. At the end of the independent reading time, the students will share their mental images with one another. Ask:

Q *How do you want other students to act while you are reading? How will that be helpful?*

Q *How will you act while you are reading?*

▶2 Model Visualizing with Independent Books

Teacher Note

Have an image in mind ahead of time so this modeling goes smoothly. (You might say, "I can picture a big puffy armchair with little white grains of salt and pieces of french fry all over the seat and french fry bags crumpled up on the floor. I'm going to stick my note here next to this description.")

Explain that as they read today, the students will use self-stick notes to mark places in their books where they visualized the story. The purpose of using the self-stick notes is to help them refer to those places when they discuss their mental images with their partners.

Model the procedure by rereading page 28 of "Dry Skin" aloud. Think aloud about your mental image and place a self-stick note in the page's margin.

3 Read Independently and Practice Visualizing

Make sure the students have books that are appropriate for their reading levels. Encourage them to read non-illustrated books, if possible, and emphasize that even if their books have pictures, you want them to imagine or picture what the words mean. Have them read independently for 15–20 minutes. Stop them at 5-minute intervals and have them use "Turn to Your Partner" to talk about the passages they marked and the mental pictures they created.

Circulate among the students and notice whether they are able to visualize images that connect to their reading. Some students may have difficulty creating mental images, especially those who are reading picture books. You might ask those students to reread descriptive words or phrases and then close the book and describe what they see in their mind, or ask them to act out part of the story briefly.

 Note

Note challenging vocabulary in the students' independent reading books and be ready to define necessary words for them as they read.

CLASS COMPREHENSION ASSESSMENT

During the discussion, notice what the students are visualizing. Ask yourself:

Q *Are the students able to describe how the text helps them visualize?*

Q *Are they using their background knowledge and/or inference to help them visualize?*

Record your observations on page 9 of the *Assessment Resource Book.*

4 Discuss the Students' Mental Pictures

Have a volunteer read aloud one or two sentences she marked and ask the class to listen carefully and try to visualize as they hear the sentences. After the reading, facilitate a brief discussion among the students by asking:

Q *What did you see in your mind when [Dana] read [her] passage?*

Q *Which words helped you create your mental image?*

Teacher Note ▶

Keep this part of the lesson moving. Select relatively fluent readers to read their sentences aloud to the class.

Have the volunteer who read the sentences share her own mental picture for the passage. Repeat this procedure with one or two other volunteers.

5 ▶ Reflect on the Partner Work

Facilitate a brief whole-class discussion of how the students did during independent reading. Ask:

Q *What did you do to be helpful during the independent reading and while you were talking with your partner? Why was that helpful?*

   Students might say:

   "I read my book and pictured the story in my mind until it was time to talk to my partner."

   "It helped our work because we weren't bothering each other during the reading time."

Tell the students that they will have more opportunities to practice visualizing in their independent reading.

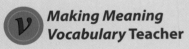

***Making Meaning Vocabulary* Teacher**

Next week you will revisit "Dry Skin" to teach Vocabulary Week 7.

Week 3

Overview

UNIT 3: VISUALIZING
Narrative Nonfiction, Poetry, and Fiction

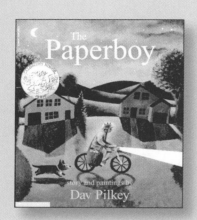

The Paperboy
by Dav Pilkey
(Scholastic, 1997)

A paperboy and his dog enjoy the quiet of the early morning as they deliver their newspapers.

ALTERNATIVE BOOKS

The Salamander Room by Anne Mazer
Fireflies! by Julie Brinckloe

Comprehension Focus

• Students *visualize* to make sense of a text.

• Students informally *use schema and inference* as they visualize.

• Students read independently.

Social Development Focus

• Students analyze the effect of their behavior on others and on the group work.

• Students relate the values of caring and helpfulness to their behavior and interactions.

• Students develop the group skills of taking turns talking and listening.

DO AHEAD

• If possible, collect some non-illustrated books for the students to read independently this week.

• Conceal the cover of *The Paperboy* (see the "Teacher Note" on page 94).

• Make copies of the Unit 3 Parent Letter (BLM3) to send home with the students on the last day of the unit. (For more information about the Parent Letters, see page xxxviii.)

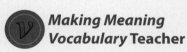

Making Meaning Vocabulary Teacher

If you are teaching Developmental Studies Center's *Making Meaning Vocabulary* program, teach Vocabulary Week 7 this week. For more information, see the *Making Meaning Vocabulary Teacher's Manual*.

Day 1

Materials

- *The Paperboy*
- "Reading Comprehension Strategies" chart and a marker
- "Resource Sheet for IDR Conferences"
- *Student Response Book,* IDR Journal section

Reading Comprehension Strategies

- making connections
- visualizing

Teacher Note ▶

Conceal the cover of *The Paperboy* before you read the book to encourage the students to create their own mental images and tap into their background knowledge and experiences. (You will show the students the first few pages, which establish the setting and context for the story but do not show any of the action.)

Read-aloud

In this lesson, the students:

- *Visualize* to enjoy and understand a story
- Read independently for up to 20 minutes
- Take turns talking and listening

1 Review Visualizing

Have partners sit together. Refer to the "Reading Comprehension Strategies" chart and remind the students that they have been using the words in stories to help them visualize or create a picture in their minds.

Explain that today they will hear another story, think about it, and talk to their partners about how they picture what is happening.

2 Introduce *The Paperboy*

Show the title page of the book and read the title and the author's name aloud. Explain that this is a book about a paperboy and his dog enjoying the quiet of the early morning as they deliver their papers. Explain that a paperboy is a boy who delivers newspapers as a job.

To help the students visualize the setting, show the illustrations on pages 1–5 and explain that the truck is dropping off the papers for the boy to deliver.

3 Read Aloud with Visualizing

Explain that you will read the story without showing the illustrations, as you did in the last few lessons. Ask the students to listen carefully and think about and visualize what is happening in the story. Explain that you will stop four times during the story and each time partners will talk about their mental pictures.

Read the book as described below.

Suggested Vocabulary

loaded down: carrying something heavy (p. 16)

route: path to all of the houses a paperboy or a delivery person delivers to (p. 18)

birdbaths: wide shallow bowls filled with water for birds to bathe in (p. 20)

fade away: disappear slowly (p. 25)

ELL Vocabulary

English Language Learners may benefit from discussing this additional vocabulary:

knows his route by heart: remembers where to go (p. 18)

Read pages 6–9 aloud twice, slowly and clearly. Stop after:

p. 9   "…but they do."

Have the students use "Think, Pair, Share" to talk about what they see happening so far. Ask:

Q   *What did you see in your mind when I read this part of the story?*

Have a few volunteers share their mental pictures with the class. As the students share, ask which words or phrases helped them create a mental picture. Reread the last sentence before the stop and continue reading to the next stop. Follow the same procedure at the next three stops:

p. 14   "And out to the garage where they quickly fold their papers, snapping on green rubber bands and placing them in a large red bag."

p. 20   "…and which cats are for growling at."

p. 27   "And his empty red bag flaps behind him in the cold morning air."

Reread page 27 and continue reading to the end of the book.

◀ **Teacher Note**

Reading the first few pages twice helps the students get a mental picture of the story.

FACILITATION TIP

This week, continue to focus on **asking a question once** without repeating or rewording it. Also, take time to reflect on your experience over the past few weeks with this technique. Does the technique feel comfortable and natural? Are you using it throughout the day? What effect has the technique had on the students' attentiveness and responsiveness during discussions? We encourage you to continue to use and reflect on this technique throughout the year.

 Discuss the Story

At the end of the story, facilitate a discussion about the book. Have the students turn to their partners to discuss the questions before sharing as a whole class.

Q *What are some of the things the paperboy does to get ready to deliver the newspapers?*

Q *What does the paperboy's dog do?*

Q *What are some of the pictures you had in your mind of the paperboy and his dog?*

Explain that in the next lesson the students will hear the story again and draw a picture of a part they see clearly in their mind.

 Reflect on Working Together

Ask:

Q *What do you like about working with a partner?*

Remind the students that the purpose of talking in pairs is to make sure everyone has a chance to share their thinking and to build their skills for working together.

If the students bring up any problems they had, facilitate a discussion about how they might avoid these problems the next time they work with a partner.

INDIVIDUALIZED DAILY READING

Confer with Individual Students

Have the students read books at their appropriate reading levels independently for 15–20 minutes.

As you confer with students today, use the questions and suggestions on the "Resource Sheet for IDR Conferences."

At the end of independent reading, have the students talk in pairs about whether or not they are enjoying their books. Circulate as the students share and identify students who might need help finding more appropriate books.

Give each student time to record the title of his book in the "Reading Log" section of his *Student Response Book*.

EXTENSION

Think About Lists

Remind the students that earlier in the lesson they talked about the "Reading Comprehension Strategies" chart. Explain that the "Reading Comprehension Strategies" chart is an example of a list. A list is a written record of a series of things that go together. Facilitate a discussion about lists and the purposes they serve by asking questions such as:

Q *What other lists do you see in the classroom? What are they used for?*

Q *What other lists can you think of that you've seen outside our class?*

Q *How are lists helpful?*

Let the students know that they will be adding more items to the list of "Reading Comprehension Strategies" as the year goes on.

ELL Note

You might want to show your English Language Learners concrete examples of lists (for example, shopping lists, to-do lists or lists of friends' names and addresses).

Day 2

Materials

- *The Paperboy*
- *Student Response Book* page 4
- Chart paper and a marker
- Crayons and markers
- "Resource Sheet for IDR Conferences"

Guided Strategy Practice

In this lesson, the students:

- *Visualize* to enjoy and understand a story
- Draw their mental images
- Connect their mental images to the text
- Read independently for up to 20 minutes
- Act in a caring way

▶1 Prepare to Reread and Draw Mental Pictures

Have partners sit together. Explain that today you will reread *The Paperboy* and the students will practice visualizing the story. After partners talk about what they saw in their minds, each student will draw a picture of part of the story.

▶2 Discuss Acting in Caring Ways

Facilitate a brief discussion about caring and kind ways to talk about other people's pictures and writing. Ask questions such as:

Q *What do we want to keep in mind when we're drawing today to make sure we act in a caring way toward one another?*

Q *Why is this important in our community?*

▶3 Reread *The Paperboy*

Read the book title and author's name aloud. Ask:

Q *What happens in* The Paperboy?

 Have the students talk in pairs then have a few volunteers briefly share with the class.

Reread *The Paperboy,* slowly and clearly, without showing the illustrations.

 Draw Mental Pictures

Explain that the students will use crayons or markers to draw a picture of a part of the story that they saw very clearly in their minds as they listened. Explain that each student will draw a picture, and then write about what is happening in it. Ask the students to think quietly about their mental pictures, and then continue to work quietly as they draw on *Student Response Book* page 4, "How I Pictured *The Paperboy*."

As the students draw, circulate among them. To help them get started, you might model doing a brief sketch on a sheet of chart paper and writing a sentence that describes the picture. Note which students need encouragement to get started and which need to add details to their drawings.

 Note

This activity is especially helpful for your English Language Learners.

◀ **Teacher Note**

Remind the students that their mental pictures are more important than their drawings. They should try their best to capture on paper what they see in their minds.

 Share and Discuss Drawings

 Have the students use "Turn to Your Partner" to discuss their drawings and writing with their partners. Remind them to think about how they can be respectful when viewing and discussing other people's drawings.

As the partners share, circulate among them. Observe the students' interactions and their responsiveness to each other's ideas. Note whether or not they are expressing interest in and appreciation for their partners' work.

 Reflect on Acting in Caring Ways

Have the students reflect on how they did acting in caring ways toward one another during the lesson. Point out examples you noticed. If you noticed problems, point these out without mentioning the students' names and discuss them using questions such as:

Q *How might it feel to have someone [put down your drawing]?*

Q *Why is it important that we try to avoid hurting one another's feelings in our community?*

Q *What can we do to make things better if we realize we have hurt someone's feelings?*

Tell the students they will have more chances to talk about their mental pictures and practice acting in caring ways.

INDIVIDUALIZED DAILY READING

7 ▶ Confer with Individual Students/Have Them Write or Draw About Visualizing

Have the students read independently for 15–20 minutes.

Continue to monitor the students' reading levels and comprehension. As you confer with individual students, refer to the "Resource Sheet for IDR Conferences" for questions and suggestions.

At the end of independent reading, have the students draw two of their mental pictures from their reading. Ask:

Q *What mental pictures come to mind as you read today?*

Q *Which two mental pictures did you find were the most helpful as you read today?*

EXTENSIONS

Stroll with *The Paperboy*

Have the students display their drawings of *The Paperboy* on their desks. Then have them stroll around to look at one another's work. As a class, discuss what the students noticed about the pictures and writing.

Show Illustrations and Retell *The Paperboy*

Have volunteers retell *The Paperboy* as you show the illustrations to the class.

ELL Note

This extension is especially helpful for your English Language Learners.

Think About Alternative Endings

Explain that one way to learn about a story is to imagine what would be different if something in the story changed. Model by saying, "I'm imagining what would happen if the boy didn't get up when he was supposed to. Delivering the papers wouldn't be so peaceful. He would have to rush to get done, and he might have some angry neighbors." Ask:

Q   *How would the story be different if the boy ran out of papers before he was done?*

Q   *What else could happen that would change the story?*

Encourage the students to think about different ways that the stories they are reading independently might end.

Day 3

Materials

- Books at appropriate levels for independent reading, including some books without illustrations
- Small self-stick notes for each student
- *Assessment Resource Book*
- Unit 3 Parent Letter (BLM3)

Independent Strategy Practice

In this lesson, the students:

- *Visualize* to enjoy and understand stories read independently
- Connect their mental images to the text
- Read independently for up to 20 minutes
- Act in helpful and caring ways

1 ▶ Review Visualizing Independently

Remind the students that in the previous lessons they learned to visualize to help them understand and enjoy texts. Explain that today they will have another chance to visualize with their independent books. Explain that they will use self-stick notes to mark places where they create mental pictures as they read. This will help them discuss their mental pictures in pairs later.

2 ▶ Read Independently and Practice Visualizing

Teacher Note

If necessary, model this procedure again for students, as you did on Day 3 of Week 2 (see page 88).

Make sure the students have texts that are appropriate for their reading level. Encourage them to read non-illustrated books, if possible. Emphasize that even if their books have pictures, they should try to imagine or picture for themselves what the words are saying. Have the students read independently for 15–20 minutes.

CLASS COMPREHENSION ASSESSMENT

Circulate among the students and notice whether they are able to visualize images that connect to the reading. Ask yourself:

Q *Are the students marking descriptive words or phrases in the text?*

continues

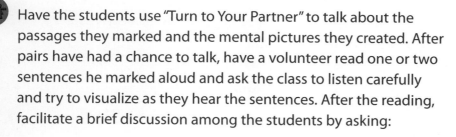

CLASS COMPREHENSION ASSESSMENT *continued*

Q *Are the students using their own experience to help them visualize?*

Record your observations on page 10 of the *Assessment Resource Book*.

3 ▶ Discuss Mental Pictures

Have the students use "Turn to Your Partner" to talk about the passages they marked and the mental pictures they created. After pairs have had a chance to talk, have a volunteer read one or two sentences he marked aloud and ask the class to listen carefully and try to visualize as they hear the sentences. After the reading, facilitate a brief discussion among the students by asking:

Q *What did you see in your mind when [Reuben] read his passage?*

Q *Which words helped you create your mental image?*

Have the volunteer who read the sentences share his own mental picture for the passage. Repeat this procedure with one or two other volunteers.

Explain that the students will think more about stories and discuss their independent reading again in the coming days. Emphasize that the students will not always be expected to mark places where they picture a story in their mind, but they will always be expected to think about the mental images they create as they read.

4 ▶ Reflect on Working Together

Review that during this unit the students focused on taking turns talking and listening and on being helpful and caring. Use "Think, Pair, Share" to have the students discuss questions such as:

Q *What is one way you have learned to be helpful to your partner?*

Teacher Note

This is the last week in Unit 3. You will need to reassign partners for Unit 4.

Grade Two | 103

Q *What is our class doing to be caring and helpful during class discussions? What do we want to work on?*

Encourage the students to continue to think about ways to be caring and helpful as they interact in the coming days.

INDIVIDUAL COMPREHENSION ASSESSMENT

Before continuing with Unit 4, take this opportunity to assess individual students' progress in *visualizing* to make sense of text. Please refer to pages 32–33 in the *Assessment Resource Book* for instructions.

EXTENSION

Make a Class Book

Read a non-illustrated book aloud to the students twice. Have partners work together to illustrate various parts of the story. View the illustrations as a class and talk about which words in the text helped them illustrate the story. Compile the students' drawings to create a class book.

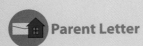

Parent Letter

Send home with each student the Parent Letter for this unit (see "Do Ahead," page 93). Periodically, have a few students share with the class what they are reading at home.

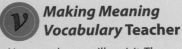

***Making Meaning Vocabulary* Teacher**

Next week you will revisit *The Paperboy* to teach Vocabulary Week 8.

Making Inferences

FICTION

During this unit, the students use inference to understand characters' feelings, motivations, and actions. They also informally explore narrative text structure, including character and plot. During IDR the students make inferences about the characters in the books they read independently. Socially, they take responsibility for their learning and behavior and develop the group skill of explaining their thinking.

Week 1 *What Mary Jo Shared* by Janice May Udry

Week 2 *Erandi's Braids* by Antonio Hernández Madrigal

Week 3 *Chester's Way* by Kevin Henkes

Week 1 Overview

UNIT 4: MAKING INFERENCES
Fiction

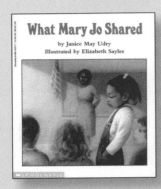

What Mary Jo Shared
by Janice May Udry, illustrated by Elizabeth Sayles
(Scholastic, 1991)

Mary Jo uses an original idea to solve the problem of what to share with her class.

ALTERNATIVE BOOKS

Luka's Quilt by Georgia Guback

Emily's Art by Peter Catalanotto

Comprehension Focus

• Students *make inferences* to understand characters' feelings, motivations, and actions.

• Students informally *explore text structure* in narrative texts, including character and plot.

• Students read independently.

Social Development Focus

• Students take responsibility for their learning and behavior.

• Students develop the group skill of explaining their thinking.

• Students participate in a check-in class meeting.

DO AHEAD

• Prior to Day 1, decide how you will randomly assign partners to work together during the unit.

• Prior to Day 2, label a sheet of chart paper "What Mary Jo Shared." Under this title, create two columns labeled "What does Mary Jo do?" and "What does this tell us about Mary Jo?" (see the example on page 113).

• Collect a variety of narrative texts for the students to read independently throughout the unit.

• Make multiple copies of the "IDR Conference Notes" record sheet from the blackline master on page BLM16. This week you will begin using these to document IDR conferences in order to track individual students' growth in their independent reading. You will continue to use these sheets throughout the program. (For more about documenting IDR conferences, see page xxvi.)

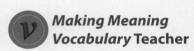

Making Meaning Vocabulary Teacher

If you are teaching Developmental Studies Center's *Making Meaning Vocabulary* program, teach Vocabulary Week 8 this week. For more information, see the *Making Meaning Vocabulary Teacher's Manual*.

Read-aloud

Materials

- *What Mary Jo Shared*
- "IDR Conference Notes" record sheets (to be used during IDR throughout the program)

In this lesson, the students:

- Hear and discuss a story
- Use examples from the story to support their thinking
- Read independently for up to 20 minutes
- Explain their thinking
- Begin working with new partners

About Making Inferences About Characters

In this unit, the students informally explore character, a key element of narrative text structure. They make inferences to understand characters' traits, relationships, and development. They come to understand that stories are about characters, the problems they face, and how they deal with those problems. (For more information about *making inferences* and *understanding text structure,* see pages xv–xvi.)

In this unit, provide a wide variety of narrative fiction and nonfiction for students to read independently.

Being a Writer™ **Teacher**

You can either have the students work with their *Being a Writer* partner or assign them a different partner for the *Making Meaning* lessons.

❶ Pair Students and Get Ready to Work Together

Assign partners, have them sit together, and make sure the students know their partners' names. Explain that for the next three weeks the students will work with the same partners. Remind the students that it is important to explain their thinking clearly to their partners. Ask:

Q *What do you want to keep in mind to be a responsible partner during today's lesson? Why is that important?*

Students might say:

"I have to say something. It can't just be my partner talking."

"If I don't understand my partner, I can ask her to repeat what she said."

"I can help my partner remember the story."

Introduce *What Mary Jo Shared*

Show the cover of *What Mary Jo Shared* and read the title and the names of the author and illustrator. Remind the students that in previous weeks they made connections to their own lives and visualized, or made pictures in their minds, to help them understand stories. Encourage the students to make connections and visualize as they listen to *What Mary Jo Shared* today.

 Read *What Mary Jo Shared* Aloud

Read the book aloud, showing the illustrations and stopping as described below.

> **Suggested Vocabulary**
>
> **clustered:** gathered (p. 13)
> **became determined:** decided (p. 16)
> **pondered:** thought about things carefully (p. 21)
>
> **ELL Vocabulary**
>
> English Language Learners may benefit from discussing additional vocabulary, including:
>
> **tag:** label (p. 6)
> **shook her head and looked at the floor:** looked down when she shook her head "no" (p. 9)
> **grasshopper:** insect that has long legs and can jump a long way (p. 11)
> **woods:** group of trees (p. 16)
> **as usual:** like always (p. 21)
> **saluted:** raised their hands to their hearts as a sign of respect (p. 22)

Stop after:

p. 15   "Mary Jo shook her head and looked at the floor."

Ask:

Q   *What has happened in the story so far?*

Have the students use "Turn to Your Partner" to discuss the question. Reread the last sentence on page 15 and continue reading to page 21. Stop after:

p. 21   "'Wait and see,' said Mary Jo."

 ELL Note

You may wish to explain that every day the students in Mary Jo's class have a chance to share, or tell about, something they have brought to class, such as a pet or a letter they received in the mail.

 ELL Note

English Language Learners may benefit from an earlier stop to discuss what is happening in the story—for example, at the end of page 9.

Ask:

Q *What do you think Mary Jo will do? What in the story makes you think that?*

 Have the students use "Turn to Your Partner" to discuss the question. Reread the last sentence on page 21 and continue reading to the end of the story.

4 ▶ Discuss the Story

Facilitate a whole-class discussion of the story using questions such as:

Q *What happens in this story?*

Q *What problems does Mary Jo face in this story? How does she solve them?*

Q *Does the story end the way you expected it to? Explain your thinking.*

Explain that all stories have characters in them—characters that face problems. Knowing this can help them think about the stories they read. Tell the students that they will continue to explore characters in stories in the coming weeks.

Teacher Note

This unit will give you an opportunity to meet with each student and practice using the "IDR Conference Notes" record sheet to conduct and document individual student conferences. Each conference should take 5–8 minutes. It is suggested that in the future units, you meet more frequently with struggling students.

INDIVIDUALIZED DAILY READING

 5 ▶ Start Using the "IDR Conference Notes" Record Sheet to Document Conferences

Have the students read books at their appropriate reading levels independently for 15–20 minutes.

Tell the students that starting this week during IDR, you will spend more time conferring, or talking with them one-on-one, about their books so that you can get to know each of them better and help them become stronger readers.

Tell the students that you will ask them to choose a book that they can read and enjoy. During the conference, you will have them read a part of the book, and then talk about what they have read.

Before conducting the first reading conference, facilitate a brief discussion about the importance of everyone else reading independently while you meet with a student.

Select a student and have him bring a book he can read to the conference. Use one or two of the questions on the "IDR Conference Notes" to guide your reading conference. Jot down the student's responses as well as any other notes that you think are important on the "IDR Conference Notes" (for example, "reads fluently and with understanding" or "does not have a strategy for attacking an unfamiliar word").

During IDR conferences, it is important for each student to be reading a book at his appropriate level. If you begin a conference and find that a student is not in an appropriate book, stop documenting the conference and help him find a different book. Document an IDR conference with the student on another day.

Pause between conferences to circulate among the students and check in with them.

At the end of independent reading, facilitate a brief discussion about how IDR conference time went. Have a few students share their reading with the class.

Day 2

Materials

- *What Mary Jo Shared*
- "What Mary Jo Shared" chart, prepared ahead, and a marker
- *Assessment Resource Book*
- "IDR Conference Notes" record sheets

Strategy Lesson

In this lesson, the students:

- *Make inferences* about characters as they hear a story
- Use examples from the story to support their thinking
- Read independently for up to 20 minutes
- Explain their thinking and listen to one another

▶ 1 Discuss Explaining Thinking Clearly

Have partners sit together. Explain that today they will hear *What Mary Jo Shared* read aloud again, and they will talk to each other about their thinking. Ask:

Q *Why will it be important for you to explain your thinking clearly to your partner today?*

Q *What can happen if partners don't explain their thinking clearly?*

Encourage them to explain their thinking clearly and tell them you will check in with them at the end of the lesson to see how they did.

▶ 2 Reread *What Mary Jo Shared*

Explain that you will reread *What Mary Jo Shared*. Ask the students to listen carefully and think about Mary Jo, what is happening to her in the story, and how she feels.

Reread the story aloud.

▶ 3 Introduce the "What Mary Jo Shared" Chart

Point out that often what a character does, says, and thinks in a story gives the reader clues about how the character feels. Explain that in today's lesson, the students will use a chart to help them think about what they know about Mary Jo's feelings.

Direct the students' attention to the "What Mary Jo Shared" chart. Have the students read each of the questions.

Refer to the left-hand column, and ask:

Q *What are some important things that Mary Jo does in the story?*

Have the students use "Turn to Your Partner" to talk about the question. Have several students share their ideas with the class. As they share, record their ideas in the "What does Mary Jo do?" column. For example:

> ### What Mary Jo Shared
>
> | What does Mary Jo do? | What does this tell us about Mary Jo? |
> |---|---|
> | - Mary Jo decides to bring an umbrella to school, but lots of students have umbrellas. | |

◀ **Teacher Note**

To keep the lesson moving, record only four or five ideas. Be sure to record ideas from the beginning, middle, and end of the story.

Remind the students that the things characters do in a story often give us clues about how they feel. Read the first entry in the left-hand column and ask:

Q *When Mary Jo does this, what does it tell you about her? How might she be feeling?*

Q *Do you agree or disagree with [Molly]? Why?*

Q *What can you add to what [Gregory] said?*

Record the students' responses in the "What does this tell us about Mary Jo?" column of the chart.

Repeat this process with two or three more of the ideas listed in the "What does Mary Jo do?" column.

Teacher Note

If the students refer only to basic emotions, such as "sad," "happy," and "mad," think aloud about other emotions Mary Jo might have. (For example, you might say, "I think Mary Jo might have felt a little frustrated or disappointed.")

Teacher Note

The students will need to infer to understand Mary Jo's feelings. For example, the students might say that Mary Jo felt sad or disappointed when she saw the umbrellas. Although these feelings are not stated explicitly, they can be inferred from clues such as "I guess that isn't a good thing to share" (page 9).

4 ▶ Introduce Making Inferences About Characters

Refer to one of the entries in the right-hand column of the chart (for example, "Mary Jo is disappointed") and point out that the story never says directly that Mary Jo is disappointed. The students used clues in the story to figure out how she is feeling. When readers use clues to figure out things about characters, they are *making inferences* about the characters.

5 ▶ Reflect on Explaining Thinking Clearly

Facilitate a brief discussion about how the students did explaining their thinking today. Ask:

Q *How did you and your partner do explaining your thinking clearly today?*

Q *What problems, if any, did you have explaining your thinking? What did you do to solve the problems? How did that help?*

INDIVIDUALIZED DAILY READING

6 ▶ Document IDR Conferences

Review the procedure for IDR conferences and continue to use the "IDR Conference Notes" record sheet to conduct and document individual conferences.

Have the students read independently for 15–20 minutes.

At the end of independent reading, facilitate a brief discussion about how IDR conference time went. Have a few students share their reading with the class.

Day 3

Materials

- "Class Meeting Ground Rules" chart
- *Student Response Book,* IDR Journal section
- "IDR Conference Notes" record sheets

Class Meeting Ground Rules

- one person talks at a time
- listen to one another

 ELL Note

If necessary, provide prompts for your students' response, such as "I need to work on…."

Class Meeting

In this lesson, the students:

- Review ground rules and procedure for a class meeting
- Analyze the ways they have been interacting
- Think about how they are handling books and materials
- Read independently for up to 20 minutes

1 Gather for a Class Meeting

Before the class meeting, make sure the "Class Meeting Ground Rules" chart is posted where everyone can see it. Review the procedures for coming to a class meeting. Have the students move into a circle with partners sitting together. Make sure all the students can see their classmates. Remind the students that they are working to create a caring and safe learning community of readers.

Review the ground rules and tell the students that at the end of the class meeting you will ask them how they think they did following the rules.

2 Discuss Taking Responsibility

Explain that the purpose of this class meeting is to check in on how the students are taking responsibility during whole-class discussions and independent reading.

Have the students use "Think, Pair, Share" to discuss:

Q *What has been going well for you during our whole-class discussions?*

Q *What do we need to work on?*

Q *What has been working well during independent reading time? What do we need to work on?*

If necessary, probe the students' thinking by asking questions such as:

Q *How are we sharing books? Putting books back in their proper place? Reading quietly?*

Students might say:

"We listen during the read-aloud."

"Some people still don't talk loud enough even when I ask them to please talk a little louder."

"Sometimes people talk during independent reading, and I can't concentrate."

Briefly discuss how the students did today following the ground rules, and adjourn the class meeting.

INDIVIDUALIZED DAILY READING

 ## 3 Document IDR Conferences/Have the Students Write in Their IDR Journals

Review the procedure for IDR conferences and continue to use the "IDR Conference Notes" record sheet to conduct and document individual conferences.

Have the students read independently for 15–20 minutes.

At the end of independent reading, have the students write a few sentences in their IDR Journals about what they like about the characters in their books.

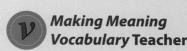
***Making Meaning Vocabulary* Teacher**

Next week you will revisit *What Mary Jo Shared* to teach Vocabulary Week 9.

Week 2

Overview

UNIT 4: MAKING INFERENCES
Fiction

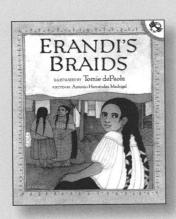

Erandi's Braids*

by Antonio Hernández Madrigal, illustrated by Tomie dePaola
(Puffin, 2001)

Erandi hopes for a new dress for her birthday. But when her mother finds holes in the fishing net, Erandi wonders how they will get the money for the things they need.

* This book is also used in Unit 9.

ALTERNATIVE BOOKS

The Story of Ruby Bridges by Robert Coles

Keep the Lights Burning, Abbie by Peter and Connie Roop

Comprehension Focus

• Students *make inferences* to understand characters.

• Students informally *explore text structure* in narrative texts, including character and plot.

• Students read independently.

Social Development Focus

• Students take responsibility for their learning and behavior.

• Students develop the group skill of explaining their thinking.

DO AHEAD

• Prior to Day 2, label a sheet of chart paper "Erandi's Braids." Under this title, create two columns labeled "What does Erandi do?" and "What does this tell us about Erandi?" (see the example on page 124).

• Prepare to model making an inference about a character in independent reading (see Day 3, Step 3 on pages 126–127).

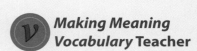 **Making Meaning Vocabulary Teacher**

If you are teaching Developmental Studies Center's *Making Meaning Vocabulary* program, teach Vocabulary Week 9 this week. For more information, see the *Making Meaning Vocabulary Teacher's Manual.*

Day 1

Read-aloud

Materials

- *Erandi's Braids*
- "IDR Conference Notes" record sheets

In this lesson, the students:

- Hear and discuss a story
- Use examples from the story to support their thinking
- Read independently for up to 20 minutes
- Explain their thinking and listen to one another

▶ 1 Get Ready to Work Together

Have partners sit together. Remind the students that they are responsible for thinking and sharing in pairs. Part of that responsibility is to make sure that they can hear and understand what their partners and classmates say.

▶ 2 Introduce *Erandi's Braids*

Show the cover of *Erandi's Braids* and read the title and the names of the author and illustrator. Explain that the main character in the story is a girl named Erandi who lives with her mother in a village in Mexico. In this story, Erandi's birthday is coming and her family doesn't have much money to buy her a gift.

▶ 3 Read *Erandi's Braids* Aloud

Read the story aloud, stopping as described on the next page.

 Note

You may want to point to the picture of Erandi on the cover and explain that a *braid* is a *hairstyle made by weaving together pieces of hair.*

ELL Note

English Language Learners may benefit from additional stops to discuss the story—for example, after pages 7, 20, and 25.

Suggested Vocabulary

huipil: (Spanish) blouse (p. 4)

tortillas: thin corn pancakes (p. 5)

embroidery: a picture or design stitched with thread to decorate cloth (p. 6)

adobe: building material made of clay mixed with straw and dried in the sun (p. 7)

fiesta: (Spanish) party (p. 8)

buenos días: (Spanish) good morning (p. 11)

procession: number of people walking together, like in a parade (p. 12)

mi hija: (Spanish) my daughter (p. 21)

huaraches: (Spanish) sandals (p. 26)

ELL Vocabulary

English Language Learners may benefit from discussing additional vocabulary, including:

pay a fortune: give a lot of money (p. 7)

tremble: shake with fear (p. 18; model trembling)

Stop after:

> **p. 16** "But she didn't say anything to Mamá."

Have the students use "Turn to Your Partner" to discuss:

Q *What is happening in the story? What makes Erandi think her mother is going to sell her braids?*

Without sharing as a class, reread the last sentence on page 16 and read to the end of the story.

4 Discuss the Story

Facilitate a whole-class discussion about the story. Ask:

Q *What is this story about?*

Q *What is Erandi's problem in this story? How is her problem solved?*

FACILITATION TIP

This week and next continue to practice **asking a question once** and using wait-time (at least 5–10 seconds) to give the students an opportunity to think before responding.

Q *How does the story end? Is that what you expected? Explain your thinking.*

Explain that in the next lesson they will think more about the story's main character, Erandi.

INDIVIDUALIZED DAILY READING

5▶ **Document IDR Conferences/Have the Students Discuss Main Characters in Their Books**

If needed, review the procedures for IDR conferences and continue to conduct and document individual conferences. Use a copy of the "IDR Conference Notes" record sheet for each individual conference.

Have the students read independently for 15–20 minutes. Ask them to think about the main characters in their book.

At the end of independent reading, have the students talk about the main characters in their book in pairs or with the class.

Day 2

Strategy Lesson

In this lesson, the students:

- Hear a story read aloud again
- Examine a character in the story
- Use examples from the story to support their thinking
- Read independently for up to 20 minutes
- Explain their thinking and listen to one another

▶1 Get Ready to Work Together

Have partners sit together. Review that in the previous lesson, the students heard and discussed the story *Erandi's Braids*. Explain that today they will hear the story again and then think and talk more about the main character, Erandi.

▶2 Reread *Erandi's Braids* Aloud

Ask the students to listen carefully as you reread the story and to think about what Erandi says, does, and thinks in the story, and what these clues tell them about her.

Reread *Erandi's Braids* without stopping.

▶3 Discuss the Story and Complete the "Erandi's Braids" Chart

Explain that the students will use a chart again to think about a story's main character.

Direct their attention to the "Erandi's Braids" chart. Point to the left-hand column and read the question, "What does Erandi do?" Ask:

Q *What are some important things that Erandi does in the story?*

Materials

- *Erandi's Braids*
- "Erandi's Braids" chart, prepared ahead (see page 119)
- "Reading Comprehension Strategies" chart
- *Student Response Book,* IDR Journal section
- "IDR Conference Notes" record sheets

◀ **Teacher Note**

Rereading the text gives the students time to listen for details, such as a character's traits or feelings, that they might have missed.

Have the students use "Turn to Your Partner" to talk about their ideas.

Have several pairs share their ideas with the class. As the pairs share, chart their ideas in the left-hand column. For example:

Erandi's Braids

What does Erandi do?	What does this tell us about Erandi?
- Erandi lets the man cut her hair.	

Point to an entry in the "What does Erandi do?" column, and ask:

Q *What does this tell us about Erandi? How does she feel in this part of the story? How do you know?*

Teacher Note ▶

During this discussion, emphasize the connection between the students' thinking and the text.

As the students share, record their responses in the "What does this tell us about Erandi?" column. (For example, you might write, "Erandi wants to help her mother buy a new fishing net.") Repeat this process with other ideas listed in the left-hand column.

4 Add to the "Reading Comprehension Strategies" Chart

Direct the students' attention to the "Reading Comprehension Strategies" chart and add *making inferences about characters* to it. Explain that when readers use clues in a story to figure things out about the characters, they are making inferences about the characters. It is an important strategy that readers use to understand stories. Explain that the students will have many chances to practice making inferences in the coming weeks.

Reading Comprehension Strategies

- visualizing

INDIVIDUALIZED DAILY READING

 Document IDR Conferences/Have the Students Write in Their IDR Journals

Have the students read independently for 15–20 minutes.

Continue to conduct and document individual conferences.

At the end of independent reading, have the students write in their IDR Journals about one of the characters in their book and why they like the character.

EXTENSION

Revisit Visualizing with *Erandi's Braids*

Several passages in *Erandi's Braids* have very vivid language. Remind the students that one of the strategies they use to help them understand what they read is *visualizing*. Read a few passages aloud, and ask the students to think about the language the author uses to describe Erandi and her village.

The following is an example of a passage that vividly describes a setting in the story:

> **p. 3** "'Erandi, it's time to wake up,' Mamá whispered. Roosters were crowing as the orange and crimson colors of dawn spread across the village of Pátzcuaro, in the hills of Mexico."

The following is an example of a passage that describes a character's feelings:

> **p. 18** "Gazing at the enormous scissors in his hand, Erandi felt her knees tremble."

 Note

Consider having your students with limited English proficiency draw a picture of their favorite character and then dictate a sentence about the character to you.

Day 3

Materials

- Narrative texts at appropriate levels for independent reading
- Small self-stick notes for each student
- Narrative text for teacher modeling in Step 3
- *Assessment Resource Book*

Independent Strategy Practice

In this lesson, the students:

- Read independently
- *Make inferences* about a main character in their independent reading
- Use examples from the story to support their thinking
- Explain their thinking

1 Review Making Inferences About Characters

Remind the students that this week they heard the story *Erandi's Braids* and talked about the main character, Erandi. They thought about things Erandi does in the story and what those things tell us about her. Point out that the students used clues in the story, such as Erandi's thoughts, actions, and words, to make inferences about her character.

Explain that today the students will again practice making inferences about characters in their independent reading. Tell them that they will read their own books for 10 minutes. Then you will ask them to reread the same section and think about what they know about a character in their book.

ELL Note

Note challenging vocabulary in the students' independent reading books and have brief discussions with individual students to define words as they read independently.

2 Read Independently Without Stopping

Ask the students to use a self-stick note to mark the place they begin reading today. Have them read independently for 10 minutes.

3 Model Making an Inference About a Character

After 10 minutes, stop the students. Review that they will reread, starting again at the self-stick note. As they read, they will use another self-stick note to mark a place where they figure out something about a character from what the character says, does, or thinks. Explain that at the end of independent reading, partners will share the clues they found about their characters.

Model the process with your own narrative text. Read a brief selection aloud, and then think aloud about what you figured out about a character and the clues in the text that helped you make the inference. Mark the clues with a self-stick note.

◀ **Teacher Note**

To prepare for this modeling, select a narrative text and preview the selection you will read aloud. The text may be one from your own reading, a book from your class library, or a read-aloud text from the *Making Meaning* program that the students heard earlier in the year. Think about the inference you will make and the clues that support it ahead of time so that the modeling will go smoothly.

 4 **Reread Independently and Talk to a Partner**

Have the students reread independently for 10 minutes. After 10 minutes, use "Turn to Your Partner" to have the students discuss:

Q   *What did you figure out about a character in your story?*

Q   *What clues in the story helped you figure that out?*

Remind each student to begin by telling her partner the title and author of her book and briefly what it is about.

CLASS COMPREHENSION ASSESSMENT

As partners share, note how the students are able to infer about characters. Ask yourself:

Q   *Are the students able to make an inference about a character?*

Q   *Can they identify clues that support their inference?*

Record your observations on page 12 of the *Assessment Resource Book*.

 5 **Reflect on Making Inferences and Working Together**

Facilitate a whole-class discussion about using the strategy *making inferences* to make sense of a character. Ask:

Q   *How does making inferences about a story character help us understand the character?*

Q *How did your partner do explaining [his] thinking clearly to you today? How did you do? How did that help your work together?*

Students might say:

"Sometimes the author doesn't tell you why a character is scared or sad. You have to figure it out from what is happening to the character."

"My partner and I explained our thinking clearly and we could understand each other."

Explain that the students will have more opportunities to make inferences about characters in stories they hear and read independently.

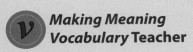

Making Meaning Vocabulary Teacher

Next week you will revisit *Erandi's Braids* to teach Vocabulary Week 10.

Week 3 Overview

UNIT 4: MAKING INFERENCES
Fiction

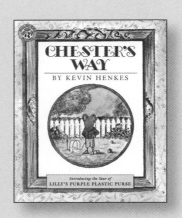

Chester's Way
by Kevin Henkes
(Mulberry, 1988)

Chester and Wilson are best friends and they share the same way of doing things, until one day Lilly moves into the neighborhood.

ALTERNATIVE BOOKS

The Name Jar by Yangsook Choi

Dear Juno by Soyung Pak

Comprehension Focus

• Students *make inferences* to understand characters.

• Students informally *explore text structure* in narrative texts, including character and plot.

• Students read independently.

Social Development Focus

• Students take responsibility for their learning and behavior.

• Students develop the group skill of explaining their thinking.

D O   A H E A D

• (Optional) Prepare to model making an inference about a character (see Day 3, Step 3 on page 139).

• Make copies of the Unit 4 Parent Letter (BLM4) to send home with the students on the last day of the unit. (For more information about the Parent Letters, see page xxxviii.)

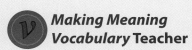

Making Meaning
Vocabulary Teacher

If you are teaching Developmental Studies Center's *Making Meaning Vocabulary* program, teach Vocabulary Week 10 this week. For more information, see the *Making Meaning Vocabulary Teacher's Manual.*

Day 1

Materials

- *Chester's Way*
- "IDR Conference Notes" record sheets

Read-aloud

In this lesson, the students:

- Hear and discuss a story
- Read independently for up to 20 minutes
- Explain their thinking

▶1 Reflect on Partner Work

Have partners sit together. Facilitate a brief discussion about what has gone well in partner work and what the students still want to work on.

Q *What is working well for you when you work with your partner?*

Q *What are some things you would like to work on today? How will that help your learning?*

▶2 Introduce *Chester's Way*

Show the cover of *Chester's Way,* and read the title and the author's name. Explain that this story is about two mice who are best friends. One day another mouse moves into the neighborhood.

▶3 Read *Chester's Way* Aloud

Remind the students that as you read they should pay careful attention to what the characters are doing. Explain that you will stop during the story so that partners can talk about what has happened so far.

Read the story aloud, showing the illustrations and stopping as described on the next page.

ELL Note

English Language Learners may benefit from additional stops— for example, after pages 9 and 23.

Suggested Vocabulary

have a mind of your own: (idiom) do things your own way (p. 7)

rarely: not often (p. 9)

duplicated: copied (p. 10)

nifty disguises: clever ways to dress to hide the way you really look (p. 16)

circled: gathered around (p. 20)

fierce: wild and scary (p. 21)

ELL Vocabulary

English Language Learners may benefit from discussing additional vocabulary, including:

diagonally: in a straight line joining opposite corners of a square or rectangle (p. 6)

double knotting: tying your shoelaces twice (p. 6)

first-aid kit: bandages and other things to care for cuts and injuries (p. 7)

pitch: ball thrown toward a hitter in baseball (p. 8)

hand signals: signs you make with your hands to let cars or other riders know where you are going (p. 8)

picnics: meals out of doors (p. 10)

sunscreen: lotion to protect skin from the sun (p. 13)

loaded squirt gun: water gun full of water (p. 17)

popping wheelies: (idiom) riding a bicycle on one wheel (p. 20)

Read pages 5–14 aloud. Stop after:

p. 14 "And then Lilly moved into the neighborhood."

Ask:

Q *What has happened in the story so far, and what do you think might happen next?*

Have the students use "Turn to Your Partner" to discuss the questions. Reread the last sentence on page 14 and continue to page 19. Stop after:

p. 19 "'Looks like it,' said Wilson."

Ask:

Q *What happens when Lilly arrives?*

Have the students use "Turn to Your Partner" to discuss the question. Reread the last sentence on page 19 and continue reading to the end of the story.

4▶ Discuss the Story

Have the students discuss their ideas about the book. Remind them that during the whole-class discussion they need to speak loudly and clearly so everyone can hear their ideas.

Ask:

Q *What happens in this story?*

Q *Who are the main characters in this story? What other characters are in the story?*

Q *How are things different at the end of the story from the way they were in the beginning?*

Let the students know that in the next lesson, they will hear parts of the story again and think more about the characters in it.

INDIVIDUALIZED DAILY READING

5▶ Document IDR Conferences/Have the Students Infer About Characters

Have the students read books at their appropriate reading levels independently for 15–20 minutes.

Continue to conduct individual conferences with the students and use an "IDR Conference Notes" record sheet to document each conference.

 At the end of independent reading, have partners talk about the characters in their books and inferences they made about the characters.

Have partners discuss questions such as:

Q *What happens in your book?*

Q *Who is the main character?*

Q *How would you describe the main character?*

Q *What happens to the character?*

Day 2

Materials

- *Chester's Way*
- "IDR Conferences Notes" record sheets

Strategy Lesson

In this lesson, the students:

- *Make inferences* about characters
- Explore an ethical issue in a story
- Read independently for up to 20 minutes
- Explain their thinking

1 Revisit *Chester's Way* and Prepare to Reread

Show the cover of *Chester's Way*. Ask:

Q *What do you remember about the story* Chester's Way?

Have a few volunteers share their thinking with the class.

Explain that you will reread parts of the story aloud, and the students will listen for clues that tell them something about the characters Chester and Wilson. Explain that you will read each part twice. The first time, they will just listen. The second time, they will raise their hands each time they hear a clue that tells them something about Chester and Wilson.

Teacher Note ▶

The students may not remember many details after hearing the story just once. Be ready to reread sections of the text or to show illustrations again during this discussion to help the students remember the story.

Teacher Note

You may want to model inferring about Chester and Wilson by reading aloud pages 8–9 of the book, stopping when you come to clues about Chester and Wilson. (For example, after reading the sentence, "Wilson wouldn't ride his bike unless Chester wanted to, and they always used hand signals," you might say, "I think that Chester and Wilson are always careful and safe because they always use hand signals.")

2 Reread and Infer About the Main Characters

Read page 10 aloud and pause. Reread this page and ask the students to raise their hands when they hear a clue about Chester and Wilson. As the students raise their hands, ask:

Q *What is the clue that tells you something about Chester and Wilson?*

Q *What do you infer about Chester and Wilson from this clue?*

When necessary, probe the students' thinking with questions such as:

Q *From what I just read, how would you describe Chester and Wilson?*

Q *What clue in the story made you think that about Chester and Wilson?*

Repeat this process with pages 18–19 and pages 26–27.

▶3 Connect the Reading to Partner Work

Remind the students that things change for Chester and Wilson when Lilly comes to their neighborhood. At first Chester and Wilson don't talk to Lilly or play with her. Facilitate a discussion using the following questions:

Q *Why do you think Chester and Wilson ignore Lilly at first?*

Q *How do you think Chester and Wilson feel about Lilly at the end of the story?*

Q *What can we learn from this story about getting to know new people?*

Tell the students that in the next lesson, they will make inferences about characters in their independent reading.

INDIVIDUALIZED DAILY READING

▶4 Document IDR Conferences/Have the Students Infer About Characters

Have the students read independently for 15–20 minutes.

Continue to conduct and document individual conferences.

At the end of independent reading, have partners talk about the characters in their books and inferences they made about the characters. Have partners discuss questions such as those on page 135.

Day 3

Materials

- Narrative texts at appropriate levels for independent reading
- "Reading Comprehension Strategies" chart
- Small self-stick notes for each student
- (Optional) Narrative text for modeling in Step 3
- *Assessment Resource Book*
- Unit 4 Parent Letter (BLM4)

Reading Comprehension Strategies

- visualizing

Independent Strategy Lesson

In this lesson, the students:

- Read independently
- *Make inferences* about a character in their independent reading
- Use examples from the story to support their thinking
- Explain their thinking

1 Review Making Inferences About Characters

Remind the students that in previous lessons they used clues in stories to learn about characters such as Mary Jo, Erandi, Chester, and Wilson. Review that when readers use clues in a story to figure out something that is not stated directly, they are making an inference. Direct the students' attention to the "Reading Comprehension Strategies" chart and remind them that *making inferences* is a powerful strategy for helping readers understand characters in stories.

Explain that today the students will practice making inferences about characters in their independent reading. They will begin by reading their own books for 10 minutes. As they read, they should identify a character in the story that they would like to talk to their partner about. After 10 minutes, they will read the section again, then share their thinking about the character in pairs.

2 Read Independently Without Stopping

Make sure each student has a narrative text at the appropriate level. Ask them to use a self-stick note to mark the place they begin reading today; then have them read independently for 10 minutes. Remind them to identify a character in their reading to discuss with their partners.

Get Ready to Reread

Stop the students, and explain that you would like them to reread, starting again at the self-stick note. Explain that as they reread you want them to think about their character and what they can figure out about the character from clues in the story. Review that clues can be something the character says, does, or thinks. Explain that you will stop them after five minutes so partners can discuss what they figured out about their characters.

 Reread Independently and Talk to a Partner

Have the students reread independently for 10 minutes, stopping them after five minutes and at the end of the 10 minutes to discuss the following questions with their partners. Remind each student to tell his partner the title and author of his book and the name of the character.

Q   *What did you figure out about your character?*

Q   *What clues in the story helped you to figure that out?*

CLASS COMPREHENSION ASSESSMENT

As partners share, circulate and ask yourself:

Q   *Are the students able to make an inference about a character?*

Q   *Can they identify clues that support their inference?*

Record your observations on page 13 of the *Assessment Resource Book*.

 Discuss Characters as a Class

At the end of the independent reading time, have one or two volunteers share their thinking about their characters with the class. Remind them each to say the title and author of the book and the name of the character.

Teacher Note ◀

If the students have difficulty inferring about characters, you might model the process again for the class using a text you previously selected. (For example, reread page 30 of *Chester's Way* aloud, stopping and using a self-stick note to mark the sentence "In winter, they never threw snowballs at each other." You might say, "I can figure out that Chester, Wilson, and Lilly like one another because they don't throw snowballs at each other.")

Probe the students' thinking by asking:

Q *What inference did you make about your character?*

Q *What did the character say, do, or think that helped you make the inference?*

6 ▶ Reflect on Taking Responsibility During Independent Reading

Facilitate a whole-class discussion about how the students took responsibility during independent reading today. Ask:

Q *What did you do to act in a responsible way during independent reading and while you were talking with your partner?*

Students might say:

"I showed my partner I was listening by looking at her when she was talking."

"I asked my partner questions when we discussed the characters in our books."

Explain that the students will continue to think about the characters in stories they hear and read independently.

Teacher Note

This is the last week in Unit 4. If you would like to spend more time on this strategy, repeat the lessons with an alternative book. See this week's Overview page for alternative books. You will reassign partners for Unit 5.

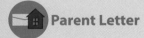
Parent Letter

Send home with each student the Parent Letter for this unit (see "Do Ahead," page 131). Periodically, have a few students share with the class what they are reading at home.

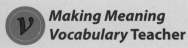
Making Meaning Vocabulary Teacher

Next week you will revisit *Chester's Way* to teach Vocabulary Week 11.

INDIVIDUAL COMPREHENSION ASSESSMENT

Before continuing with Unit 5, take this opportunity to assess individual students' progress in *making inferences* about characters. Be aware that while students can often make appropriate inferences, they may be unable to recognize when they make them. This is to be expected, as this kind of metacognition develops slowly over time. The goal of this unit is to help the students begin to understand that characters reveal themselves in stories through the things they say, do, and think. Please refer to pages 34–35 in the *Assessment Resource Book* for instructions.

Unit 5

Wondering

FICTION

During this unit, the students use wondering to understand a story. They continue to infer and make predictions, referring to the story to support their thinking. During IDR, the students use wondering to help them comprehend the stories they read independently. They relate the value of responsibility to their behavior and develop the group skills of sharing their thinking with one another and using a prompt to give reasons for their thinking. In Week 2, they have a check-in class meeting.

Week 1 *The Incredible Painting of Felix Clousseau* by Jon Agee
The Ghost-Eye Tree by Bill Martin Jr. and John Archambault

Week 2 *Galimoto* by Karen Lynn Williams

Week 3 *The Paper Crane* by Molly Bang

Week 1

Overview

UNIT 5: WONDERING
Fiction

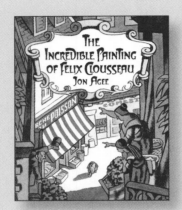

The Incredible Painting of Felix Clousseau
by Jon Agee
(Farrar, Straus & Giroux, 1988)

Unusual paintings make a painter famous.

The Ghost-Eye Tree
by Bill Martin Jr. and John Archambault, illustrated by Ted Rand
(Henry Holt, 1988)

A brother and sister are fearful of a tree they pass on their way to get a pail of milk on a dark, windy night.

ALTERNATIVE BOOKS

I Have an Olive Tree by Eve Bunting
Solomon the Rusty Nail by William Steig

Comprehension Focus

- Students use *wondering* to understand a story.

- Students make predictions and *infer*.

- Students refer to the story to support their thinking.

- Students read independently.

Social Development Focus

- Students relate the value of responsibility to their behavior.

- Students develop the group skills of sharing their thinking with one another and using a prompt to give reasons for their thinking.

DO AHEAD

- Prior to Day 1, decide how you will randomly assign partners to work together during this unit.

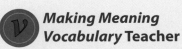

Making Meaning Vocabulary Teacher

If you are teaching Developmental Studies Center's *Making Meaning Vocabulary* program, teach Vocabulary Week 11 this week. For more information, see the *Making Meaning Vocabulary Teacher's Manual.*

Day 1

Materials

- *The Incredible Painting of Felix Clousseau*
- "IDR Conference Notes" record sheets

Read-aloud/Strategy Lesson

In this lesson, the students:

- *Wonder* about a story read aloud
- Refer to the story to support their thinking
- Read independently for up to 20 minutes
- Share their thinking and listen to one another
- Begin working with new partners

About Wondering

The purpose of this unit is to wonder about stories, building on the students' understanding of character and plot. *Wondering* is a strategy that good readers use to construct understanding. Students build this understanding through teacher modeling and making their own "I wonder" statements about the read-aloud book and their independent reading books. (For more information about *wondering*, please see page xv.)

Being a Writer™ **Teacher**

You can either have the students work with their *Being a Writer* partner or assign them a different partner for the *Making Meaning* lessons.

▶1 Pair Students and Get Ready to Work Together

Randomly assign new partners and ask pairs to sit together. Remind the students that they have been talking about books and listening to one another's ideas. Doing this helps readers understand and enjoy books. First in pairs, and then as a class, discuss:

Q *What are some things you would like your new partner to do to show that [she] is listening?*

▶2 Introduce *The Incredible Painting of Felix Clousseau* and Model Wondering

Show the cover of *The Incredible Painting of Felix Clousseau* and read the title and author's name aloud. Point to Felix Clousseau on the cover and explain that he is a painter who lives in Paris, France, and paints incredible—*incredible* means *amazing*—pictures.

Note

You may want to explain to the students that when you *wonder* about something, you *are curious* or *want to know more* about it.

Model wondering by thinking aloud about the title and the illustration on the cover. (For example, you might say, "I wonder what makes Felix's paintings incredible.") Ask:

Q *What do you wonder about this story?*

> **Students might say:**
>
> "I wonder what his paintings will be like."
>
> "I wonder if it will be a funny story."
>
> "I wonder why the people are waving to him."

Explain that you will stop during the reading to have partners talk about what is happening in the story and what they are wondering about.

 Read Aloud and Stop and Wonder

Read the story aloud, showing the illustrations and stopping as described on the next page.

Suggested Vocabulary

armor: metal covering for the body, used as a defense (p. 8)

outrageous: shocking (p. 10)

stunned: shocked (p. 13)

genius: very smart or talented person (p. 14)

hailed: greeted enthusiastically (p. 16)

commissioned: ordered (p. 16)

baroness: noblewoman (p. 18)

chaos: complete confusion (p. 21)

seized: taken by force (p. 25)

notorious: well-known, usually for something bad (p. 26)

ferocious: very fierce (p. 28)

ELL Vocabulary

English Language Learners may benefit from discussing additional vocabulary, including:

an unknown painter: a painter no one had heard of or knew about (p. 6)

ridiculous: very silly (p. 10)

But that was only half of it: There is a lot more to know (p. 15)

was on the loose: was stealing jewels and the police had not caught him (p. 26)

Read pages 5–13. Stop after:

p. 13 "The judges were stunned."

Ask:

Q *What has happened so far?*

Have one or two students share. Then ask:

Teacher Note ▶

If the students have difficulty generating "I wonder" statements, model several like those in the "Students might say" note. Be ready to continue modeling during the reading until the students seem comfortable generating "I wonder" statements on their own.

Q *What do you wonder about the story at this point?*

Have the students use "Think, Pair, Share" to discuss the question. Have two or three volunteers share with the class. Ask the students to begin their sharing with the prompt "I wonder…."

Students might say:

"I wonder if he'll win the prize."

"I wonder if someone is behind the painting."

"I wonder if he has magic paint."

Without stopping to discuss the statements, reread the sentence on page 13 and continue reading to the next stop. Repeat this process at each stop:

p. 25 "Clousseau's paintings were seized…all except one."

p. 28 "The crown was saved."

Continue reading to the end of the story. Ask:

Q *What do you wonder about the ending of the story?*

Have the students use "Turn to Your Partner" to discuss the question. Have two or three volunteers share with the class.

Students might say:

"I wonder who painted him since he came out of the picture."

"I wonder if the whole town was a painting."

"I wonder if he might be magic because he came out of the picture."

Discuss the Story as a Class

 Use "Turn to Your Partner" to have the students talk about what they are still wondering about the story. Then facilitate a whole-class discussion. Ask:

Q   *What is this story about?*

Q   *What do you think of this story? Did you like it? Why? Why not?*

Tell the students they will use wondering again in the next lesson.

 Reflect on Group Work

Facilitate a brief discussion about how the students showed their partners that they were listening.

INDIVIDUALIZED DAILY READING

 Document IDR Conferences

Have the students independently read books at their reading level for 20 minutes.

Use the "IDR Conference Notes" record sheet to conduct and document individual conferences.

At the end of independent reading, have partners discuss their books. Circulate as the pairs talk and ask questions such as:

Q   *What is happening in the story?*

Q   *What do you wonder about the story?*

EXTENSION

Reread the Story

Reread *The Incredible Painting of Felix Clousseau* aloud. As a class, discuss any additional things the students wonder about the story.

FACILITATION TIP

During this unit, we invite you to focus on **pacing** whole-class discussions so that they are lively and focused. A class discussion should be long enough to allow thinking and sharing, but short enough to sustain the attention of all the students. Good pacing during a discussion requires careful observation of all the students—not just those responding—and the timely use of pacing techniques such as:

- Use wait-time before calling on anyone to respond.

- Call on only a few students to respond to a question, even if others have their hands up.

- If many students want to respond, use "Turn to Your Partner" to give partners an opportunity to share with each other. Then call on two or three students to share with the whole class.

- If a discussion goes off topic, restate the question.

 Note

When conferring with students with limited English proficiency, pay close attention to nonverbal evidence of comprehension, such as pointing to characters in story illustrations or acting out story events. During the conference, you may wish to provide the students with a chance to draw to demonstrate comprehension.

Day 2

Materials

- *The Ghost-Eye Tree*
- Scratch paper and a pencil
- Chart paper and a marker
- "IDR Conference Notes" record sheets

Read-aloud/Strategy Practice

In this lesson, the students:

- *Wonder* about a story
- Read independently for up to 20 minutes
- Share their thinking with one another

▶ **1 Review Wondering and Working Together**

Have partners sit together. Remind them that in the last lesson they heard *The Incredible Painting of Felix Clousseau* and talked in pairs about what they wondered as they listened to the story. Explain that today they will listen to another story and talk to their partners about what they wonder as they listen. Ask:

Q *How does listening to your partner's ideas help you wonder?*

Q *What can you do to make sure you are both offering ideas?*

▶ **2 Introduce *The Ghost-Eye Tree***

Show the cover of *The Ghost-Eye Tree* and read the title and the names of the authors and illustrator aloud. Tell the students that this is a story about a walk a brother and sister take to get a bucket of milk. Explain that you will read the story aloud and stop during the reading to have partners talk about what they are wondering about the story. Ask:

Q *Often, one of the first things a reader does is wonder about the title and the illustration on the cover of the book. What do you wonder about the title* The Ghost-Eye Tree?

Teacher Note

At the end of today's lesson, you will create a chart with several of the students' "I wonder" statements in preparation for tomorrow's lesson. Jot down some of the statements you hear the students making on a sheet of scratch paper. You will select among these statements when you create the chart. (See the "Teacher Note" on page 150.)

Have the students use "Turn to Your Partner" to discuss the question.

> ***Students might say:***
>
> "I wonder why the tree is called the ghost-eye tree."
>
> "I wonder if it is a magical tree."

Have two or three volunteers share their ideas with the class.

3 ▶ Read *The Ghost-Eye Tree* Aloud and Stop and Wonder

Read *The Ghost-Eye Tree* aloud, showing the illustrations and stopping as described below.

Suggested Vocabulary

dreaded: feared (p. 3)

muttering: speaking in a quiet, unclear way (p. 11)

ELL Vocabulary

English Language Learners may benefit from discussing additional vocabulary, including:

Don't hang back!: Don't stay where you are because you're afraid! (p. 5)

a fooly: imaginary; make-believe (p. 8)

gasping: taking in breath suddenly (p. 22)

Read pages 3–15, and stop after:

> **p. 15** "'Help me carry the milk.'"

Ask:

Q *What has happened so far?*

 Have the students use "Turn to Your Partner" to discuss the question. Then ask:

Q *What do you wonder about the story at this point?*

 Have the students use "Turn to Your Partner" to discuss this question. Have two or three volunteers share what they wonder with the class. Remind them to start with the prompt "I wonder…."

◀ **Teacher Note**

To maintain the flow of the lesson, have only two or three students share at each stop. Accept the students' "I wonder" statements without discussion. Hearing others' statements gives students examples of things they might wonder about as they hear a story.

Without discussing the "I wonder" statements, reread the last sentence on page 15 and continue reading. Follow the same procedure at the next stop:

p. 22   "We set the bucket down…flopped on the ground… gasping…for breath…"

Reread the last sentence on page 22, and continue reading to the end of the book. Ask:

Q *What do you still wonder?*

Students might say:

"I wonder if the sister is also scared."

"I wonder why the sister says 'here's your dumb hat.'"

"I wonder if the ghost-eye tree is a real tree."

Teacher Note ▶

If the students wonder about things that are unconnected to the story, help them to connect their questions to the text by asking, "What in the book makes you wonder that?"

4 ▶ **Discuss the Story as a Class**

Facilitate a brief class discussion, using questions such as:

Q *Why do you think they were afraid of the tree?*

Q *Why do you think the sister went back for her brother's hat?*

Q *How does this story make you feel? What parts made you feel [excited]?*

5 ▶ **Reflect on Working Together**

Help the students think about how they worked together today. Ask:

Q *How did you and your partner do making sure that you both shared ideas? What could you do differently next time to make it go better?*

Teacher Note

In preparation for the Day 3 lesson, select four or five of the students' "I wonder" statements that you recorded on scratch paper today, and write them on a sheet of chart paper entitled "I Wonder About *The Ghost-Eye Tree*." If possible, select both statements that are addressed in the story and those that are not addressed.

INDIVIDUALIZED DAILY READING

 Document IDR Conferences

Have the students read independently for 20 minutes.

Use the "IDR Conference Notes" record sheet to conduct and document individual conferences.

At the end of independent reading, have the students talk with their partners about their books. Circulate as the students discuss their books and ask questions such as:

Q *What is happening in the story?*

Q *What do you wonder about the story?*

Allow time for any student who has finished a book to record it in his "Reading Log."

If time permits, have a few students share with the class what they discussed with their partners.

Day 3

Strategy Lesson

Materials

- *The Ghost-Eye Tree*
- "I Wonder About *The Ghost-Eye Tree*" chart, prepared ahead (see the "Teacher Note" on page 150)
- *Assessment Resource Book*
- "IDR Conference Notes" record sheets
- *Student Response Book,* IDR Journal section

 Note

Observe your English Language Learners and, if you see them struggling, consider providing extra support by modeling the use of the prompt.

In this lesson, the students:

- Refer to the story to support their thinking
- Read independently for up to 20 minutes
- Learn a prompt to give reasons for their thinking

▶ 1 Introduce and Model Giving Reasons for Your Thinking

Have partners sit together. Explain that today you will reread *The Ghost-Eye Tree* and they will revisit some of the things they wondered about the story yesterday.

Explain that during today's discussion you would like the students to focus on giving a reason for their thinking whenever they share. Write the prompt "I think _____, because _____" where everyone can see it, and briefly model using the prompt. (For example, you might say, "I think giving a reason for my thinking is a good idea, because it helps everyone understand my thinking.")

Encourage the students to use the prompt when they share today, and tell them that you will check in with them at the end of the lesson.

▶ 2 Review "I Wonder" Statements

Refer to the "I Wonder About *The Ghost-Eye Tree*" chart and read the "I wonder" statements aloud. Remind the students that these are some of the things they wondered as they heard the story. Ask the students to keep these questions in mind as you reread the story. Tell them that after you read, partners will talk about whether or not the "I wonder" statements on the chart are discussed in the story.

3 ▶ Reread *The Ghost-Eye Tree*

Reread the story aloud, showing the illustrations as you read.

4 ▶ Discuss "I Wonder" Statements

Read an "I wonder" statement from the chart. Ask:

Q *Is this answered in the book? How?*

 Have the students use "Turn to Your Partner" to discuss the question.

> **CLASS COMPREHENSION ASSESSMENT**
>
> As partners discuss the "I wonder" statements, circulate among them and ask yourself:
>
> **Q** *Are the students using the "I wonder" statements to discuss the book?*
>
> **Q** *Are they using evidence from the text to support their thinking?*
>
> Record your observations on page 14 of the *Assessment Resource Book*.

Have a few volunteers share their thinking with the class. Remind the students to use the prompt "I think _____, because _____" as they talk.

Use the same procedure to discuss the other "I wonder" statements. During this discussion, explain that it is normal for some "I wonder" statements to be addressed in a story, while others might not be. Whether they are addressed or not, wondering during reading helps readers be more active thinkers as they read.

5 ▶ Reflect on Giving Reasons for Your Thinking

Briefly discuss how the students did using the prompt "I think
_____ , because _____" as they talked today. Encourage
them to continue to use the prompt whenever they are sharing
their thinking during the school day.

INDIVIDUALIZED DAILY READING

6 ▶ Document IDR Conferences/Have the Students Write in Their IDR Journals

Ask the students to notice what they wonder as they read today.
Explain that at the end of IDR they will write about what they like
about their book.

Have the students read independently for 20 minutes.

Use the "IDR Conference Notes" record sheet to conduct and
document individual conferences.

At the end of independent reading, have the students write in
their IDR Journals about what they like about their books. You
might want to write the prompt "I like this book because…." where
everyone can see it.

ELL Note

You may want to have your
English Language Learners draw
a picture of what they like about
their reading. Depending on their
fluency levels, consider having
them dictate a sentence to you.

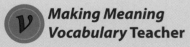

Making Meaning Vocabulary **Teacher**

Next week you will revisit
*The Incredible Painting of
Felix Clousseau* to teach
Vocabulary Week 12.

UNIT 5: WONDERING
Fiction

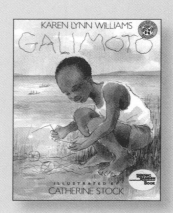

Galimoto
by Karen Lynn Williams, illustrated by Catherine Stock
(Mulberry, 1991)

A boy searches for wires to make a toy car, called a galimoto.

ALTERNATIVE BOOKS

Dream Wolf by Paul Goble
Our Gracie Aunt by Jacqueline Woodson

Comprehension Focus

- Students use *wondering* to understand a story.

- Students make predictions and *infer*.

- Students refer to the text to support their thinking.

- Students read independently.

Social Development Focus

- Students relate the value of responsibility to their behavior.

- Students develop the group skills of sharing their thinking with one another and using a prompt to give reasons for their thinking.

- Students have a check-in class meeting.

DO AHEAD

- Prepare to model wondering in independent reading (see Day 3, Step 2 on page 163).

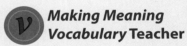

Making Meaning Vocabulary Teacher

If you are teaching Developmental Studies Center's *Making Meaning Vocabulary* program, teach Vocabulary Week 12 this week. For more information, see the *Making Meaning Vocabulary Teacher's Manual.*

Day 1

Materials

- *Galimoto*
- Scratch paper and a pencil
- Chart paper and a marker
- "IDR Conference Notes" record sheets

Read-aloud/Strategy Lesson

In this lesson, the students:

- *Wonder* about a story
- Read independently for up to 20 minutes
- Share their thinking with one another

▶ 1 Get Ready to Work Together

Ask partners to sit together. Remind the students that they have been listening to stories and talking in pairs and with the class about what they wonder about the stories. Explain that today they will listen to a story and wonder about it before, during, and after the reading. Remind them that they will be responsible for thinking on their own and explaining their thinking to their partners and the class.

▶ 2 Introduce *Galimoto*

Show the cover of *Galimoto* and read the title and names of the author and illustrator aloud. Ask:

Q *What do you wonder about the story?*

Have two or three volunteers share their ideas with the class.

> **Students might say:**
>
> "I wonder if *galimoto* is a thing or a boy."
>
> "I wonder what *galimoto* means."

Explain that *Galimoto* is a story about a boy named Kondi who walks around his town collecting things. He meets and talks to several people—Ufulu, Kondi's brother; Gift, Kondi's friend; and Munde, Gift's sister. Write the characters' names on the board.

Explain that you will read the story aloud, stopping in the middle and at the end to have partners talk about what they are wondering.

Teacher Note

As you did last week, you will create a chart with several of the students' "I wonder" statements in preparation for this week's Day 2 lesson. During today's lesson, jot down some of the students' statements on a sheet of scratch paper. You will select among these statements when you create the chart. (See the "Teacher Note" on page 159.)

3 ▶ Read *Galimoto* Aloud and Stop and Wonder

Read *Galimoto* aloud, showing the illustrations as you read and stopping as described below.

Suggested Vocabulary

flour mill: building containing machinery for grinding grain into flour (p. 12)

maize: corn (p. 12)

spokes: thin metal rods that connect the rim, or outside, of a wheel to the hub, or center (p. 18)

ELL Vocabulary

English Language Learners may benefit from discussing additional vocabulary, including:

clever: good at doing or making things; smart (p. 10)

playthings: toys (p. 15)

sturdy: strong (p. 23)

Stop after:

> **p. 10**   "'…Take the wires.'"

Ask:

Q   *What has happened so far?*

 Have the students use "Turn to Your Partner" to discuss the question. Then ask:

Q   *What do you wonder about the story so far?*

Have the students use "Turn to Your Partner" to discuss the question. Have two or three volunteers share what they wonder with the class. Without stopping to discuss the questions, reread the last paragraph on page 10 and continue reading. Follow the same procedure at the next two stops:

> **p. 21**   "'Thief, thief,' they chanted, pointing at Kondi."

> **p. 28**   "'Perhaps tomorrow I shall make my galimoto into an ambulance or an airplane or a helicopter.'"

Teacher Note

In preparation for the Day 2 lesson, select four or five of the students' "I wonder" statements that you recorded on scratch paper today, and write them on a sheet of chart paper entitled "I Wonder About *Galimoto*." If possible, select both statements that are addressed in the story and those that are not addressed.

4 ▶ Discuss the Story in Pairs and as a Class

 Have the students use "Think, Pair, Share" to discuss:

Q *What are some problems in this story? How are they solved?*

Q *Kondi likes to make galimotos. If you were to build a galimoto, what would you like to build?*

Remind the students to use the prompt. "I think _____, because _____."

Tell the students that they will revisit the story again tomorrow.

INDIVIDUALIZED DAILY READING

5 ▶ Document IDR Conferences/Have the Students Discuss "I Wonder" Statements

Have the students read books at appropriate reading levels independently for 20 minutes.

Use the "IDR Conference Notes" record sheet to conduct and document individual conferences.

 At the end of independent reading, have partners discuss their books. Circulate as the students talk and ask questions such as:

Q *What is happening in the story?*

Q *What do you wonder about the story?*

Have a few volunteers share their ideas with the class, and model writing two or three of their "I wonder" statements where everyone can see them. Tell the students that they will write their own statements during the next IDR period.

ELL Note

You may wish to help your English Language Learners choose books at the right level by asking them to pick from a limited number of appropriate books that you have selected.

Day 2

Strategy Lesson

In this lesson, the students:

• Refer to the story to support their thinking

• Read independently for up to 20 minutes

• Share their thinking with one another

• Use a prompt to give reasons for their thinking

▶1 Review the "I Wonder" Statements

Have partners sit together. Show the cover of *Galimoto* and remind the students that they wondered about the book in the previous lesson. Read the statements on the "I Wonder About *Galimoto*" chart aloud, and explain that these are some of the things they wondered about. Explain that as they listen to the story again you would like them to think about whether or not these "I wonder" statements are addressed in the story.

▶2 Reread *Galimoto*

Reread *Galimoto* aloud, without stopping.

▶3 Discuss the "I Wonder" Statements

Read an "I wonder" statement from the chart. Ask:

Q *Is this answered in the book? How?*

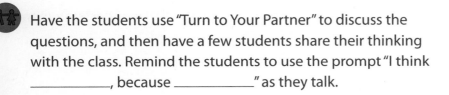

Have the students use "Turn to Your Partner" to discuss the questions, and then have a few students share their thinking with the class. Remind the students to use the prompt "I think _____, because _____" as they talk.

Materials

• *Galimoto*

• "I Wonder About *Galimoto*" chart, prepared ahead (see the "Teacher Note" on page 159)

• *Student Response Book*, IDR Journal section

FACILITATION TIP

This week continue to focus on **pacing** class discussions so that they are long enough to allow thinking and sharing but short enough to sustain the students' attention. See page 147 for a list of specific techniques.

Use the same procedure to discuss the other "I wonder" statements. During this discussion, remind the students that some of their "I wonder" statements may be addressed in the story, while others might not. Remind them that whether or not the questions are addressed, wondering helps readers be more active thinkers as they read.

4 ▶ Reflect on Giving Reasons for Thinking

Briefly discuss how the students did using the prompt "I think _____, because _____" as they talked today. Encourage them to continue to use the prompt whenever they share their thinking during the school day.

INDIVIDUALIZED DAILY READING

5 ▶ Have the Students Write "I Wonder" Statements in Their IDR Journals

Explain that at the end of IDR, each student will write an "I wonder" statement about her reading in her IDR Journal. Ask the students to notice what they wonder about their books as they read today.

Have the students read books at appropriate reading levels independently for up to 20 minutes.

At the end of independent reading, model an "I wonder" statement by reading part of a story aloud, thinking aloud about something you wonder, and writing an "I wonder" statement on the chalkboard where everyone can see it. Ask the students to write their own statements in their IDR Journals, starting with the words "I wonder."

If time allows, have a few students share their "I wonder" statements with the class.

ELL Note

You may need to model several "I wonder" statements for your English Language Learners.

Day 3

Independent Strategy Practice

In this lesson, the students:

- Stop and *wonder* about stories read independently
- Share their thinking with one another
- Have a check-in class meeting

1 Review Wondering

Have partners sit together. Remind the students that this week they heard *Galimoto* read aloud, and stopped and wondered to help them better understand and discuss the story. Explain that today the students will wonder about stories they read independently.

2 Model Wondering with Independent Reading

Model wondering when reading independently by using a narrative text of your own and a self-stick note. Examine the book cover and read a few sentences aloud. Then wonder aloud about a question that comes to mind. Write a question mark on your self-stick note and place it in your book at the place where you thought of the question. Distribute the self-stick notes, and have the students write question marks on the notes. Explain that they will use the notes to mark places in their books where they wonder about something or where a question comes to mind.

3 Read Independently

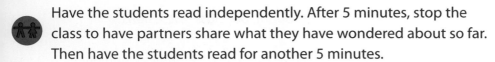

Have the students read independently. After 5 minutes, stop the class to have partners share what they have wondered about so far. Then have the students read for another 5 minutes.

Materials

- Narrative text to model wondering in independent reading (see Step 2)
- Books at appropriate levels for independent reading
- Small self-stick notes for each student
- *Assessment Resource Book*
- "Class Meeting Ground Rules" chart
- Scratch paper and a pencil

◀ **Teacher Note**

As the students work, circulate and notice whether they are marking places where they have questions.

4 Discuss the Independent Reading

At the end of independent reading time, use "Turn to Your Partner" to have the students talk about what they wondered about their books.

> ### CLASS COMPREHENSION ASSESSMENT
>
> Circulate among the students and ask yourself:
>
> **Q** *Are the students wondering about characters and events in their stories?*
>
> Record your observations on page 15 of the *Assessment Resource Book.*

Have several volunteers share what they wondered with the class. Probe the students' thinking by asking:

Q *What in the story made you wonder about that?*

Q *What do you still wonder about?*

Explain that during the next lesson the students will have more opportunities to wonder about stories.

5 Have a Brief Check-in Class Meeting

Tell the students they will have a brief check-in class meeting, and have them move into a circle with partners sitting together. Review the "Class Meeting Ground Rules" chart. Explain that the topic of today's meeting will be ways to improve class discussions. First in pairs, and then as a class, discuss:

Q *What are we doing well during our class discussions?*

Q *What things do we want to focus on to improve during our class discussions?*

Class Meeting Ground Rules

- one person talks at a time

Remind the students to use the prompt "I think _____, because _____" as they share. Jot down on scratch paper a few notes for yourself to use during future class discussions to remind the students of what they agreed to work on.

Briefly discuss how the students did following the "Class Meeting Ground Rules" and adjourn the meeting.

◀ **Teacher Note**

In the time period following a class meeting, it is important to hold the students accountable for things they agreed to work on. Use your notes to regularly remind the students what they agreed to and to check in with them about how they are doing.

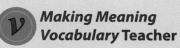

**Making Meaning
Vocabulary Teacher**

Next week you will revisit *Galimoto* to teach Vocabulary Week 13.

Week 3

Overview

UNIT 5: WONDERING
Fiction

The Paper Crane
by Molly Bang
(Mulberry, 1985)

A popular roadside restaurant loses its customers when a highway is built to replace the old road. When the restaurant owner receives a special gift in exchange for his kindness, his fortune is changed.

ALTERNATIVE BOOKS

Sylvester and the Magic Pebble by William Steig

Spinky Sulks by William Steig

Comprehension Focus

• Students use *wondering* to understand a story.

• Students make predictions and *infer.*

• Students refer to the text to support their thinking.

• Students read independently.

Social Development Focus

• Students relate the value of responsibility to their behavior.

• Students develop the group skills of sharing their thinking with one another and using a prompt to give reasons for their thinking.

DO AHEAD

• Make copies of the Unit 5 Parent Letter (BLM5) to send home with the students on the last day of the unit.

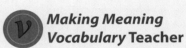

Making Meaning
Vocabulary Teacher

If you are teaching Developmental Studies Center's *Making Meaning Vocabulary* program, teach Vocabulary Week 13 this week. For more information, see the *Making Meaning Vocabulary Teacher's Manual.*

Day 1

Read-aloud

Materials

- *The Paper Crane*
- "Reading Comprehension Strategies" chart
- Scratch paper and a pencil
- Chart paper and a marker

In this lesson, the students:

- *Wonder* about a story
- Read independently for up to 20 minutes
- Share their thinking with one another
- Use a prompt to give reasons for their thinking

Reading Comprehension Strategies

- making connections

- wondering

1 ▶ Discuss Wondering and Add to the "Reading Comprehension Strategies" Chart

Have partners sit together. Refer to the "Reading Comprehension Strategies" chart and remind the students that they have been listening to stories and talking to their partners about what they wondered as they listened. Explain that wondering about what you are reading is a strategy that readers use to make sense of stories. Write *wondering* on the chart, and point out that this is another strategy the students will use this year to make sense of what they read.

Explain that today you will read a story aloud and the students will have another chance to wonder about the story before, during, and after the reading.

2 ▶ Introduce *The Paper Crane*

Show the cover of *The Paper Crane* and read the title and author's name. Read the summary on the back cover aloud. Ask:

Q *What do you wonder about this story?*

Have two or three volunteers share their ideas with the class.

ELL Note

You may want to explain that a crane is a kind of bird. Use the illustrations on the front and back covers of the book to help the students understand that in the story the stranger folds a piece of paper into the shape of a bird.

Students might say:

"I wonder what the magic in the paper crane is."

"I wonder if the crane is going to come alive."

"I wonder who the stranger is."

Explain that you will stop in the middle and at the end of the story to have partners talk about what they wonder.

 ## Read *The Paper Crane* Aloud and Stop and Wonder

Read *The Paper Crane* aloud, showing the illustrations and stopping as described below.

Suggested Vocabulary

host: person who welcomes you into their home or shop (p. 11)
crane: type of bird (p. 12)
overjoyed: very happy (p. 23)

ELL Vocabulary

English Language Learners may benefit from discussing additional vocabulary, including:

highway: main road (p. 6; refer to the illustration)
manner: way someone behaves (p. 9)
company: guests or visitors (p. 19)

Stop after:

p. 12 "With these words the stranger left."

 Use "Turn to Your Partner" to discuss:

Q *What do you wonder about the story so far?*

Have two or three volunteers share what they wonder. Without stopping to discuss the statements, reread the last sentence on page 12 and continue reading to the next stop. Repeat this process at each stop:

p. 23 "The owner knew him at once and was overjoyed."

p. 28 "He climbed on the back of the crane, and they flew out of the door and away."

Teacher Note

At the end of today's lesson, you will create a chart with several of the students' "I wonder" statements in preparation for tomorrow's lesson. Jot down some of the students' statements on a sheet of scratch paper. Select among these statements when you create the chart. (See the "Teacher Note" on page 170.)

p. 31 "But neither the stranger nor the dancing crane has ever been seen again."

Students might say:

"I wonder if the stranger is going to give the owner another magical gift."

"I wonder why the man flew away with the crane."

"I wonder if the man goes where people need help."

4 ▶ Discuss the Story

First in pairs and then as a class, discuss the following questions. (You may want to substitute some of the students' "I wonder" statements for the questions.)

Remind the students to give reasons for their thinking.

Q *Why do you think the stranger gave the restaurant owner such a wonderful gift?*

Q *Why do you think the stranger took back the crane?*

5 ▶ Reflect on Working Together

Facilitate a brief discussion about how the students worked together today. Ask:

Q *How does hearing others share what they wonder help you think more about the story?*

Students might say:

"Sometimes when I hear someone talk about part of the story, it reminds me of what happened in the story."

"When I hear someone wonder about something in the story, I start to wonder about it too."

Tell the students that in the next lesson, they will listen to the story again and discuss whether what they wonder is addressed in the story.

FACILITATION TIP

Reflect on your experience over the past three weeks with **pacing** class discussions. Do the pacing techniques feel comfortable and natural? Do you find yourself using them throughout the school day? What effect has your focus on pacing had on the students' participation in discussions? We encourage you to continue to focus on pacing class discussions during the remainder of the school year.

Teacher Note

In preparation for the Day 2 lesson, select four or five of the students' "I wonder" statements that you recorded on scratch paper today, and write these on a sheet of chart paper entitled "I Wonder About *The Paper Crane*." If possible, select both statements that are addressed in the story and those that are not addressed.

INDIVIDUALIZED DAILY READING

6 ▶ **Review the "Reading Comprehension Strategies" Chart/Read Independently**

Refer to the "Reading Comprehension Strategies" chart and review the strategies on it. Encourage the students to use these strategies to make sense of their reading.

Have the students read books at appropriate reading levels independently for 20 minutes.

As the students read, circulate among them and talk to individual students about their reading. Ask questions such as:

Q *What is your book about? What's happening in your book right now?*

Q *Are you wondering about anything so far? If so, what?*

Q *What do you know about the main character? Why do you think that?*

Q *What strategies are you using to help you understand the story?*

At the end of independent reading, have a few students share what they read with the whole class. Ask questions such as:

Q *What is happening in your story?*

Q *What is a reading comprehension strategy on the chart you used when reading today? How did it help you understand your story?*

Day 2

Materials

- *The Paper Crane*
- "I Wonder About *The Paper Crane*" chart, prepared ahead (see the "Teacher Note" on page 170)
- "IDR Conference Notes" record sheets
- *Student Response Book,* IDR Journal section

Strategy Practice

In this lesson, the students:

- Refer to the story to support their thinking
- Read independently for up to 20 minutes
- Share their thinking with one another
- Use a prompt to give reasons for their thinking

▶1 Review "I Wonder" Statements

Have partners sit together. Show the cover of *The Paper Crane* and remind the students that in the previous lesson they wondered before, during, and after the read-aloud. Explain that today they will listen to the story again and think about whether what they wondered is addressed in the story.

Read the "I wonder" statements on the "I Wonder About *The Paper Crane*" chart aloud. Explain that these are some of the things the students wondered about when they heard the story. Ask the students to keep these ideas in mind as you reread the story. Explain that at the end of the rereading, partners will discuss whether the story talks about what they wondered.

▶2 Reread *The Paper Crane*

Reread the story aloud without stopping.

▶3 Discuss the "I Wonder" Statements

Read an "I wonder" statement from the chart. Ask:

Q *Is this answered in the book? How?*

Have the students use "Turn to Your Partner" to discuss the question; then have a few students share their thinking with the class. Remind the students to use the prompt "I think _____, because _____" as they talk.

Use the same procedure to discuss the other "I wonder" statements.

 ## 4 Reflect on Rereading

Review the day's lesson. Remind the students that rereading is an important technique that readers use to think more deeply about a story. Point out that when they heard *The Paper Crane* again and discussed whether what they wondered was explained in the story, they were thinking more deeply about the story.

Ask:

Q *What did you think about during the second reading of* The Paper Crane *that you didn't think about during the first reading?*

Encourage the students to use rereading when they read independently to help them think more deeply about the story.

INDIVIDUALIZED DAILY READING

 ## 5 Document IDR Conferences/Have the Students Write "I Wonder" Statements in Their IDR Journals

Ask the students to notice what they wonder as they read today. Explain that at the end of IDR they will write "I wonder" sentences in their IDR Journals.

Have the students read independently for 20 minutes.

Use the "IDR Conference Notes" record sheet to conduct and document individual conferences.

At the end of IDR, ask the students to write one or two "I wonder" statements in their IDR Journals. If time allows, have a few students share their "I wonder" statements with the class.

Teacher Note

This is the last week in which the "IDR Conference Note" record sheets will appear in the Materials list; however, you should continue to use these sheets during IDR conferences for the rest of the year.

 Note

Depending on your students' level of fluency, consider having them tell you what they are wondering about.

The following books contain instructions for making paper cranes: *Origami Classroom* or *Easy Origami* by Dokuotei Nakano, or *Spread Your Wings and Fly* by Mary Chloe Saunders. You can also visit your library for books or search the Internet for instructions.

If making paper cranes is too difficult for your second-graders, you may want to demonstrate folding the crane or show a folded crane. Then, model folding simpler figures for the students to make.

EXTENSIONS

Make Paper Cranes

Read *Sadako and the Thousand Paper Cranes* by Eleanor Coerr. Discuss how the paper crane became a symbol of peace. Model making a paper crane, and have each student make one.

Join a Thousand Cranes Peace Project

As an ongoing project, have the class make a thousand cranes as an expression of hope for world peace. You may send the cranes to any of several peace organizations that you can find on the Internet.

Day 3

Independent Strategy Practice

In this lesson, the students:

- *Wonder* about stories read independently
- Refer to the stories to support their thinking
- Explain their thinking

Materials

- *The Paper Crane*
- Books at appropriate levels for independent reading
- Small self-stick notes for each student
- *Assessment Resource Book*
- Unit 5 Parent Letter (BLM5)

1 ▶ Review Wondering

Have partners sit together. Remind the students that this week they heard *The Paper Crane* and thought about whether or not their "I wonder" statements were explained in the story.

2 ▶ Prepare to Wonder During Independent Reading

Explain that today the students will wonder about stories they read independently. Review using self-stick notes to mark places where they wonder. Distribute the self-stick notes, and have the students use them to mark places in their books where they wonder about something or where a question comes to mind.

3 ▶ Read Independently

Have the students read independently for up to 15 minutes. Circulate and ask the students what they are reading and what they wonder. Stop the students at 5-minute intervals to talk with their partners about their wondering.

4 ▶ **Discuss the Independent Reading**

  First in pairs, and then as a class, discuss:

Q *As you read today, what did you wonder about?*

Q *What was happening in the story when you wondered that?*

Q *Did the book answer what you wondered? How?*

Review with the students what they have learned in this unit. Remind them that wondering about stories helps readers better understand what they are reading. Tell the students to note questions they have or what they wonder about during their reading throughout the day.

5 ▶ **Reflect on Working Together**

  Have the students use "Think, Pair, Share" to discuss:

Q *How has your partner helped you to become a better reader?*

Ask a few volunteers to share their ideas with the class.

Teacher Note

This is the last week of Unit 5. You will reassign partners for Unit 6.

INDIVIDUAL COMPREHENSION ASSESSMENT

Before continuing with Unit 6, take this opportunity to assess individual students' progress in using wondering to understand text. Please refer to pages 36–37 in the *Assessment Resource Book* for instructions.

SOCIAL SKILLS ASSESSMENT

Take this opportunity to assess your students' social development using the "Social Skills Assessment" record sheet on pages 2–3 of the *Assessment Resource Book*.

This assessment will occur again after Unit 7.

 Parent Letter

Send home with each student the Parent Letter for this unit (see "Do Ahead," page 167). Periodically, have a few students share with the class what they are reading at home.

 Making Meaning Vocabulary **Teacher**

Next week you will revisit *The Paper Crane* to teach Vocabulary Week 14.

Wondering

FICTION AND NARRATIVE NONFICTION

During this unit, the students explore the difference between fiction and nonfiction texts and identify what they learn from nonfiction text. They use schema and wondering to make sense of texts. During IDR, the students practice monitoring their own reading and write about their independent reading in their IDR Journals. Socially, they develop the group skill of contributing ideas that are different from other people's ideas and they continue to relate the value of responsibility to their behavior.

Week 1 *The Tale of Peter Rabbit* by Beatrix Potter
Beatrix Potter by Alexandra Wallner

Week 2 *The Art Lesson* by Tomie dePaola
**"Draw, Draw, Draw": A Short Biography
of Tomie dePaola**

Week 1

Overview

UNIT 6: WONDERING
Fiction and Narrative Nonfiction

The Tale of Peter Rabbit
by Beatrix Potter
(Frederick Warne, 1987)

This classic tale describes Peter Rabbit's adventures in Mr. McGregor's garden.

Beatrix Potter
by Alexandra Wallner
(Holiday House, 1995)

This book describes the life of Beatrix Potter and how the tale of Peter Rabbit became a story that children still enjoy today.

ALTERNATIVE BOOKS

Author: A True Story by Helen Lester

Monet by Mike Venezia

Comprehension Focus

• Students explore the difference between fiction and nonfiction texts.

• Students identify what they learn from text.

• Students use *wondering* to make sense of text.

• Students read independently.

Social Development Focus

• Students relate the value of responsibility to their behavior.

• Students develop the group skill of contributing ideas that are different from other people's ideas.

DO AHEAD

• Prior to Day 1, decide how you will randomly assign partners to work together during the unit.

• Prepare the "Thinking About My Reading" chart for self-monitoring during IDR (see Day 1, Step 7 on page 186).

• Collect nonfiction texts that the students can examine and read independently (see "About Nonfiction" on page 187).

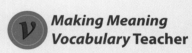

**Making Meaning
Vocabulary Teacher**

If you are teaching Developmental Studies Center's *Making Meaning Vocabulary* program, teach Vocabulary Week 14 this week. For more information, see the *Making Meaning Vocabulary Teacher's Manual.*

Read-aloud

Materials

- *The Tale of Peter Rabbit*
- Scratch paper and a pencil
- "Thinking About My Reading" chart, prepared ahead (see "Do Ahead," page 181)

***Being a* Writer™ Teacher**

You can have the students work with their *Being a Writer* partner or assign them a different partner for the *Making Meaning* lessons.

Teacher Note

The edition of *The Tale of Peter Rabbit* suggested for this week is a new version of the original 1902 edition. It is very small and the students will have difficulty seeing the illustrations during the read-aloud. Before and after today's lesson, give the students opportunities to look at the illustrations on their own.

The students will also hear a biography of Beatrix Potter this week. If possible, collect other books by Beatrix Potter for them to read independently.

In this lesson, the students:

- Begin working with new partners
- Hear and discuss a story
- Read independently for up to 20 minutes
- Share their thinking

▶1 Pair Students and Get Ready to Work Together

Randomly assign partners and have them sit together. Explain that for the next two weeks they will work with these partners.

Tell the students that they will be talking with their partners about books they hear read aloud. Ask:

Q *What did you do the last time you worked with a partner that will help you work with your new partner?*

▶2 Introduce *The Tale of Peter Rabbit*

Show the cover of *The Tale of Peter Rabbit* and explain that it was the first story Beatrix Potter wrote and illustrated. She wrote it and many similar books 100 years ago, and children still enjoy reading them. Explain that you will read a story about Beatrix Potter's life in the next lesson.

Explain that you will stop during the reading of *The Tale of Peter Rabbit* to have partners talk about the story.

Read *The Tale of Peter Rabbit* Aloud

Read the story aloud, showing the illustrations and stopping as described on the next page.

Teacher Note

◀ If the students had a chance to see the book before the read-aloud, you might want to read without showing the illustrations.

Suggested Vocabulary

mischief: playful behavior that may bother or harm others (p. 13)

implored him to exert himself: begged him to try and get up (p. 33)

sieve: container with lots of small holes in it (p. 34; refer to the illustration on p. 35)

hoe: gardening tool with a long handle and a thin blade (p. 49)

fortnight: two weeks (p. 54)

ELL Vocabulary

English Language Learners may benefit from discussing additional vocabulary, including:

lane: narrow (not wide) road (p. 10)

Peter gave himself up for lost: Peter was sure he would be caught (p. 36)

wriggled out just in time: escaped just moments before Mr. McGregor caught him (p. 38)

upsetting: knocking over (p. 44; refer to the illustration)

damp: wet (p. 47)

caught sight of him: saw him (p. 50)

Stop after:

> **p. 10**   "'…he was put in a pie by Mrs. McGregor.'"

Ask:

Q *What does Mrs. Rabbit mean when she says that their father had an accident?*

Have a few students share with the class. Reread page 10 and continue reading to the next stopping point:

> **p. 18**   "But Peter, who was very naughty, ran straight away to Mr. McGregor's garden, and squeezed under the gate!"

Ask:

Q *What has happened so far, and what do you think will happen next?*

 Have the students use "Turn to Your Partner" to discuss the question. Without stopping to share as a class, reread page 18 and continue reading to the next stop. Follow this procedure at the next three stopping points:

p. 30 "It was a blue jacket with brass buttons, quite new."

p. 41 "He went back to his work."

p. 49 "His back was turned towards Peter, and beyond him was the gate!"

Continue reading to the end of the book.

4 ▶ Discuss the Story

As a class, discuss:

Q *What part of the story did you like best?*

As the students respond, reread the parts of the story they mention and show the illustrations.

5 ▶ Wonder About Beatrix Potter

Remind the students that in the next lesson they will hear a true story about Beatrix Potter's life. Ask:

Q *After hearing* The Tale of Peter Rabbit *and seeing the illustrations, what are some things you wonder about the author, Beatrix Potter? What would you like to find out about her?*

FACILITATION TIP

During this unit, we encourage you to **avoid repeating or paraphrasing** students' responses. Repeating what students say when they speak too softly or paraphrasing them when they don't speak clearly teaches the students to listen to you but not to one another. Help the students learn to take responsibility by asking one another to speak up or by asking a question if they don't understand what a classmate has said.

Students might say:

"I wonder if she enjoyed writing children's books."

"I wonder if she had a pet rabbit."

"I wonder if she only wrote books about animals."

"I wonder if she was married and had children of her own."

Tell the students that some of their questions might be addressed in the book about Beatrix Potter they will hear in the next lesson.

◀ **Teacher Note**

Record a few of the students' "I wonder" statements on scratch paper. In particular, record questions that might be answered in Beatrix Potter's biography.

6 ▶ **Reflect on Working Together**

Facilitate a brief discussion about how partners worked together. Ask questions such as:

Q *What worked well for you and your new partner today?*

Q *What do you want to keep working on?*

Tell the students that they will have more opportunities to work with their partners.

INDIVIDUALIZED DAILY READING

7 ▶ **Teach Self-monitoring**

Before the students read independently, explain that today you will stop them periodically during IDR to have them think about how well they are understanding their own reading. Tell them that good readers pause while reading to think about what they are reading and how well they are understanding. Direct their attention to the question on the following page, which you have written on a piece of chart paper labeled "Thinking About My Reading."

Thinking About My Reading

- What is happening in my story right now?

- Does the reading make sense?

- How many words on the page I just read are new to me?

- How many words don't I know?

- Would it be better to continue reading this book or get a new book?

Read each of the charted questions aloud. Explain that these questions will help the students know whether their books are right for them. Explain that when you stop them you would like them to think about each of these questions quietly before continuing to read. When they realize that they are not understanding, they need to reread. If they don't understand after the second reading, they may need to get a new book.

Have the students read independently for up to 20 minutes. Stop them at 10-minute intervals, read the questions on the chart aloud, and have them monitor their comprehension by thinking about the questions.

As the students read, circulate among them and ask individual students to read a selection aloud for you and tell you what it is about. Use the questions on the chart to help struggling students practice monitoring their own comprehension.

At the end of independent reading, have the students talk about how the questions on the chart helped them monitor their own comprehension.

Day 2

Read-aloud/Strategy Lesson

In this lesson, the students:

* Compare fiction and nonfiction
* Identify what they learn from a nonfiction text
* *Wonder* about the text
* Read independently for up to 20 minutes
* Share their thinking

About Nonfiction: Wondering

The purpose of this unit and the two that follow is to introduce the students to nonfiction text and help them make sense of nonfiction using the reading comprehension strategies they have learned in earlier units. These strategies include *making connections* to information the students already know, *wondering* about topics they read about, and *visualizing* what authors describe. The units' primary goal is for the students to use comprehension strategies to make sense of what they read, rather than to recall the many facts presented in the books.

In this unit the students informally compare nonfiction and fiction, think about what they are learning from nonfiction texts, and use *wondering* to think more about the texts.

If possible, provide a variety of narrative nonfiction (biographies and autobiographies) and expository text for the students to read independently. Expository texts include books and magazines like *Ask, Discover, Ranger Rick,* and *Scholastic News.* For information about Developmental Studies Center's Individualized Daily Reading Libraries, see page xxvii and visit Developmental Studies Center's website at www.devstu.org.

1 Introduce Nonfiction

Have partners sit together. Remind them that yesterday they heard *The Tale of Peter Rabbit.* Explain that this story is called *fiction* because it has make-believe characters, places, and things that happen. Write *fiction: make-believe stories* on the board. Direct the students' attention to some of the other fiction books you displayed and point out that these books are also fiction.

Materials

* *Beatrix Potter* (pages 4–21)
* "I wonder" statements you recorded on scratch paper on Day 1
* Scratch paper and a pencil
* Variety of fiction and nonfiction books
* "Thinking About My Reading" chart

◀ Teacher Note

Display a few nonfiction and fiction texts where all the students can see them. Select texts that at least some of your students have read or heard.

Explain that during the coming weeks the students will hear and read books about real people, animals, and things. Explain that these books are called *nonfiction*. Write *nonfiction: books about real people, places, and things* on the board. Direct the students' attention to the nonfiction books you displayed, briefly describing each one. (For example, you might say, "*Reptiles* is a nonfiction book that gives lots of information about snakes, such as where they live and what they eat.")

ELL **Note**

Your English Language Learners will benefit from previewing *Beatrix Potter* prior to today's read-aloud.

2 ▶ Introduce *Beatrix Potter* and Build Background Knowledge

Show the cover of *Beatrix Potter* and read the title and author's name aloud. Explain that this is a true story about Beatrix Potter, the author of *The Tale of Peter Rabbit*. Point out that a nonfiction book that tells the story of a person's life is called a *biography*.

Explain that Beatrix was born in England around 150 years ago. Beatrix loved science, animals, and drawing. She often drew pictures and wrote about animals.

Read aloud some of the "I wonder" statements that you jotted down at the end of the previous lesson. Ask the students to listen for answers to their questions.

3 ▶ Read *Beatrix Potter* Aloud with Brief Section Introductions

Teacher Note ▶

This week's read-aloud contains a lot of factual information that the students might have difficulty following. To support them, you will introduce each section briefly before you read it. This will help focus the students' listening on the main ideas discussed in that section.

Explain that today you will read the first part of the book aloud and that you will stop during the reading to have partners talk about what they are learning about Beatrix's life.

Suggested Vocabulary

governesses: women who take care of other people's children (p. 4)

fond of: liked very much (p. 6)

boarding school: school at which the students live (p. 10)

companion: person who accompanies another (p. 10)

bronchitis: illness of the throat and lungs (p. 12)

rheumatic fever: a children's disease that is no longer common (p. 12)

enlarge: make bigger (p. 18)

> **ELL Vocabulary**
>
> English Language Learners may benefit from discussing additional vocabulary, including:
>
> **studio:** room where someone makes art (p. 8; refer to the illustration)
>
> **strict:** having a lot of rules that must be followed (p. 12)
>
> **rewriting the story:** writing the story again and making changes to it (p. 18)
>
> **Beatrix got her way:** Beatrix did not have to make the pictures bigger (p. 20)

Explain that the first part of the book describes Beatrix and her brother Bertram's lives as children. Start reading on page 4, showing the illustrations as you read. Stop after:

> **p. 6**   "Beatrix was especially fond of two pet mice named Hunca Munca and Appley Dapply, and a rabbit named Peter."

Ask:

Q *What did you learn about Beatrix as a child?*

Have the students use "Turn to Your Partner" to discuss the question; then ask a few volunteers to share with the class.

◄ Teacher Note

You might want to reread pages 4–6 before discussing the question.

Explain that the next part of the book tells about Beatrix's interest in painting. Ask the students to listen for what they learn about this. Reread the last sentence before the stop and continue reading to the next stop:

> **p. 9**   "Her years of practice made her an excellent painter."

Ask:

Q *What did you learn about Beatrix Potter's interest in painting?*

Have the students use "Turn to Your Partner" to discuss the question; then ask a few volunteers to share with the class.

Explain that the next part of the book tells about Beatrix's good friend Annie Carter, and how Beatrix came to write *The Tale of Peter Rabbit*. Reread the last sentence on page 9 and continue reading to the next stop:

> **p. 15**   "She didn't think about writing other stories because she was more interested in making drawings and keeping notes on science."

Ask:

Q *What have you learned about how Beatrix got the idea for* The Tale of Peter Rabbit*?*

Have two or three pairs share what they learned.

Briefly paraphrase page 16. Read the last paragraph on page 16 and continue to read to the next stopping point:

> **p. 21**   "The book was very popular and made a lot of money for her."

Ask:

Q *What did you learn from the part of the story I just read?*

▶4 Discuss What the Students Learned and Wonder

Remind the students that today they learned about Beatrix Potter's life from her childhood to the age of 36. Ask:

Q *What did you learn about Beatrix Potter that surprised you?*

Students might say:

"I was surprised that she was alone a lot and didn't have many friends."

"I think it is funny that her parents hired a friend for her."

"I was surprised that her parents did not let her live alone."

Remind the students that *wondering* is a strategy that can help them think about what they are reading.

Teacher Note ▶

Page 16 of the book contains information that is not directly related to how Beatrix Potter wrote and published *The Tale of Peter Rabbit*. To maintain the students' focus on how the author wrote her book, we suggest that you briefly paraphrase page 16.

 Note

You might prompt the students to begin their response by saying, "I learned...."

Ask:

Q *Based on what you know so far about Beatrix Potter, what do you wonder about her?*

Tell the students that some of their questions might be answered in the next lesson, when they hear the rest of *Beatrix Potter.*

◀ **Teacher Note**

Record a few of the students' "I wonder" statements on scratch paper. In particular, record questions that might be addressed in the last part of the book.

5 ▶ Reflect on Working Together

Briefly discuss how partners worked together. Point out ways you noticed the students contributing to their partner conversations and listening to one another.

INDIVIDUALIZED DAILY READING

6 ▶ Practice Self-monitoring

Have the students read nonfiction independently for up to 20 minutes.

Stop the students at 10-minute intervals and have them monitor their comprehension by thinking about the questions on the "Thinking About My Reading" chart.

As the students read, circulate among them and ask individual students to read a selection aloud to you and tell you what it is about. Use the questions on the chart to help struggling students practice monitoring their own comprehension.

At the end of independent reading, have the students talk about how the questions on the chart helped them monitor their own comprehension.

Thinking About My Reading

- What is happening in my story right now?

Day 3

Materials

- *Beatrix Potter* (pages 22–31)
- Your jotted "I wonder" statements from Days 1 and 2
- *Assessment Resource Book*
- *Student Response Book,* IDR Journal section

Read-aloud/Strategy Lesson

In this lesson, the students:

- Identify what they learn from a nonfiction text
- *Wonder* about the text
- Read independently for up to 20 minutes
- Contribute ideas that are different from other people's ideas

▶1 Introduce and Briefly Model Contributing Different Ideas

Have partners sit together. Review that this year they have learned several skills to help them work with their partners, such as explaining their thinking and listening carefully to each other.

Explain that today the students will learn a new skill: contributing ideas that are different from their partners' ideas. Point out that this skill is especially useful when reading nonfiction books with lots of information, such as *Beatrix Potter*. If each partner contributes different ideas, then together the pair can remember more information.

Choose a volunteer to act as your partner. Show the cover of *Beatrix Potter* and ask:

Q *What do you remember about Beatrix Potter from the first part of the book?*

Listen as your partner talks; then model contributing a different idea. (For example, you might say, "You remembered that Beatrix was lonely as a child because she didn't have any friends. In addition to what you said, I learned that she first wrote about Peter Rabbit in a letter to Noel, who was Annie's son.")

Ask partners to briefly practice the skill by taking turns telling each other different things they remember from the first part of the book.

 Read the Rest of *Beatrix Potter* Aloud with Brief Section Introductions

Explain that you will read the rest of the book aloud today, and the students will learn about Beatrix's life after she became famous for writing *The Tale of Peter Rabbit*.

Suggested Vocabulary

tales: stories (p. 22)

proposed: asked her to marry him (p. 25)

disapproved: didn't think it was a good idea (p. 26)

museums: places where interesting objects of art, history, or science are displayed (p. 28)

tourists: people who travel and visit places for pleasure (p. 28)

private: quiet, keeping to oneself (p. 30)

modest: not boastful; she did not brag (p. 30)

ELL Vocabulary

English Language Learners may benefit from discussing additional vocabulary, including:

disturb: frighten; annoy (p. 28)

 ELL Note

English Language Learners might benefit from viewing accompanying illustrations before hearing the text.

Remind the students that at the end of the first day's reading, Beatrix had just become famous and wealthy because of her book, *The Tale of Peter Rabbit*. Explain that the next part of the book tells about Beatrix's time at Hilltop Farm in the countryside of England. Reread page 21 and continue reading to the following stopping point:

p. 22   "Finally, Beatrix was doing what she wanted and was happy."

Ask:

Q   *What have you learned about Beatrix in this part of the story?*

 Have the students use "Turn to Your Partner" to discuss the question. Remind them to share different ideas. Then ask a few volunteers to share their ideas with the class.

Wondering
Fiction and Narrative Nonfiction

Unit 6 ▶ Week 1 ▶ Day 3

Explain that the last part of the book talks about Beatrix's marriage. Reread page 22 and continue reading to the next stopping point:

> **p. 26** "Her eyesight was getting weak, and she preferred spending her time with her animals and farming."

First in pairs, and then as a class, discuss:

Q *What new information have you learned about Beatrix Potter?*

Have two or three pairs share what they learned. Reread the last sentence on page 26 and continue reading to the end of the book.

CLASS COMPREHENSION ASSESSMENT

As the students share, ask yourself:

Q *Have the students learned new things about Beatrix Potter from the reading?*

Q *Are partners contributing different ideas?*

Record your observations on page 17 of the *Assessment Resource Book.*

3 Discuss the Book and What the Students Wonder

Facilitate a brief whole-class discussion about what the students learned and what they wonder. Ask questions such as:

Q *In what ways did Beatrix use her own life to help her write her stories?*

Q *What was the most surprising or interesting thing that you learned about Beatrix Potter?*

Read aloud and discuss one or two of the "I wonder" statements that you jotted down on Days 1 and 2 to connect the students' questions with information in the text. Point out that they could read other books or magazines or use the Internet to find out more about Beatrix Potter.

Teacher Note

If you want to shorten this reading, you might paraphrase, rather than read, pages 24–25.

Reflect on Contributing Different Ideas

Briefly discuss how the students did contributing ideas that were different from their partners' ideas. Ask questions such as:

Q *What did you and your partner do to contribute different ideas?*

Q *Were you able to remember more of the book together by contributing different ideas? Give us an example.*

Explain that partners will have more opportunities to practice contributing different ideas in the next lesson.

INDIVIDUALIZED DAILY READING

5 **Practice Self-monitoring/Have the Students Write in Their IDR Journals**

Have the students read nonfiction independently for up to 20 minutes.

As the students read, circulate among them and ask individual students to read a selection aloud for you. Use the questions on the "Thinking About My Reading" chart to help struggling students practice monitoring their own comprehension.

At the end of independent reading, have the students write in their IDR Journals about their reading.

 Note

Consider having your English Language Learners draw, rather than write, about an interesting part of their reading.

EXTENSIONS

Read Other Tales by Beatrix Potter

Read other stories by Beatrix Potter, and have the students discuss the tales and their connections to her life. (For example, she had a pet bunny named Bounce, and she wrote a story about a bunny.)

Learn More About Beatrix Potter

Read other stories about Beatrix Potter. Biographies of Potter for young readers are: *Beatrix Potter* by Elizabeth Buchan, *My Dear Noel: The Story of a Letter from Beatrix Potter* by Jane Johnson, *Beatrix Potter (Tell Me More)* by John Malam, and *Beatrix Potter (Lives and Times)* by Jayne Woodhouse.

v *Making Meaning*
Vocabulary **Teacher**

Next week you will revisit *Beatrix Potter* to teach Vocabulary Week 15.

Week 2

Overview

UNIT 6: WONDERING
Fiction and Narrative Nonfiction

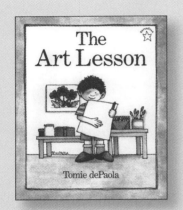

The Art Lesson
by Tomie dePaola
(PaperStar, 1999)

This autobiographical tale recounts Tomie dePaola's early love of drawing.

"Draw, Draw, Draw": A Short Biography of Tomie dePaola

This article describes the life of author and illustrator Tomie dePaola.

ALTERNATIVE BOOKS

Now One Foot, Now the Other by Tomie dePaola

The Baby Sister by Tomie dePaola

Comprehension Focus

- Students identify what they learn from nonfiction text.

- Students use *wondering* to make sense of text.

- Students read independently.

Social Development Focus

- Students relate the value of responsibility to their behavior.

- Students develop the group skill of contributing ideas that are different from other people's ideas.

DO AHEAD

- Collect books written or illustrated by Tomie dePaola (including other autobiographical stories) for the students to read independently.

- Prepare a chart with the title "What We Wonder About Tomie dePaola" (see Day 2, Step 2 on page 204).

- Make copies of the Unit 6 Parent Letter (BLM6) to send home with the students on the last day of the unit.

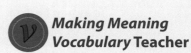

Making Meaning Vocabulary Teacher

If you are teaching Developmental Studies Center's *Making Meaning Vocabulary* program, teach Vocabulary Week 15 this week. For more information, see the *Making Meaning Vocabulary Teacher's Manual.*

Day 1

Read-aloud

In this lesson, the students:

- Identify what they learn from a nonfiction text
- *Wonder* about and *make personal connections* to a text
- Read independently for up to 20 minutes
- Contribute ideas that are different from other people's ideas

Materials

- *The Art Lesson*
- Variety of books written and/or illustrated by Tomie dePaola
- "Thinking About My Reading" chart

▶ 1 Review Biographical Nonfiction and Build Background Knowledge

Have partners sit together. Review that last week the students listened to a biography of Beatrix Potter, and that a biography is a nonfiction story that tells about someone's life. Explain that today they will hear a story called *The Art Lesson,* by Tomie dePaola. Tomie based the story on his own childhood.

Refer to the books you have displayed and explain that these are books that have been written and/or illustrated by Tomie dePaola. Briefly show a few and ask the students whether they are familiar with any of them.

Teacher Note ▶

In this lesson, the students will hear a story about Tomie dePaola's childhood interest in art. To introduce the lesson, display a few of his books where all the students can see them. Try to select books that are familiar to some of your students. If possible, read a couple of the books prior to this lesson.

▶ 2 Introduce *The Art Lesson*

Show the cover of *The Art Lesson* and explain that it is a story about a boy who loves to draw. Read the first paragraph on the back cover aloud.

Explain that you will stop during the reading to have partners talk about what they are learning and wondering.

Read *The Art Lesson* Aloud and Wonder

Read *The Art Lesson* aloud, showing the illustrations and stopping as described below.

Suggested Vocabulary

barber shop: place to get a haircut (p. 9)
school property: materials that belong to the school (p. 22)
paper monitor: child in charge of passing out paper in the classroom (p. 25)

ELL Vocabulary

English Language Learners may benefit from discussing additional vocabulary, including:

carpenters: people who make things out of wood (p. 14)
couldn't wait: was very excited (p. 15)
not pleased: angry (p. 22)

Stop after:

> **p. 14** "But, when the painters came, his dad said, 'That's it, Tommy. No more drawing on the walls.'"

Ask:

Q *What have you learned about Tommy so far?*

Have two or three students share their ideas with the class. Then ask:

Q *What are you wondering at this point in the story?*

Have the students use "Turn to Your Partner" to discuss the question. Remind them to try to come up with questions that are different from their partners' questions. Have one or two students share with the class. Reread the last sentence and continue reading to the next stopping point:

> **p. 18** "…and she always carried a big box of thick colored chalks."

Ask:

Q *Now what are you wondering?*

 Have the students use "Turn to Your Partner" to discuss the question. Have one or two students share with the class. Reread page 18 and continue reading to the next stopping point:

> **p. 23** "And Joe was right. They only got ONE piece of paper."

Ask:

Q *How do you think Tommy feels at this point? What do you think will happen next?*

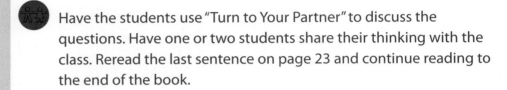 Have the students use "Turn to Your Partner" to discuss the questions. Have one or two students share their thinking with the class. Reread the last sentence on page 23 and continue reading to the end of the book.

▶ 4 **Discuss the Story and Make Connections**

Facilitate a whole-class discussion using questions such as:

Q *What part of the story did you like best?*

Q *What was Tommy's problem when he went to school? How was it solved?*

Q *Have you ever felt or acted like Tommy does in this story?*

As the students respond, reread the passages they mention and show the corresponding illustrations.

▶ 5 **Reflect on Working Together**

Facilitate a brief discussion about how partners worked together. Ask:

Q *How did you and your partner do contributing ideas that were different from each other's? Give us some examples.*

Tell the students that they will hear a short biography of Tomie dePaola in the next lesson. Invite them to look at and read other books by Tomie dePaola on their own.

FACILITATION TIP

This week continue to **avoid repeating or paraphrasing** the students' responses. Help them to learn to participate responsibly in class discussions by asking one another to speak up or by asking a question if they don't understand what a classmate has said.

INDIVIDUALIZED DAILY READING

▶6 **Practice Self-monitoring/Document IDR Conferences**

Have the students read nonfiction books independently for up to 20 minutes.

Use the "IDR Conference Notes" record sheet to conduct and document individual conferences. As you confer with each student, ask her to stop and use the questions on the "Thinking About My Reading" chart to think about how well she is understanding the reading. If the student is struggling, decide if she should reread the text or select a new book.

At the end of independent reading, have the students share their reading with the class. Ask questions such as:

Q *What do you like about what you read?*

Q *What surprised you in your reading?*

EXTENSION

Read Other Autobiographical Stories by Tomie dePaola

Read other autobiographical stories by Tomie dePaola and have the students discuss the stories and make personal connections. Some other stories based on his life are *Nana Upstairs & Nana Downstairs; The Baby Sister; Tom;* and *Now One Foot, Now the Other.*

 Note

Before the students begin to read, preview the questions you will ask them at the end of independent reading. For example, you might tell them that you'll ask them to talk about what they liked about what they read and what surprised them in their reading.

---

*Thinking About
My Reading*

- *What is happening in my story right now?*

Day 2

Read-aloud/Strategy Lesson

Materials

- "Draw, Draw, Draw" (see pages 209–211)
- *The Art Lesson*
- "What We Wonder About Tomie dePaola" chart and a marker
- *Assessment Resource Book*
- "Thinking About My Reading" chart

In this lesson, the students:

- Identify what they learn from a nonfiction text
- *Wonder* about the text
- Read independently for up to 20 minutes
- Contribute ideas that are different from other people's ideas

1 ▶ Review *The Art Lesson*

Have partners sit together. Show the cover of *The Art Lesson* and remind the students that Tomie dePaola based this story on his own childhood. Leaf through the pages of the book and show the illustrations. Ask:

Q *What did we learn about the character Tommy in this book?*

Have a few students share. Remind them to contribute different ideas.

2 ▶ Introduce "Draw, Draw, Draw" and Wonder

Explain that today they will hear a short biography of Tomie dePaola called "Draw, Draw, Draw." Remind the students that a biography is nonfiction—it is a true story about a person's life. Ask:

Q *What are some things you wonder about Tomie dePaola?*

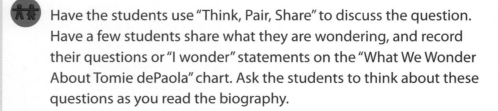

Have the students use "Think, Pair, Share" to discuss the question. Have a few students share what they are wondering, and record their questions or "I wonder" statements on the "What We Wonder About Tomie dePaola" chart. Ask the students to think about these questions as you read the biography.

Explain that you will stop during the reading to have partners talk about what they are learning. This biography does not have illustrations so they can use their imaginations to visualize as you read.

 Read "Draw, Draw, Draw" Aloud

Read "Draw, Draw, Draw" aloud, stopping as described below.

Suggested Vocabulary

appears: shows up (p. 209)

family legend: family story passed down from one generation to the next (p. 209)

was determined: had his mind made up (p. 209)

deep fried: cooked in fat, like french fries (p. 209)

tap dancing: dancing with special shoes that make clicking noises (p. 209)

performing onstage: dancing or acting for an audience on a stage (p. 209)

hire: give a person a job (p. 210)

reveals: tells (p. 210)

fabulous: wonderful (p. 211)

ELL Vocabulary

English Language Learners may benefit from discussing additional vocabulary, including:

active: moving around a lot (p. 209)

famous: known about by a lot of people (p. 209)

letter of advice: letter telling Tomie how he could get better at drawing (p. 210)

Read the first five paragraphs and stop after:

> **p. 209** "…and continued until he grew up, often performing onstage."

Ask:

Q *What did you learn about Tomie as a child?*

 Have the students use "Turn to Your Partner" to discuss the question. Then ask a few volunteers to share their ideas.

Teacher Note

If possible, show the students a photograph of Tomie dePaola. The book *Tomie dePaola: His Art & His Stories* by Barbara Elleman contains several photographs.

ELL

CLASS COMPREHENSION ASSESSMENT

As the students contribute to this discussion, ask yourself:

Q *Are the students' ideas connected to the text?*

Q *Are partners contributing different ideas?*

Record your observations on page 18 of the *Assessment Resource Book.*

Reread the last sentence before the stop and continue reading. Stop after:

p. 210 "One was Arnold Lobel, who wrote and illustrated the *Frog and Toad* series."

Ask:

Q *What did you learn about Tomie in the part that I just read?*

Have the students use "Turn to Your Partner" to discuss the question. Then ask a few volunteers to share their ideas. Reread the last sentence and continue reading to the end of the biography.

At the end of the reading, turn to the last page of *The Art Lesson* and point out the symbol of the white bird with a pink heart. Tell the students that they might look for this symbol when they read other stories by Tomie dePaola.

▶ 4 Discuss What the Students Learned and Wonder

Facilitate a brief whole-class discussion about what the students learned and wondered.

Ask:

Q (Refer to the "What We Wonder About Tomie dePaola" chart.) *What did we learn about Tomie dePaola that could help us answer some of the questions we had?*

Q *What did you learn about Tomie dePaola that surprised you?*

5 Reflect on Working Together

Briefly discuss how partners worked together. Point out ways you noticed students contributing ideas that were different from their partners'.

> ### INDIVIDUAL COMPREHENSION ASSESSMENT
>
> Before continunuing with Unit 7, take this opportunity to assess individual students' progress using *wondering* to understand text. Please refer to pages 38–39 in the *Assessment Resource Book* for instructions.

INDIVIDUALIZED DAILY READING

6 Practice Self-monitoring/Document IDR Conferences

Have the students read nonfiction books independently for up to 20 minutes.

Use the "IDR Conference Notes" record sheet to conduct and document individual conferences.

As you confer with each student, ask him to stop and use the questions on the "Thinking About My Reading" chart to think aut how well he is understanding the reading.

At the end of independent reading, have the students share what they read with their partners. Ask each student to begin by telling his partner the title of his book. Then have the students share one thing they learned today from their reading. If time allows, have a few students share what they learned with the class.

> ### Thinking About My Reading
>
> - What is happening in my story right now?

EXTENSION

Learn More About Tomie dePaola

Use the questions on the "What We Wonder About Tomie dePaola" chart to learn more about him. *Tomie dePaola: His Art & His Stories* by Barbara Elleman contains additional information, photographs of Tomie and his family, and examples of his illustrations and paintings.

Article

"Draw, Draw, Draw": A Short Biography of Tomie dePaola

Tomie dePaola was born on September 15, 1934, in Meriden, Connecticut, where his father worked as a barber. His parents named him Thomas Anthony dePaola after his two grandfathers. His Irish grandpa, Tom Downey, was a hero of Tomie's. He appears in many of the author's books, including *Now One Step, Now the Other*, and *Tom*. His Italian grandpa, Antonio dePaola, died before Tomie was born.

Why does Tomie spell his name the way he does? A family legend says that before he was born, Tomie's mother joked to her cousin that she thought the active baby might grow up to be a dancer. Her cousin, Morton Downey, a famous singer, knew that Mrs. dePaola was planning to name her son Thomas. According to the story, Morton said that if little Tommy was going to be famous, he would have to spell his name "differently." So Tomie did, and he is—famous, that is.

Tomie was the second child in a family of four children. Maureen, who was born after Tomie, was his favorite. His book *The Baby Sister* tells how happy Tomie was when she was born. The two loved making puppets together and putting on shows for their family. The grown-up brother and sister are still close friends.

DePaola describes himself as a stubborn little boy. He was determined to learn to cook and insisted on creating his own recipes. He says, "I found out that flour and water and ketchup, deep fried, didn't taste very good, but I had to discover that for myself."

Besides doing artwork, Tomie loved reading, putting on shows, and dancing, just as his mother predicted. He began taking tap dancing lessons at age five and continued until he grew up, often performing onstage.

continues

"Draw, Draw, Draw": A Short Biography of Tomie dePaola
continued

As a boy, Tomie had many great teachers. The ones he loved best were Beulah Bowers, the art teacher he describes in *The Art Lesson*, his fifth grade teacher, Rose Mulligan, who read aloud to the class every day, and Miss Leah, his tap dancing teacher.

When he was in fourth grade, Tomie sent one of his pictures to Walt Disney, the famous cartoonist who created Mickey Mouse. Tomie was sure that Mr. Disney would see what a good artist he was and hire him to help make Disney cartoons. Disney sent the boy's picture back with a letter of advice. He told Tomie to keep his early artwork and practice. Tomie paid attention to this advice. He drew all the time. DePaola says that when children write to him today he takes their letters very seriously, because he knows how important good advice can be.

Tomie's twin cousins, Franny and Fuffy McLaughlin, went to an art college called Pratt Institute. After high school, Tomie went there, too. For him, art school was "heaven on earth." His teachers encouraged him to "keep your eyes open and draw, draw, draw." Some of Tomie's friends at Pratt also went on to create popular children's books. One was Arnold Lobel, who wrote and illustrated the *Frog and Toad* series.

Even though he practiced all the time, it took many years for Tomie to get his first job as a book illustrator, drawing the pictures for a nonfiction book called *Sound*, written by Lisa Miller.

Soon Tomie began writing his own books instead of just illustrating other writers' work. Many of his books are based on his own life. In *The Art Lesson* he describes his beloved art teacher, Mrs. Bowers, and the box of 64 crayons that he received as a birthday gift. *Nana Upstairs & Nana Downstairs* tells about Tomie's Irish grandma and great-grandma. *Oliver Button Is a Sissy* reveals

continues

Article

"Draw, Draw, Draw": A Short Biography of Tomie dePaola
continued

that as a boy Tomie was terrible at sports, though he was a fabulous tap dancer.

Tomie dePaola also writes and illustrates religious stories, folktales, and made-up stories with funny characters such as Strega Nona, Big Anthony, and Bill and Pete, pals who happen to be a crocodile and a bird. "All of my characters seem to be parts of me," says dePaola.

Today Tomie dePaola lives in New London, New Hampshire. To make an art studio, he fixed up a large 200-year-old barn. Though he has no children, he has many nieces and nephews. He also has four dogs named Madison, Markus, Morgan, and Moffat.

The symbol for dePaola's company, Whitebird Inc., is a little white bird with a pink heart on its chest. This symbol appears in many of his books. When Tomie dePaola signs his name, he often adds a little pink heart to his signature.

Day 3

Materials

- Space for the class to sit in a circle
- "Class Meeting Ground Rules" chart
- "Thinking About My Reading" chart
- *Student Response Book,* IDR Journal section
- Unit 6 Parent Letter (BLM6)

Class Meeting
Ground Rules

- one person talks
  at a time

FACILITATION TIP

Reflect on your experience **avoiding repeating or paraphrasing** students' responses. Is the practice beginning to feel natural? Are you integrating it into class discussions throughout the day? What effect is the use of this technique having on the students? We encourage you to continue to use this practice as you facilitate class discussions.

Class Meeting

In this lesson, the students:

- Participate in a class meeting
- Analyze the ways they have contributed to the reading community
- Read independently for up to 20 minutes
- Share their thinking with one another

▶1 Gather for a Class Meeting

Tell the students that they are going to have a class meeting today to check in on how they are doing creating a safe and caring reading community. Have them move to the circle, with partners sitting together, and briefly review the ground rules.

▶2 Reflect on the Reading Community

Remind the students that they have been working to create a reading community in their classroom where everyone feels welcome, safe, and respected. Ask them to think about how they have contributed to building their community.

After a few moments of individual reflection, use the following questions to facilitate a whole-class discussion:

Q *What is one thing you've done that has helped to make our class a caring community?*

Q *What are some examples you've seen of your classmates acting in caring ways?*

Q *Are you feeling safe and respected in our reading community? If yes, why? If not, what suggestion do you have for creating a safer and more respectful community?*

During the discussion, ask the students not to use names when giving examples and to avoid blaming or accusing others. Use "Turn to Your Partner" as needed during this discussion to increase participation, especially if you are hearing from only a few students. You can also use "Turn to Your Partner" if many students want to speak at the same time.

Explain that you would like the students to think of one thing they will do to make others feel respected in the reading community. Tell them that you will check in with them again about how they are contributing to the community.

 3 Adjourn the Class Meeting

Refer to the "Class Meeting Ground Rules" chart and ask:

Q *How do you think we did using the ground rules during today's class meeting?*

Q *What do you think we still need to work on?*

Have the students briefly review the procedure for returning to their desks and adjourn the meeting.

Teacher Note

This is the last week in Unit 6. If the students need more practice with identifying what they have learned from a text and using wondering, repeat Days 1 and 2 of this week using an alternative book. Alternative books are listed in the Week 2 Overview.

You will reassign partners for Unit 7.

INDIVIDUALIZED DAILY READING

 4 Review Self-monitoring/Have the Students Write in Their IDR Journals

Refer to the "Thinking About My Reading" chart and review the questions. Remind the students that it is important to check their reading comprehension as they are reading.

Have the students read independently for up to 20 minutes. As the students read, circulate among them and ask questions such as:

Q *What is your book about?*

Q *What are you learning about [frogs] from this book? What do you wonder about [frogs]?*

Thinking About
My Reading

- What is happening in my
* story right now?*

Note

If the students are struggling to write, have them draw or act out what they learned from their reading.

 Parent Letter

Send home with each student the Parent Letter for this unit (see "Do Ahead," page 199). Periodically, have a few students share with the class what they are reading at home.

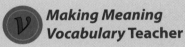 ***Making Meaning Vocabulary* Teacher**

Next week you will revisit "Draw, Draw, Draw" to teach Vocabulary Week 16.

Q *If you don't understand what you are reading, what do you do? How is this helpful?*

At the end of independent reading, have the students write about what they learned in their IDR Journals.

Unit 7

Wondering

EXPOSITORY NONFICTION

During this unit, the students continue to identify what they
learn from nonfiction. They use the comprehension strategy of
wondering to help them to make sense of nonfiction. They also
informally explore expository features to help them make sense
of texts. During IDR, the students read nonfiction independently
and wonder to help them make sense of the text. Socially, they
share their partners' thinking during whole-class discussions and
reflect on how they are taking responsibility for their behavior.

Week 1 *It Could Still Be a Worm* by Allan Fowler
  Plants that Eat Animals by Allan Fowler

Week 2 *Fishes (A True Book)* by Melissa Stewart

Week 3 *POP! A Book About Bubbles* by Kimberly Brubaker Bradley

Week 1 Overview

UNIT 7: WONDERING
Expository Nonfiction

It Could Still Be a Worm
by Allan Fowler
(Children's Press, 1996)

This book is a simple introduction to the earthworm, roundworm, flatworm, and other kinds of worms.

Plants that Eat Animals
by Allan Fowler
(Children's Press, 2001)

A variety of carnivorous plants, including the Venus's-flytrap, sundew, pitcher plant, and bladderwort, are described.

ALTERNATIVE BOOKS

It Could Still Be a Butterfly by Allan Fowler

It Could Still Be a Flower by Allan Fowler

Comprehension Focus

• Students identify what they learn from the texts.

• Students use *wondering* to make sense of the texts.

• Students informally *explore text features* of expository nonfiction.

• Students read independently.

Social Development Focus

• Students share their partners' thinking with the class.

• Students relate the value of responsibility to their behavior.

DO AHEAD

• Prior to Day 1, decide how you will randomly assign partners to work together during the unit.

• Collect nonfiction books at various reading levels for independent reading (see Day 3).

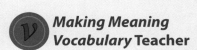

Making Meaning Vocabulary Teacher

If you are teaching Developmental Studies Center's *Making Meaning Vocabulary* program, teach Vocabulary Week 16 this week. For more information, see the *Making Meaning Vocabulary Teacher's Manual.*

Read-aloud

Materials

- *It Could Still Be a Worm*

Being a Writer™ **Teacher**

You can either have the students work with their *Being a Writer* partner or assign them a different partner for the *Making Meaning* lessons.

Teacher Note ▶

If the students have difficulty answering this question, suggest some ideas like those in the "Students might say" note.

In this lesson, the students:

- Use *wondering* to help them understand nonfiction
- Identify what they learn from a nonfiction text
- Read independently for up to 20 minutes
- Share their partners' thinking
- Relate the value of responsibility to their behavior

1 ▶ Pair Students and Get Ready to Work Together

Randomly assign new partners and have them sit together. Explain that for the next few weeks you will be asking the students to share their partners' thinking with the class.

Ask and briefly discuss:

Q *What will you have to do to be ready to share your partner's thinking with the class?*

Students might say:

"I will have to listen carefully when my partner is talking."

"I might have to ask her a question to make sure I understood her."

"I might repeat what my partner said to check to make sure I got it right."

2 ▶ Review Biographies and Introduce Another Kind of Nonfiction

Remind the students that in previous lessons they listened to two biographies, or nonfiction stories about people's lives. The biographies told the stories of Beatrix Potter and Tomie dePaola.

Tell the students that today they will listen to another type of nonfiction that gives true information about topics such as animals, plants, places, and weather; for example, the nonfiction book you will read to them today gives information about worms.

 ### 3 Introduce *It Could Still Be a Worm* and Wonder

Show the cover of *It Could Still Be a Worm* and read the title and author's name aloud. Point out that since nonfiction books tell about real things, many are illustrated with photographs rather than with drawings or paintings. Show a few of the photos, such as the sea worm photo on the cover and the earthworm photo on page 3. Briefly discuss:

Q *What do you think you know about worms?*

Q *Based on what you know, what do you wonder about them?*

Tell the students that you will stop several times during the read-aloud so partners can talk about what they are learning from the book. After you have read the book, they will share with the class what they learned and what they wonder about worms.

4 Read Aloud with Brief Section Introductions

Read *It Could Still Be a Worm* aloud, showing the photographs and stopping as described on the next page.

Suggested Vocabulary

segments: parts or sections (p. 4)
bristles: stiff hairs (p. 5)
attract the fish: make the fish come (p. 13)
dull: not bright (p. 16)
crops: plants grown on farms (p. 23)
moisture: wetness (p. 25)
wormcasts: worms' solid waste (p. 26)

ELL Vocabulary

English Language Learners may benefit from discussing additional vocabulary, including:

automobile: car (p. 8)

Note

English Language Learners will benefit from previewing the photographs and hearing the text prior to the lesson.

Teacher Note

Make sure the students understand that they will not share with the class at each stop. This maintains the flow of the text and cultivates the habit of students' relying on a partner— rather than the teacher or the whole class—to confirm and support their thinking.

Teacher Note ▶

Today's read-aloud contains a lot of factual information, which the students might have difficulty following. To support the students, you will briefly introduce each section before you read it. This will help to focus the students on the main ideas discussed in that section. You may have to read each passage twice before having partners discuss it.

Tell the students that the first part you will read tells about the sizes of different worms. Begin reading and stop after:

> **p. 8**   "…like this giant Australian earthworm."

Ask:

Q *What did you learn about different worms' sizes?*

Have the students use "Turn to Your Partner" to discuss the question.

After a minute, tell the students that the next part you will read tells about places where worms can live. Resume reading and stop after:

> **p. 15**   "…a sea worm or a ribbon worm."

Have the students use "Turn to Your Partner" to discuss:

Q *What did you learn about places where worms can live?*

After a minute, tell the students that the next part tells what different worms look like. Resume reading and stop after:

> **p. 20**   "…young insects that haven't yet grown into their adult form."

Have the students use "Turn to Your Partner" to discuss:

Q *What did you find out about what worms can look like?*

After a minute, tell the students that the last part of the book tells some ways that worms can be harmful and helpful. Resume reading and stop after:

> **p. 28**   "…and still be a worm."

Have the students use "Turn to Your Partner" to discuss:

Q *How can worms be harmful and helpful to people, plants, and animals?*

Discuss What the Students Learned and Wonder

Show pages 30–31, the "Words You Know" section. Briefly point out that some nonfiction books include sections like this one that use photos or pictures to explain the meanings of words from the book. Use these photos to help the students recall what they learned from *It Could Still Be a Worm.*

Tell the students that you will ask them some questions and they will talk with in pairs about them. Explain that later you will ask them to share their partners' thinking with the class, so it is important to listen carefully. Have the students use "Turn to Your Partner" to discuss:

Q *What did you learn about worms from this book that interested or surprised you?*

Q *What are you still wondering about worms?*

Students might say:

"My partner is wondering if worms have eyes."

"My partner is wondering how worms can be cut in half and still live."

"My partner was surprised by the part about worms being cut in half and still living. We didn't know that worms can still live after being cut in half."

Reflect on Working Together

Ask and discuss as a whole class:

Q *Did you and your partner remember different information from the book? How did that help your learning today?*

Tell the students that they will hear another nonfiction book tomorrow.

Teacher Note

If necessary, probe the students' thinking with questions such as:

Q *How long or short can worms be?*

Q *Where can worms live?*

Q *Why are worms important to people, animals, and plants?*

Grade Two | 221

INDIVIDUALIZED DAILY READING

 Model Previewing a Text Before Reading

Remind the students that they have been practicing pausing to check how well they are understanding what they are reading. Another strategy that good readers use is to look at the cover, read the information on the back of the book, and preview the book by looking through the pages to help them get acquainted with the book before reading it. Model previewing a book for the students. Tell them that looking over a nonfiction book before reading is especially helpful.

Ask the students to take the time to look over their books today before starting to read, even if they have already begun reading.

Have the students read nonfiction books independently for up to 20 minutes. As they read, circulate and ask individual students questions such as:

Q *What did you notice about your book when you looked it over before you started to read? How was this helpful to you?*

At the end of independent reading, give the students time to share with the whole class what they read and what information they learned from previewing their books.

Help the students reflect on their independent reading by asking questions such as:

Q *What did you do to take responsibility for yourself during independent reading?*

Q *What do you think is working well during independent reading? What do you want to do differently next time to help the independent reading time go well?*

 Note

You might prompt your English Language Learners to begin their response by saying "I took responsibility for myself when I…."

EXTENSION

Revisit Visualizing

Several passages in *It Could Still Be a Worm* are good ones for the students to visualize. Remind the students that *visualizing* is one of the strategies readers use to help them understand what they are reading. Have them close their eyes and picture, or visualize, the following passages:

p. 8 "Or a worm could be longer than an automobile and still be a worm—like this giant Australian earthworm."

p. 10 "A small farm might have more worms than a big city has people."

p. 19 "If [earthworms] are cut into two or more pieces, each piece can live by itself as a whole worm."

After reading each of these passages, have the students discuss their mental images, first in pairs and then as a class. Then ask each student to select one of the passages and draw a picture of her mental image. Have partners compare their drawings. As a class, discuss how visualizing helped them better understand the text.

Day 2

Materials

- *Plants that Eat Animals*
- *Student Response Book, IDR Journal section*

Read-aloud/Strategy Lesson

In this lesson, the students:

- Identify what they learn from a nonfiction text
- Use *wondering* to help them understand nonfiction
- Read independently for up to 20 minutes
- Share their partners' thinking
- Relate the value of responsibility to their behavior

1 ▶ Review the Previous Lesson

Gather the class with partners sitting together. Review that in the previous lesson, the students listened to a nonfiction book about worms and talked in pairs and with the class about what they learned and wondered. Explain that today they will listen to a book that gives information about unusual kinds of plants.

2 ▶ Introduce *Plants that Eat Animals*

Show the cover of *Plants that Eat Animals* and read the title and author's name aloud. Ask:

Q *When you hear the title of this book,* Plants that Eat Animals, *what do you wonder about?*

Students might say:

"I wonder what kinds of plants eat animals."

"I wonder how the plants trap the animals."

"I wonder how the plant knows there is an animal on it."

Have a few volunteers share their ideas with the class.

3 Use "Words You Know" to Help Structure the Read-aloud

Show pages 30–31 to the students. Point to each picture, read the name of each plant, and write the names *bladderwort, pitcher plant, sundew plant,* and *Venus's-flytrap* where everyone can see them.

Tell the students that they will learn about each of these plants from today's read-aloud. Remind them to listen carefully to learn how each kind traps and eats animals. Explain that you will stop a few times during the read-aloud to give partners a chance to discuss what they learn.

ELL Note

This will be especially helpful for your English Language Learners.

4 Read Aloud with Brief Section Introductions

Read *Plants that Eat Animals* aloud, showing the photographs, reading the accompanying captions, and stopping as described below. Before you read about each type of plant, point to its name on the list you wrote during Step 3.

> **Suggested Vocabulary**
>
> **minerals:** things in food that are needed by people, animals, and plants to stay strong and healthy (p. 3)
>
> **wetlands:** land where there is a lot of water in the soil (p. 7)
>
> **boggy:** wet and spongy (p. 12)
>
> **ELL Vocabulary**
>
> English Language Learners may benefit from discussing additional vocabulary, including:
>
> **pitcher:** container with an open top for holding and pouring liquid (p. 18)

Read page 3 aloud. Stop and ask:

Q *What do all plants need to grow? Where do most plants get what they need?*

Have one or two students respond to each question. Then reread page 3 and continue reading. At the end of page 5, tell the students that the next section you will read tells how a Venus's-flytrap gets its food. Read and stop after the caption:

◀ Teacher Note

Be ready to reread passages if necessary.

> **p. 11** "A Venus's-flytrap traps a cricket."

Ask:

Q *How does a Venus's-flytrap catch and eat insects?*

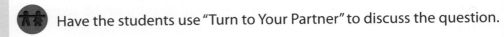 Have the students use "Turn to Your Partner" to discuss the question.

After a minute, tell the students that the next part you will read tells about sundew plants. Resume reading and stop after:

> **p. 17**   "The sundew is ready for another meal."

 Have the students use "Turn to Your Partner" to discuss:

Q *How does a sundew catch and eat its food?*

After a minute, tell the students that the next part of the book tells about pitcher plants, another kind of insect-eating plant. Resume reading and stop after the caption:

> **p. 23**   "Flytrap pitcher plant"

 Have the students use "Turn to Your Partner" to discuss:

Q *How do pitcher plants catch and kill their prey?*

After a minute, tell the students that the next section of the book tells about bladderwort plants. Resume reading and stop after:

> **p. 27**   "…it opens up and sucks the animal inside."

 Have the students use "Turn to Your Partner" to discuss:

Q *How do bladderworts catch their food?*

After a minute, resume reading and continue reading to the end of the book.

▶5 Discuss as a Whole Class

Facilitate a whole-class discussion about what the students learned from the book. Have the students use "Turn to Your Partner" to discuss the following questions. Ask the students to be ready to share their partners' thinking during the whole-class discussion.

Q *What was the most interesting thing you learned about plants that eat animals?*

Q *What are you still wondering about plants that eat animals?*

Students might say:

"My partner is wondering if a human can drink the liquid from a pitcher plant."

"My partner is wondering whether the plants can eat any small animal."

"My partner and I thought the Venus's-flytrap was the most interesting. We liked how the book describes how it traps insects."

Explain that in the coming weeks the students will continue to read and listen to nonfiction books.

6 Reflect on Sharing Their Partners' Thinking

Review that the students shared their partners' thinking about what they are still wondering about plants that eat animals. Ask and briefly discuss:

Q *What did you have to do to be ready to share your partner's thinking with the class?*

Explain that the students will have more opportunities to share their partners' thinking with the class in the next few days. Tell the students that in the coming weeks they will hear and read more nonfiction books.

INDIVIDUALIZED DAILY READING

7 Read Independently and Share Books

Have the students independently read nonfiction books for up to 20 minutes. Explain that at the end of IDR today they will each share with their partner a picture or photograph from the book they are reading and talk about the images.

FACILITATION TIP

During this unit, we invite you to practice responding neutrally with interest during class discussions. To **respond neutrally** means to refrain from overtly praising (e.g., "Great idea" or "Good job") or criticizing (e.g., "That's wrong") the students' responses. Although it may feel more natural to avoid criticism rather than praise, research shows that both kinds of response encourage students to look to you, rather than themselves, for validation. To build the students' intrinsic motivation, try responding with genuine curiosity and interest (e.g., "Interesting—say more about that") while avoiding statements that communicate judgment, whether positive or negative.

As the students read, circulate among them. Stop and ask individual students to talk about the photograph or picture they will share. Ask questions such as:

Q *What is your book about?*

Q *Which picture are you going to share with your partner? Tell me about it.*

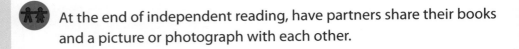 At the end of independent reading, have partners share their books and a picture or photograph with each other.

Day 3

Independent Strategy Practice

In this lesson, the students:

- Read nonfiction books independently
- Identify what they learn from a nonfiction text
- Share their thinking with one another

1 ▶ Review the Week

Have partners sit together. Remind the students that in the past couple of weeks they heard nonfiction books and talked about what they learned from the books and what they wondered. Review that nonfiction books tell about real people, places, events, or things. Explain that today the students will think about what they learn as they read nonfiction books independently.

2 ▶ Read Independently Without Stopping

Have the students use a self-stick note to mark the place where they begin to read.

Have them read independently for 5 minutes.

3 ▶ Reread Independently and Identify Information Learned

Stop the students after 5 minutes. Tell them that they will reread, starting again at the self-stick note, to find something interesting or surprising that they want to share in pairs.

Have the students return to their self-stick note and reread that section of the book for 5 minutes. Circulate as the students work. Notice whether they are able to identify what they learn from their reading.

Materials

- Nonfiction books at appropriate levels for independent reading
- A small self-stick note for each student
- *Assessment Resource Book*
- *Student Response Book* page 5

Teacher Note

Today the students will practice rereading. They will read a section of the text independently twice, once for surface understanding and again to identify something to share in pairs. You will ask the students to read for 5 minutes; then stop and reread the section, paying close attention to what they learn.

 Note

Note challenging vocabulary in the students' books and have brief discussions with individual students to define words as they read.

4 ▶ Discuss in Pairs What the Students Learned

 Stop the students after 5 minutes. Have each student share with his partner the title of the book and one thing that was interesting or surprising in it.

> ### CLASS COMPREHENSION ASSESSMENT
>
> Circulate among the students and ask yourself:
>
> **Q** *Are the students able to identify and describe something interesting or surprising they learned from their text?*
>
> Record your observations on page 19 of the *Assessment Resource Book.*

 ELL Note

Consider having your English Language Learners draw pictures, rather than write sentences, about what they learned.

5 ▶ Write About What the Students Learned

Have the students turn to *Student Response Book* page 5, "What I Learned," and explain that you would like them to write one or two sentences in their own words about what they learned from their reading.

6 ▶ Discuss Independent Reading as a Class

Have a few volunteers share something they learned from their reading. Remind each student to say the title of the book before sharing. Ask questions such as:

Q *What new or interesting information did you learn from your book?*

Q *What are you wondering about what you have read?*

Share your observations of ways partners worked together, and explain that partners will continue to talk about what they are learning and what they are wondering about in their independent reading books.

 ***Making Meaning Vocabulary* Teacher**

Next week you will revisit *It Could Still Be a Worm* and *Plants that Eat Animals* to teach Vocabulary Week 17.

Week 2 **Overview**

UNIT 7: WONDERING
Expository Nonfiction

Fishes (A True Book)
by Melissa Stewart
(Children's Press, 2001)

This book describes the behavior, physical traits, and life cycles of fish.

ALTERNATIVE BOOKS

It Could Still Be a Butterfly by Allan Fowler
It Could Still Be a Flower by Allan Fowler

Comprehension Focus

• Students identify what they learn from the texts.

• Students use *wondering* to make sense of the texts.

• Students informally *explore text features* in expository nonfiction.

• Students read independently.

Social Development Focus

• Students share their partners' thinking with the class.

• Students relate the value of responsibility to their behavior.

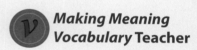

Making Meaning Vocabulary Teacher

If you are teaching Developmental Studies Center's *Making Meaning Vocabulary* program, teach Vocabulary Week 17 this week. For more information, see the *Making Meaning Vocabulary Teacher's Manual*.

Day 1

Materials

- *Fishes* (pages 3–9)
- Scratch paper and a pencil

Read-aloud

In this lesson, the students:

- Use *wondering* to help them understand nonfiction
- Identify what they learn from a nonfiction text
- Read independently for up to 20 minutes
- Share their partners' thinking
- Relate the value of responsibility to their behavior

▶ 1 Get Ready to Work Together

Gather the class with partners sitting together. Remind the students that they have been sharing their partners' thinking with the class. Explain that they will have more opportunities to share their partners' thinking this week.

ELL Note

You may wish to explain that both *fish* and *fishes* can be used to mean more than one fish.

▶ 2 Introduce *Fishes* and Explore Expository Text Features

Show the cover of *Fishes* and read the title and author's name aloud. Explain that the photo on the cover shows a school of fish called "French grunts." Display the copyright page and explain that you learned what the photo shows by reading information on this page, which also tells which company published the book (Children's Press) and when it was published (2001).

Next show the table of contents on page 3. Explain that a table of contents gives information about the topics in a book and the pages where these topics can be found. Read a few of the chapter titles aloud.

Ask:

Q *What do you think you will learn about fishes from this book?*

Have one or two students share their ideas, and then explain that you will read the first chapter, "What Is a Fish?" As before, you will stop during the reading to give partners a chance to share what they are learning from the book.

3 Read the First Chapter of *Fishes* Aloud

Read the first chapter of *Fishes* aloud, showing the photographs, reading the accompanying captions, and stopping as described below.

Read the first sentence on page 5 aloud twice and have the students use "Think, Pair, Share" to briefly discuss what they think of when they hear the word *fish*. Have a few volunteers share what they discussed with the class. Then read pages 4–5 aloud.

Tell the students that the next part of the chapter tells where fish live and how large or small they can be. Resume reading and stop after:

p. 7   "…about the size of the eraser on a pencil."

Ask, and have the students use "Turn to Your Partner" to discuss:

Q   *What did you find out about fishes in the part I just read?*

After a moment, tell the students that the next part you will read tells about fishes' bodies. Resume reading and stop after:

p. 9   "The white area behind this hogfish's mouth is its gills."

Ask and have the students use "Turn to Your Partner" to discuss:

Q   *What did you learn about fishes' bodies?*

4 Discuss What the Students Learned

Facilitate a whole-class discussion about what the students learned about fish. Use questions such as:

Q   *What did you hear about fish that you already knew?*

Q   *What new or surprising information about fish did you learn?*

ELL Note

English Language Learners will benefit from previewing the book prior to the read-aloud.

FACILITATION TIP

Continue to focus on **responding neutrally** with interest during class discussions by refraining from overtly praising or criticizing the students' responses. Instead, build the students' intrinsic motivation by responding with genuine curiosity and interest, for example:

• *Interesting—say more about that.*

• *What you said makes me curious. I wonder…*

• *Your idea is [similar to/different from] what [Lupe] said. How is it [similar/different]?*

5 ▶ Discuss What the Students Are Wondering

Tell the students that you will ask a question and the students will talk in pairs about it. Explain that later you will ask the students to share their partners' thinking with the class, so it is important to listen carefully. Have the students use "Turn to Your Partner" to discuss:

Q *Now that you have learned some information about fish, what are you wondering about them?*

Have a few volunteers share their partners' thinking with the class.

As the students share, jot down some of their questions on scratch paper, making particular note of those about fishes' bodies because you will read about this topic on Day 2. Tell them that some of their questions may be answered in the next lesson, when they will hear a chapter of *Fishes* titled "A Fish's Body."

INDIVIDUALIZED DAILY READING

6 ▶ Read Independently/Document IDR Conferences

Have the students independently read nonfiction books at appropriate reading levels for up to 20 minutes. As the students read, circulate among them and monitor whether they are reading books at appropriate reading levels. Ask individual students to read part of their book to you and explain what they have read. If a book seems too difficult or too easy for a student, help her select a more appropriate book. Continue to use the "IDR Conference Notes" record sheet to conduct and document individual conferences.

At the end of independent reading, facilitate a whole-class discussion by asking questions such as:

Q *What is something you learned today from your reading?*

Q *What is something you are wondering?*

Q *What is one thing you did today to take responsibility for yourself during independent reading?*

Day 2

Strategy Lesson

In this lesson, the students:

- Use *wondering* to help them understand nonfiction
- Identify what they learn from a nonfiction text
- Read independently for up to 20 minutes
- Share their thinking and listen to one another

1 Review the Previous Lesson

Have partners sit together. Show the photo on page 9 of *Fishes* and remind the students that in the previous lesson they learned what a fish's gills and backbone are for. If necessary, reread page 8 to help the students recall what they learned about these body parts.

2 Introduce Chapter 3, "A Fish's Body"

Show page 3, the table of contents page. Point to and read the title of the third chapter aloud: "A Fish's Body." Ask a volunteer what page it begins on (page 20). Tell the students that today you will skip ahead to this chapter so they can continue to learn about fishes' bodies.

Show pages 20–21 and read the chapter title aloud. Use the notes you jotted down on Day 1 to remind the students of any questions they had about fishes' bodies. Suggest that this chapter may answer some of their questions.

Explain that you will stop during the reading to give the students opportunities to talk about information they are learning.

Materials

- *Fishes* (pages 3 and 20–29)
- Your jotted questions from Day 1
- *Student Response Book* page 6

3 ▸ Read Aloud with Brief Section Introductions

Read pages 20–29 of *Fishes* aloud, stopping as described below.

Suggested Vocabulary

narrow: not wide; thin (p. 23)

cruise: travel smoothly and easily (p. 23)

broad: wide (p. 23)

shingles: flat pieces of wood that are put in overlapping rows to cover roofs and outside walls (p. 23)

suit of armor: metal suit of clothes used as protection in battle (p. 24)

grasp: hold (p. 25)

algae: small plants without roots or stems that grow under water (p. 27)

coral: colonies of tiny sea creatures (p. 27)

mussels: sea creatures that have a two-part, usually black, shell (p. 28)

ELL Vocabulary

English Language Learners may benefit from discussing additional vocabulary, including:

slim: thin (p. 23)

nostrils: openings used for breathing and smelling (p. 26)

Tell the students that the first part of the chapter tells about fishes' fins. Read pages 20–21 aloud and stop to point out the labeled photograph on page 21. Read the labels aloud and have two or three volunteers tell how a fish uses each kind of fin. Then reread pages 20–21 and continue reading. Stop after:

> **p. 23** "…but they are better at turning quickly."

 Have the students use "Turn to Your Partner" to discuss:

Q *What did you learn about fishes' fins?*

Signal for the students' attention and tell them that the next part you will read tells about fishes' scales. Resume reading and stop after:

> **p. 25** "You can tell a fish's age by counting the number of growth rings on its scales."

Have the students use "Turn to Your Partner" to discuss:

Q *What did you learn about fishes' scales?*

Signal for the students' attention and point out that fish have some body parts—such as fins, tails, and scales—that people don't have. However, they have other parts—such as eyes—that people have, too. Tell the students that the next part you will read tells about fishes' eyes, mouths, and teeth.

Skip the last paragraph on page 25 that continues onto page 26, and resume reading with the second paragraph on page 26. Continue reading and stop after:

> **p. 28** "Fishes with sharp, pointed teeth hunt other fishes."

 Have the students use "Turn to Your Partner" to discuss:

Q *What did you learn about fishes' eyes, mouths, and teeth?*

Signal for the students' attention and tell the students that the last part of the chapter tells what different-sized fish eat. Resume reading and stop after:

> **p. 29** "A large koi carp is about to swallow a small goldfish."

 Have the students use "Turn to Your Partner" to discuss:

Q *What do small, medium-sized, and large fishes eat?*

 4 Discuss and Write About What the Students Learned and Wonder

Facilitate a brief whole-class discussion of the chapter. Use the photos, labels, and captions to review the facts in it. Ask:

Q *What was the most interesting or surprising thing you learned from this chapter?*

Use the notes you jotted down on Day 1 to briefly review what the students wondered about fish. Ask:

Q *What are you still wondering about fish?*

ELL **Note**

If necessary, model writing sample sentences on the board (for example, "I learned that big fish eat smaller fish" or "I wonder if sharks ever try to eat fish that are bigger than they are").

You might have your students with limited English proficiency draw pictures rather than write sentences.

Have the students turn to *Student Response Book* page 6, "What I Learned and Wonder About *Fishes*." Explain that each student will write one thing they learned and one thing they wondered about as they listened to the book.

 Share Writing as a Class

Have volunteers read to the class the sentences they wrote in their *Student Response Books*. Be ready to reread parts of the text or show photos that support what the students wrote.

Tell the students that you will not read the rest of *Fishes* aloud, but that it will be available for independent reading.

INDIVIDUALIZED DAILY READING

 Read Independently and Wonder

Have the students independently read nonfiction books for up to 20 minutes. Explain that at the end of IDR today each student will tell his partner about the book he is reading and what he is still wondering about.

As the students read, circulate among them. Stop and ask individual students to talk about the book they are reading and what they are wondering about. Ask questions such as:

Q *What is your book about?*

Q *What are you still wondering about?*

At the end of independent reading, have partners share their books and what they are wondering about.

Help the students reflect on their independent reading time by asking questions such as:

Q *What did you do to take responsibility for yourself during independent reading?*

EXTENSIONS

Learn More About Fish

Use the additional resources listed on pages 44–45 in *Fishes* to have the students find out more about fish. As a class, discuss answers to the students' questions and other interesting information they learn during their search.

Explore an Index

Display page 47 of the book and explain that this page, the index, tells where to look in *Fishes* for information on topics like feelers, moray eels, and seahorses. Point out that the topics are listed in alphabetical order. Read aloud some of the items listed and invite volunteers to pick one or two for the class to look up and read together.

Day 3

Materials

- Nonfiction books at appropriate levels for independent reading
- A small self-stick note for each student
- *Student Response Book* page 7
- *Assessment Resource Book*

 Note

Note challenging vocabulary in the students' independent reading books and have brief discussions with individual students to define words as they read independently.

Independent Strategy Practice

In this lesson, the students:

- Read nonfiction books independently
- Identify what they learn from a nonfiction text
- Relate the value of responsibility to their behavior

▶ 1 Review the Week

Have partners sit together. Remind the students that they have been listening to nonfiction books and talking in pairs about what they learned and wondered as they listened.

Explain that today the students will continue to think about what they learn and wonder as they read independently. Explain that they will each read a section of their independent reading book twice.

▶ 2 Read Independently Without Stopping

Have the students use a self-stick note to mark the place where they begin to read. Have them read independently for 5 minutes.

Circulate as the students work. Notice whether they are able to identify questions that come to mind based on what they learn from their reading. Ask individual students:

Q *What are you wondering about [popcorn]?*

Q *What part of your book made you wonder about that?*

Reread Independently and Identify What the Students Learned and Wonder

Stop the students after 5 minutes. Tell them that they will reread, starting again at the self-stick note. Ask them to find an interesting piece of information to share with their partners. Encourage them to also pay attention to "I wonder…" statements or questions that come to mind as they read.

Have the students reread for 5 minutes.

 Discuss in Pairs What the Students Learned and Wonder

Stop the students after 5 minutes. Have each student share with her partner the title of the book, something she learned from her reading, and something she wonders about the book's topic.

 Write About What They Learned and Wonder

Have the students turn to *Student Response Book* page 7, "What I Learned and Wonder" and explain that you would like them to write one or two sentences in their own words about what they learned and wonder from their reading.

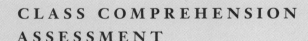

CLASS COMPREHENSION
ASSESSMENT

Circulate among the students as they work. Ask yourself:

Q *Are the students able to identify and describe what they have learned?*

Q *Do they wonder about things that are connected to their texts?*

Record your observations on page 20 of the *Assessment Resource Book.*

6 ▶ **Discuss Independent Reading as a Class**

Have a few volunteers each share something they learned and something they wonder about their book's topic. Remind each student to say the title of the book before sharing. Ask questions such as:

Q *What new or interesting information did you learn from your book?*

Q *What are you wondering about what you have read?*

7 ▶ **Reflect on Working Together**

Facilitate a brief discussion about how the students took responsibility for themselves. Ask:

Q *What did you do to act in a responsible way during independent reading time? Why is that important?*

Teacher Note

If you want to give the students more experience thinking about what they learned and wonder in independent reading, repeat this lesson using an alternative book and *Student Response Book* page 7.

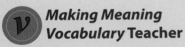

Making Meaning Vocabulary Teacher

Next week you will revisit *Fishes* to teach Vocabulary Week 18.

Week 3

Overview

UNIT 7: WONDERING
Expository Nonfiction

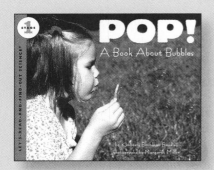

POP! A Book About Bubbles
by Kimberly Brubaker Bradley, photographs by Margaret Miller (HarperTrophy, 2001)

The book explains how bubbles are made, why they are always round, and why they pop.

ALTERNATIVE BOOKS

Big Blue Whale by Nicola Davies

Inside an Ant Colony by Allan Fowler

Comprehension Focus

• Students identify what they learn from a nonfiction text.

• Students use *wondering* to make sense of the text.

• Students read independently.

Social Development Focus

• Students share their partners' thinking with the class.

• Students relate the value of responsibility to their behavior.

DO AHEAD

• Prepare to model wondering in independent reading (see Day 3, Step 2 on page 255).

• Make copies of the Unit 7 Parent Letter (BLM7) to send home with the students on the last day of the unit.

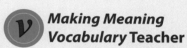

Making Meaning Vocabulary Teacher

If you are teaching Developmental Studies Center's *Making Meaning Vocabulary* program, teach Vocabulary Week 18 this week. For more information, see the *Making Meaning Vocabulary Teacher's Manual.*

Day 1

Materials

- *POP! A Book About Bubbles* (pages 5–15)
- "Reading Comprehension Strategies" chart

Read-aloud/Strategy Lesson

In this lesson, the students:

- Identify what they learn from a nonfiction text
- *Wonder* about the text
- Read independently for up to 20 minutes
- Share their partners' thinking
- Relate the value of responsibility to their behavior

1 ## Get Ready to Work Together

Have partners sit together. Explain that the students will listen to another nonfiction book this week and share their thinking in pairs. Remind the students that readers sometimes make connections and wonder as they read to better understand a book. Explain that the students will use these strategies as they listen to today's read-aloud.

2 ## Introduce *POP!*

Show the cover of *POP! A Book About Bubbles.* Read the title and names of the author and photographer aloud. Ask:

Q *Have you ever blown bubbles? Tell us about it.*

Have a few students share their experiences with the class.

3 ## Read the First Half of *POP!* Aloud

Tell the students that the first part of the book tells what bubbles are and how you can make them. Read pages 5–15 of *POP! A Book About Bubbles* aloud, showing the photographs and stopping as described on the next page.

ELL Note

English Language Learners may benefit from previewing pages 5–15 and hearing the suggested vocabulary briefly defined prior to the read-aloud.

Suggested Vocabulary

wand: thin stick or rod (p. 5; refer to the photograph)
solution: mixture made up of something dissolved in liquid (p. 5)
shimmers: shines (p. 6)
corn syrup: sweet, sticky liquid (p. 10)

Stop after:

p. 9 "All bubbles are round."

Ask:

Q *Based on what you heard, what are you wondering about bubbles?*

Have a couple of students share their thinking with the class.

Reread the last sentence on page 9 and continue reading to the bottom of page 10. Stop and tell the students you will reread page 10, and ask them to listen carefully for how bubbles are made. Reread page 10 and ask:

Q *What did you learn about how bubbles are made?*

Have one or two students share their thinking with the class.

Reread the last sentence on page 10 and continue reading to the end of page 15.

4 ▶ Discuss the Reading as a Class

Have the students use "Turn to Your Partner" to discuss the following question. Ask the students to be ready to share their partners' thinking.

Q *We talked at the beginning of the lesson about blowing bubbles. Does anything in the book remind you of experiences you have had or things you have noticed while blowing bubbles?*

Signal for the students' attention, and have a few students share their partners' thinking.

Explain that you will read the second half of the book tomorrow.

INDIVIDUALIZED DAILY READING

▶ 5 **Review the "Reading Comprehension Strategies" Chart**

Refer to the "Reading Comprehension Strategies" chart and review the strategies on it. Encourage the students to use these strategies to make sense of their reading.

Have the students read nonfiction books independently for up to 20 minutes.

As the students read, circulate among them and talk to individuals about their reading. Ask questions such as:

Q *What is your book about? What's happening in your book right now?*

Q *Are you wondering about anything so far? If so, what?*

Q *What strategies are you using to help you understand the reading?*

At the end of independent reading, have the students share what they read as a whole class. Ask questions such as:

Q *What is a reading comprehension strategy on the chart you used when reading today? Where did you use it? How did it help you understand the story?*

EXTENSION

Make and Observe Bubbles

Use the instructions on page 32 of *POP!* to have the students make and observe bubbles. You may want to begin by having pairs read page 32 together; then as a class discuss the ingredients needed and the steps for making the bubble solution. After the students have made and observed their bubbles, discuss their observations and relate them to the information in the book.

Reading Comprehension Strategies

- making connections

Day 2

Read-aloud/Strategy Lesson

In this lesson, the students:

- Identify what they learn from a nonfiction text
- *Wonder* about the text
- Read independently for up to 20 minutes
- Share their partners' thinking
- Relate the value of responsibility to their behavior

1 ▶ **Review the First Half of *POP!***

Remind the students that in the last lesson they used *wondering* and *making connections* to learn about bubbles in the book *POP!* Tell them that today they will use *visualizing* to help them remember the first half of the book.

Ask the students to close their eyes and think about blowing bubbles as you read pages from the first half of the book. Read pages 6 and 9 to the students while they have their eyes closed. Briefly discuss:

Q *What did you see in your mind?*

Tell the students that you will read the second half of the book today and that you would like them to think about new things they learn about bubbles.

2 ▶ **Read the Second Half of *POP!***

Read pages 16–30, stopping as described on the next page.

Suggested Vocabulary

evenly: equally; the same amount (p. 19)

shrink: become smaller (p. 20)

stream: steady flow (p. 29)

Materials

- *POP! A Book About Bubbles* (pages 6, 9 and 16–30)

 Note

English Language Learners may benefit from previewing pages 16–31 and hearing the suggested vocabulary words briefly defined prior to the read-aloud.

Stop at the end of page 20. Tell the students that you will reread the section, and ask them to listen for new things they learn about bubbles. Reread pages 16–20. Ask:

Q *What new things did you learn about bubbles from these pages?*

Have one or two students share their thinking with the class. Reread the last two sentences on page 20 and continue reading to the next stop:

> **p. 23**   "…higher and higher, then *pop!*"

Q *What are you wondering right now about bubbles in soda?*

Have one or two students share their thinking with the class. Reread the sentence on page 23 and continue reading to the next stop:

> **p. 24**   "Water and juice aren't sticky like soap solution, so the bubbles pop right away."

Q *What are you wondering right now?*

Have one or two students share their thinking with the class. Reread the last sentence on page 24 and continue reading to the next stop:

> **p. 26**   "Wherever they aren't touching the glass or each other, they will be round."

Have one or two students share their thinking with the class. Reread the last sentence on page 26 and continue reading to the end of the page 30.

▶ 3 Discuss *POP!* in Pairs and as a Class

As a class, discuss the following questions.

Q *What new things did you learn about bubbles in today's reading?*

Q *What are you still wondering about bubbles?*

Have the students use "Turn to Your Partner" to discuss the following question. Ask the students to be ready to share their partners' thinking during the whole-class discussion.

Q *What are some things that you would like to try with bubbles after hearing this book?*

4 ▶ Reflect on Sharing Their Partners' Thinking

Review that the students shared their partners' thinking today during the class discussion. Ask and briefly discuss:

Q *What did you do to make sure you understood your partner's thinking?*

Students might say:

"I had to listen to my partner very carefully."

"I asked my partner to repeat what she said."

"I checked with my partner to make sure I understood him."

Encourage the students to continue to listen carefully to their partners any time they work in pairs. Explain that they will have an opportunity to think about what they are learning and to wonder in their independent reading.

INDIVIDUALIZED DAILY READING

5 ▶ Read Independently and Wonder

Have the students read nonfiction books for up to 20 minutes. Explain that at the end of IDR today they will each tell their partner about the book they are reading and what they are still wondering about.

As the students read, circulate among them. Stop and ask individual students to talk about the books they are reading and what they are wondering about. Ask questions such as:

Q *What is your book about?*

Q *What are you still wondering about?*

FACILITATION TIP

Reflect on your experience over the past three weeks with **responding neutrally** with interest during class discussions. Does this practice feel natural to you? Are you integrating it into class discussions throughout the school day? What effect is it having on the students? We encourage you to continue to try this practice and reflect on the students' responses as you facilitate class discussions in the future.

At the end of independent reading, have partners share their books and what they are wondering about.

Help the students reflect on their independent reading by asking questions such as:

Q *What did you do to take responsibility for yourself during independent reading?*

EXTENSION

Bubble Experiments

Use the instructions on page 33 of *POP!* and conduct the experiments with bubbles to answer these questions:

Q *Are bubbles always round?*

Q *How slow can you blow?*

Have the students predict answers and work in pairs to confirm or reject their predictions. As a class, discuss the outcomes of the experiments.

Day 3

Independent Strategy Practice

In this lesson, the students:

*   Read nonfiction texts independently
*   *Wonder* about the texts
*   Identify what they learn from the texts
*   Share their thinking

1 ▶ Review the Week

Have partners sit together. Remind the students that this week they listened to *POP! A Book About Bubbles* and talked about questions they had about bubbles. They also shared their thinking with one another and shared their partners' thinking with the whole class. Explain to the students that at the end of the lesson they will talk about how partners worked together throughout this unit.

2 ▶ Model Wondering Before Reading Nonfiction Text

Explain that before they begin to read today, partners will talk about what they wonder about the topics of their independent reading books.

Model wondering before reading by briefly introducing the nonfiction text you selected. Examine the cover of the book and look at several pages, commenting on photographs or illustrations. Then read the first two or three sentences in the book and wonder aloud.

Model writing several "I wonder" statements where everyone can see them.

Materials

*   Nonfiction text for teacher modeling
*   A variety of nonfiction books at appropriate levels for independent reading
*   *Student Response Book* page 8
*   *Assessment Resource Book*
*   Unit 7 Parent Letter (BLM7)

◀ **Teacher Note**

Have the questions you will ask in mind ahead of time so this modeling goes smoothly.

Wonder Before Reading Independently

 Have each student look at the front and back covers and the photographs or illustrations in his book and wonder quietly to himself about its topic. After a few moments, have partners share what they are wondering with one another.

4 **Write "What I Wonder Before Reading" Statements**

Have the students turn to *Student Response Book* page 8, "What I Wonder Before Reading." Tell them that they each will write one or two "I wonder" statements about the topic of their book in their own *Student Response Book*. Refer to the statements you modeled writing and briefly review them.

Have each student write her statements in her *Student Response Book*.

CLASS COMPREHENSION ASSESSMENT

Circulate among the students as they work. Ask yourself:

Q *Are the students able to wonder about a topic prior to reading?*

Q *Is their wondering connected to what they are previewing?*

Record your observations on page 21 of the *Assessment Resource Book*.

---

5 **Read Independently**

Have the students independently read their nonfiction texts for 10–15 minutes.

 6 **Discuss Independent Reading as a Class**

 First in pairs, and then as a class, discuss questions such as:

Q *What did you wonder about before you began reading?*

Q *Were your questions answered in the book? If so, explain.*

Q *What other questions do you have now that you've read some of the book?*

Tell the students that looking over a book before reading gives them an idea about what the book will be about.

 Reflect on Working Together

Teacher Note

This is the last week of Unit 7. You will reassign partners for Unit 8.

Facilitate a brief discussion about how partners worked together during the past three weeks. Ask questions such as:

Q *Why is it important to listen to your partner during "Turn to Your Partner"?*

Q *What were some ways you acted responsibly during reading time?*

Q *What will you do [the same way/differently] the next time you work with a partner?*

 Give the students time to thank their partners.

INDIVIDUAL COMPREHENSION ASSESSMENT

Before continuing with Unit 8, take this opportunity to assess individual students' progress in thinking about what they are learning and using *wondering* to help them understand nonfiction text. Please refer to pages 40–41 in the *Assessment Resource Book* for instructions.

SOCIAL SKILLS ASSESSMENT

Take this opportunity to assess your students' social development using the "Social Skills Assessment" record sheet on pages 2–3 of the *Assessment Resource Book*.

 Parent Letter

Send home with each student the Parent Letter for this unit (see "Do Ahead," page 247). Periodically, have a few students share with the class what they are reading at home.

 ***Making Meaning Vocabulary* Teacher**

Next week you will revisit *POP! A Book About Bubbles* to teach Vocabulary Week 19.

Unit 8

Exploring Text Features

EXPOSITORY NONFICTION

During this unit, the students read expository nonfiction, including books, articles, and functional texts, and explore text features to learn more about a topic. During IDR, the students read expository texts independently and think about what they are learning. Socially, they analyze and discuss ways they take responsibility for their behavior and learning.

Week 1 *Snails* by Monica Hughes

Week 2 *Bend and Stretch: Learning About Your Bones and Muscles* by Pamela Hill Nettleton

Week 3 "Ice Cream Mania!"
"Giant Panda, Red Panda"
"Classic Smoothie"
"The City Zoo: Hours, Feeding Times, and Activity Times"

UNIT 8: EXPLORING TEXT FEATURES
Expository Nonfiction

Snails
by Monica Hughes
(Raintree, 2004)

This book describes the physical characteristics of snails, how they move, and how they survive.

ALTERNATIVE BOOKS

Ladybugs by Monica Hughes

Spiders by Monica Hughes

Comprehension Focus

• Students *explore text features* of expository texts.

• Students identify what they learn from a text.

• Students read independently.

Social Development Focus

• Students take responsibility for their learning and behavior.

• Students participate in a class meeting.

DO AHEAD

• Prior to Day 1, decide how you will randomly assign partners to work together during the unit.

• Prior to Day 1, prepare a chart with the title "Expository Text Features."

• Make the transparency of the "Index from *Snails*" (BLM13) for Day 2.

• Collect a variety of expository texts for the students to read independently and examine on Day 2. (See "About Expository Text" on page 262. For information about Developmental Studies Center's Individualized Daily Reading Libraries, see page xxvii and visit Developmental Studies Center's website at www.devstu.org.)

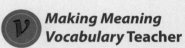

***Making Meaning
Vocabulary* Teacher**

If you are teaching Developmental Studies Center's *Making Meaning Vocabulary* program, teach Vocabulary Week 19 this week. For more information, see the *Making Meaning Vocabulary Teacher's Manual.*

Read-aloud

Materials

- *Snails*
- "Expository Text Features" chart, prepared ahead, and a marker
- *Student Response Book* page 9

In this lesson, the students:

- *Explore text features*
- Identify what they learn from a text
- Read independently for up to 20 minutes
- Take responsibility for their behavior

About Expository Text

During the next three weeks, the students will read expository texts and examine various text features. Collect enough examples of expository texts so that each student has at least one to examine. Use textbooks and trade books of various reading levels that contain examples of a range of features, including tables of contents; indexes; headings; photos, drawings, and labels; text boxes; and bold and colored type.

Being a Writer™ **Teacher**

You can either have the students work with their *Being a Writer* partner or assign them a different partner for the *Making Meaning* lessons.

▶ 1 Pair Students and Get Ready to Work Together

Randomly assign partners and have them sit together. Review that the students have been working on listening to one another, sharing their partners' ideas, looking at the person who is talking in whole-class discussions, and contributing ideas that are different from others' ideas. Explain that all of these skills have helped them take responsibility for their learning and behavior. Explain that the students will continue to work on these skills and think about how they are taking responsibility for their learning and behavior.

Teacher Note ▶

During this week's lessons, observe the students as they interact with one another and take note of students acting responsibly. You will share your observations with the students throughout the week.

Explain that you will check in during the week to see how they are taking responsibility for themselves when they participate in discussions in pairs and with the class.

Introduce Expository Text

Remind the students that in previous lessons they talked to their partners about what they learned and wondered as they listened to the nonfiction books *It Could Still Be a Worm, Plants That Eat Animals, Fishes,* and *POP! A Book About Bubbles.* Explain that these books are a special type of nonfiction called expository nonfiction. Tell the students that expository texts give information. Explain that this week the students will hear and read more expository nonfiction and will look closely at a few of the special features found in expository texts.

 Introduce *Snails*

Remind the students that expository books often look different from books that tell stories. They often include features that help the reader locate information in the text and understand the topic better. Explain that for the next several weeks the students will read expository texts, learn new information, and explore text features.

Show the cover of *Snails* and read the title aloud. Turn to the title page and read the title and the author's name aloud. Ask:

Q *Have you ever seen a snail? Where? Tell us about it.*

Have a few students share their experiences with the class.

 Explore the Table of Contents and Start the "Expository Text Features" Chart

Show the students page 3 of *Snails* and remind them that this feature is called the "table of contents." Review that the table of contents tells the reader the names of the chapters and the pages where the chapters can be found. Explain that the names of the chapters are sometimes called chapter headings.

Tell the students that they will be exploring the text features in *Snails* this week and that you will list the text features they notice on the "Expository Text Features" chart. Direct the students' attention to the chart. Write *table of contents* and *chapter headings* below the chart's name.

 Note

English Language Learners will benefit from previewing the text and the illustrations prior to the lesson.

Have the students turn to *Student Response Book* page 9 and have them look at the table of contents. Point out that most tables of contents are organized in a list at the front of the book, but in some books they might be organized differently.

Ask the students to follow along as you read the table of contents aloud. First in pairs, and then as a class, have the students discuss:

Q *After looking at the table of contents, what do you think you'll learn about snails?*

Q *On which pages might we find information about [what snails eat]?*

> **Students might say:**
>
> "We might learn about snails' bodies."
>
> "We might learn about where snails live."
>
> "We'll find out what snails eat by looking at page 18."
>
> "There's probably information about what snails eat on page 19 also."

Have a few volunteers share their thinking.

5 ▶ Read *Snails* Aloud

Read *Snails* aloud, showing the photographs but not reading the labels, and stopping as described on the next page.

> **Suggested Vocabulary**
>
> **mucus:** slimy fluid (p. 13)
> **predators:** animals that hunt other animals for food (p. 21)
> **hibernate:** sleep through the winter (p. 22)
>
> **ELL Vocabulary**
>
> English Language Learners may benefit from discussing additional vocabulary, including:
>
> **slimy:** slippery and wet feeling (p. 5)

Teacher Note ▶

If the students have difficulty answering this question, offer some suggestions like those in the "Students might say" note.

Teacher Note ▶

Tomorrow the students will explore the text features in *Snails,* including the labeled photographs.

Read pages 4–7, pointing out the chapter headings. Stop after:

> **p. 7** "Other snails live in water."

Ask:

Q *Based on what you heard, what did you learn about snails?*

Have a couple of students share their thinking with the class.

Tell the students that the next part of the book tells about snails' bodies and how they move. Resume reading, pointing out the chapter headings, and stop after:

> **p. 13** "They slide along on trails of slimy mucus."

 Ask and have the students use "Turn to Your Partner" to discuss:

Q *What did you find out about snails in the part that I just read?*

Signal for attention and explain to the students that the next part you will read tells about where snails might be found and how they survive. Resume reading, pointing out the chapter heading, and stop after:

> **p. 22** "They go inside their shells and close them with mucus."

 Ask and have the students use "Turn to Your Partner" to discuss:

Q *What did you find out about snails in the part that I just read?*

6 ▶ Discuss the Reading

 First in pairs, and then as a class, have the students discuss the following questions. As the students respond, be ready to reread passages aloud and show the photographs again to help them recall what they heard.

Q *What did you learn about snails from the reading?*

Q *What was the most interesting thing you learned about snails?*

Q *What else would you like to know about snails?*

Remind the students that readers will often use the table of contents to find sections or chapters that contain information they want to learn more about.

Explain that tomorrow the students will continue to explore expository text.

INDIVIDUALIZED DAILY READING

 Document IDR Conferences

Have the students read nonfiction books independently for up to 20 minutes.

Use the "IDR Conference Notes" record sheet to conduct and document individual conferences.

At the end of independent reading, have the students discuss their reading first in pairs, and then as a class. Ask questions such as:

Q *What is your book about?*

Q *What information did you learn today?*

Allow time for any student who has finished a book today to record it in the "Reading Log" section of her *Student Response Book*.

 ELL Note

You may want to have your English Language Learners draw pictures about their books in their "Reading Logs."

Day 2

Strategy Lesson

In this lesson, the students:

- *Explore text features*
- Identify what they learn from a text
- Read independently for up to 20 minutes
- Take responsibility for their behavior

1 ▶ **Review the Previous Lesson and Add to the "Expository Text Features" Chart**

Have partners sit together. Show the cover of *Snails* and review that the students looked closely at the table of contents and learned new information about snails. Show pages 12–13 and remind the students that many expository texts are illustrated with photographs rather than drawings or paintings. Ask:

Q *After looking at this picture, what do you remember about how snails move?*

Have one or two students share their thinking. Show pages 14–15 and ask:

Q *After looking at this picture, what do you remember about where you might find snails?*

Have one or two students share their thinking. Show pages 16–17 and point out that some of the photographs in this book have labels. Reread page 16, reading the label last, pointing to it as you read it. Explain that a label gives the reader more information about a topic by providing details about the photograph.

Show the students the photographs on pages 4–5, 8, 11, and 21 and read the labels to the students. Explain that noticing photographs and reading any labels will help the students make sense of the text. Add *photographs* and *labels* to the "Expository Text Features" chart.

Materials

- *Snails*
- "Expository Text Features" chart and a marker
- "Index from *Snails*" transparency (BLM13)
- "Reading Comprehension Strategies" chart and a marker
- *Assessment Resource Book*

Teacher Note

During today's lesson, observe the students as they interact with one another and take note of responsible behaviors you see. You will share your observations with the students later in the lesson.

Explain that today the students will explore several text features often found at the end of expository nonfiction books.

2▶ Briefly Explore the Bolded Words and Glossary in *Snails*

Show the students page 24 of *Snails* and explain that this page contains other text features sometimes found at the end of expository nonfiction books.

Point to the glossary and explain that a glossary is a list of words the author thinks readers might need to know to understand the book. Point out that it is organized like a dictionary; it lists the words in alphabetical order and tells what each word means.

Model using the glossary by showing page 22 and pointing out the bolded words. Explain that when a word is in bold print the meaning of the word can usually be found in the glossary. Read the first sentence on page 22, locate the word *hibernate* in the glossary, and read the definition. Follow the same procedure for the word *mucus*. Add *glossary* and *bolded words* to the "Expository Text Features" chart.

3▶ Introduce the Index of *Snails*

Show the index on page 24; then show the "Index from *Snails*" transparency and explain that it is a copy of the index in *Snails*. Explain that many nonfiction books have an index. Explain that readers can use an index to help them find specific information about topics mentioned in the book.

Explain that an index is a list of words related to the subject of a book. The number after a word in the index is the page number where readers can find information about that topic.

Have the students follow along as you read the index aloud. Have the students use "Think, Pair, Share" to discuss:

Q *What do you notice about the index?*

Have a few volunteers share their thinking.

> *Students might say:*
>
> "The words are in alphabetical order."
>
> "Some words have one page number and some have more than one."
>
> "Some of the words are used in the labels."

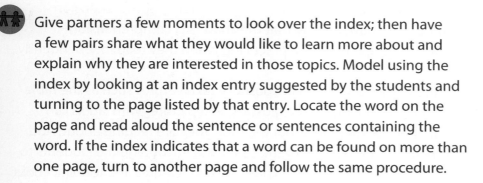

4 ▶ Explore the Index as a Class

Tell the students that they will look at the transparency of the index in pairs and together select one or two entries in the index related to a topic they want to learn more about.

Give partners a few moments to look over the index; then have a few pairs share what they would like to learn more about and explain why they are interested in those topics. Model using the index by looking at an index entry suggested by the students and turning to the page listed by that entry. Locate the word on the page and read aloud the sentence or sentences containing the word. If the index indicates that a word can be found on more than one page, turn to another page and follow the same procedure.

Tell the students that the index in a nonfiction book helps readers quickly find all the places in the book where a topic or a word is mentioned. Explain that readers often use the index if they have a question about a specific topic or want to find out more about it. Add *index* to the "Expository Text Features" chart.

5 ▶ Briefly Discuss the Text

First in pairs, and then as a class, discuss the following questions:

Q *After looking at the text features in* Snails, *what new information did you learn?*

Q *Which text feature was the most interesting to you? Why?*

◀ Teacher Note

If the students have difficulty answering the question, offer some suggestions like those in the "Students might say" note.

As you listen to pairs talk, ask yourself:

Q *Do the students recognize text features?*

Q *Are the students able to make sense of the text features?*

Record your observations on page 22 of the *Assessment Resource Book.*

Reading Comprehension Strategies

- making connections

---

6 ▶ **Add to the "Reading Comprehension Strategies" Chart**

Direct the students' attention to the "Reading Comprehension Strategies" chart. Review that the chart lists comprehension strategies they should be practicing when they read independently.

Remind the students that expository text features such as the table of contents, the index, the glossary, and pictures with labels can help them learn more about the topic they are reading about. Add *recognizing text features* to the chart, and encourage the students to continue to look for more expository text features and to think about how those features help them understand what they are reading.

Save the "Expository Text Features" chart for use in Week 2.

7 ▶ **Discuss Taking Responsibility**

Without mentioning names, point out ways you noticed students taking responsibility during partner and whole-class discussions, and then ask:

Q *How does [looking at the person who is talking] during a whole-class discussion show you are being responsible?*

Q *When have you taken responsibility for your behavior?*

Students might say:

"I was responsible when I shared my partner's thinking."

"I took responsibility for my behavior when I added an idea that was different from my partner's idea."

"I was responsible when I listened to my partner's ideas."

If necessary, discuss any problems the students had working in pairs and ways to avoid such problems in the future.

INDIVIDUALIZED DAILY READING

 Read Independently/Document IDR Conferences

Have the students read nonfiction books independently for up to 20 minutes. Ask the students to pay attention to what information they are learning from their reading. Explain that at the end of IDR, the students will discuss in pairs what they learned today.

Use the "IDR Conference Notes" record sheet to conduct and document individual conferences.

 At the end of independent reading, have the students discuss in pairs what they learned today from their nonfiction books. Ask and have partners briefly discuss:

Q *What information did you learn today?*

EXTENSION

Draw and Label a Picture of an Animal

Explain that each student will draw a picture of an animal and label the picture. Give the students an opportunity to think about and to talk in pairs about their favorite animal. First in pairs, and then as a class, have the students discuss questions such as:

Q *What is your favorite animal?*

Q *What is something interesting about your favorite animal?*

 Note

This activity will reinforce vocabulary development for your English Language Learners.

Q *Where does your favorite animal live?*

Q *What are some special characteristics of your favorite animal?*

Have the students draw pictures of their favorite animals and label important features about the animals. For example, if a student draws a picture of a bear, he might label the bear's claws with the word "claws" and the bear's snout with the word "snout." Collect the students' papers and put them together into a class book of "Favorite Animals."

Day 3

Class Meeting

In this lesson, the students:

- Review the ground rules and procedure for a class meeting
- Analyze the ways they have been interacting
- Read independently for up to 20 minutes
- Share their thinking

1 ▶ Have a Check-in Class Meeting

Have the students move into a circle for a class meeting and review the class meeting ground rules.

Remind the students that they have been building a safe and supportive reading community this school year. Explain that having a safe and supportive classroom community allows the students to share their thinking and agree and disagree comfortably with each other. Explain that the purpose of today's meeting is to discuss how they, as individuals, are contributing to the reading community, and if they need to do anything differently or do something else to help create a sense of community in the classroom.

As you did on Day 2, describe some responsible behaviors you noticed during partner and whole-class discussions this week. Ask the students to think about how they have interacted responsibly with their partners and other classmates in the past few weeks. First in pairs, and then as a class, have the students discuss:

Q *What have you done to take responsibility during partner and whole-class discussions?*

Q *What can you do in the coming days to make sure you are being responsible?*

Materials

- Space for the class to sit in a circle
- "Class Meeting Ground Rules" chart

Class Meeting Ground Rules

- one person talks at a time
- listen to one another

Teacher Note

Remind the students to use the discussion prompts they have learned, namely:

- *I agree with _____ because…*
- *I disagree with _____ because…*
- *In addition to what _____ said, I think…*

Students might say:

"I took responsibility by asking my partner and classmates questions when I didn't understand something they said."

"In addition to what [Lucas] said, I asked people to repeat what they said if I couldn't hear them."

"My partner made an effort to contribute different ideas to our discussions and that helped me learn more about what we were talking about. I think he was taking responsibility when he brought up new ideas."

"I'm going to work on listening more closely to what my partner says, and then contribute new ideas to our conversation."

As the students share, facilitate the conversation by asking questions such as:

Q *[Kiley] said [she] took responsibility for [her] learning when [she] asked her partner questions]. Why is that a responsible thing to do?*

Q *Why is it important to contribute your thinking to your partner conversations?*

Q *What can we do to be sure we [ask our classmates questions when we don't understand] in the coming weeks?*

▶2 Review the Class Meeting

Ask the students to analyze how they did today with following the class meeting ground rules. Ask questions such as:

Q *What do you think we need to continue to work on? Why?*

Q *What can you do to add to the next class meeting? How is that taking responsibility?*

Remind the students to take every opportunity in the coming weeks to take responsibility for their own behavior. Then adjourn the meeting.

INDIVIDUALIZED DAILY READING

 ## Read Independently and Discuss Text Features

Have the students read expository texts at their appropriate reading
levels independently for up to 20 minutes. Ask the students to pay
particular attention to the text features and to be ready to share
those features in pairs at the end of IDR.

 At the end of independent reading, have partners discuss what they
learned and any text features they noticed. As a class, discuss the
different text features in the students' books.

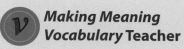 ***Making Meaning
Vocabulary* Teacher**

Next week you will revisit *Snails*
to teach Vocabulary Week 20.

UNIT 8: EXPLORING TEXT FEATURES
Expository Nonfiction

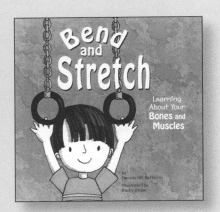

Bend and Stretch: Learning About Your Bones and Muscles
by Pamela Hill Nettleton, illustrated by Becky Shipe
(Picture Window Books, 2004)

This book is a simple introduction to bones and muscles and
how they work.

ALTERNATIVE BOOKS

Breathe In, Breathe Out: Learning About Your Lungs
by Pamela Hill Nettleton

Think, Think, Think: Learning About Your Brain
by Pamela Hill Nettleton

Comprehension Focus

- Students *explore text features* in expository texts.

- Students identify what they learn from a text.

- Students *use schema* to make sense of nonfiction.

- Students read independently.

Social Development Focus

- Students take responsibility for their learning and behavior.

- Students reflect on how their behavior affects others.

DO AHEAD

- Collect a variety of expository texts for the students to examine and read on Day 3 (see "About Expository Text" on page 262).

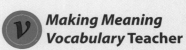

Making Meaning Vocabulary Teacher

If you are teaching Developmental Studies Center's *Making Meaning Vocabulary* program, teach Vocabulary Week 20 this week. For more information, see the *Making Meaning Vocabulary Teacher's Manual.*

Day 1

Read-aloud

In this lesson, the students:

- *Explore text features*
- Identify what they learn from a text
- Read independently for up to 20 minutes
- Take responsibility for their behavior

Materials

- *Bend and Stretch*
- "Expository Text Features" chart from Week 1 and a marker
- "Thinking About My Reading" chart

▶ 1 **Get Ready to Work Together**

Have partners sit together. Remind the students that they have been working on taking responsibility for their learning and behavior. Explain that this week they will have more opportunities to think about how they take responsibility for themselves when they participate in discussions with their partners and with the class.

▶ 2 **Introduce *Bend and Stretch* and Add to the "Expository Text Features" Chart**

Remind the students that in previous lessons they heard an expository text called *Snails.* Tell them that this week they will hear and read another expository text. Remind the students that expository texts give factual information and often include text features that provide the reader with more information.

 Note

English Language Learners will benefit from previewing the text and the illustrations prior to the lesson.

Show the cover of *Bend and Stretch* and read the title and the author's name aloud. Then show the students the back cover of *Bend and Stretch* and read the summary paragraph. Explain that books often include a summary of the book on the back cover to let readers know what the book is about. Direct the students' attention to the "Expository Text Features" chart, and add *a summary on the back of the book* to the chart. Encourage the students to get in the habit of reading the back cover when they are choosing a book to read.

Tell the students that they will be exploring the text features in *Bend and Stretch* this week.

Introduce Diagrams in Expository Nonfiction

Remind the students that in previous weeks they learned more information about topics by looking at photos with captions and labels. Open the book to pages 10–11, and point out the picture on page 11. Explain that photos cannot always show all of the details the author wants, so some expository texts use diagrams. Explain that the diagram on page 11 shows what the rib cage looks like inside our bodies. Show the diagram on page 13, and point out that diagrams can also have labels. Explain that they will find diagrams in many expository texts. Add *diagrams* to the "Expository Text Features" chart.

Explain that text features like diagrams help the reader make sense of the information in books. Encourage the students to look for diagrams as well as other text features as you read aloud from *Bend and Stretch* today.

Read *Bend and Stretch* Aloud

Read *Bend and Stretch* aloud, showing the illustrations but not reading the information in the text boxes. Stop as described below.

◀ **Teacher Note**

Tomorrow the students will explore the text features in *Bend and Stretch* including the text boxes.

> ### Suggested Vocabulary
>
> **bundles:** groups (p. 5)
> **flexible:** able to bend (p. 6)
> **mend:** heal or become better (p. 16)

Read pages 3–9. Stop after:

p. 9   "Bone marrow's job is to make new blood cells."

Ask:

Q *What did you find out about bones in the part that I just read?*

Have a couple of students share their thinking with the class.

Tell the students that the next part of the book tells about how bones and muscles work together. Resume reading and stop after:

p. 15   "That's why basketball players have big arm muscles."

Ask and have the students use "Turn to Your Partner" to discuss:

Q *What did you find out about bones and muscles in the part that I just read?*

Have a couple of students share their thinking with the class.

After a moment, tell the students that the next part you will read tells about how you can take care of your bones and muscles. Resume reading and stop after:

p. 21 "Reach for the sky!"

 Ask and have the students use "Turn to Your Partner" to discuss:

Q *What did you find out about taking care of your bones and muscles in the part that I just read?*

Have a couple of students share their thinking with the class.

 5 ▶ Discuss the Reading

Facilitate a whole-class discussion using the following questions. As the students respond, be ready to reread passages aloud and show illustrations again to help the students recall what they heard.

Q *What did you learn about bones and muscles from the reading?*

Q *What did you hear about bones and muscles that surprised you?*

Q *What else would you like to know about bones or muscles?*

Explain that the students will hear more about bones and muscles in the next lesson.

INDIVIDUALIZED DAILY READING

 ## Practice Self-monitoring

Draw the students' attention to the "Thinking About My Reading" chart and review the questions on the chart. Explain that today during independent reading you want them to use the questions on the "Thinking About My Reading" chart to monitor their comprehension.

Have the students read nonfiction texts independently for up to 20 minutes. Use the "IDR Conference Notes" record sheet to conduct individual conferences.

At the end of independent reading, have the students share their reading with the class. Ask questions such as:

Q *What is your book about?*

Q *What surprised you in your reading?*

> *Thinking About My Reading*
>
> - *What is happening in my story right now?*

Day 2

Materials

- *Bend and Stretch*
- "Expository Text Features" chart and a marker

Read-aloud/Strategy Lesson

In this lesson, the students:

- *Explore text features*
- Identify what they learn from a text
- Read independently for up to 20 minutes
- Take responsibility for their behavior

▶1 Review the Previous Lesson and Add to the "Expository Text Features" Chart

Have partners sit together. Show the cover of *Bend and Stretch* and review that in the previous lesson the students learned new information about bones and muscles and looked at diagrams. Show pages 4–5 and point to the text box on page 5. Explain that text boxes are another feature found in some expository nonfiction. Explain that text boxes give the reader more information, or interesting facts, about what is on the page. Direct the students' attention to the "Expository Text Features" chart and add *text boxes*.

Tell the students that you will reread parts of *Bend and Stretch,* and this time you will include the information from the text boxes. Encourage the students to listen for new information about bones and muscles as you read.

▶2 Reread *Bend and Stretch* and Discuss Text Boxes

Reread pages 5, 7, and 9, including the information in the text boxes. Stop after:

> **p. 9** "On the outside, bones are smooth."

Ask:

Q *What new information did you learn about bones in the part
I just read?*

Have a couple of students share their thinking with the class.

Reread pages 11 and 15, including the information in the text boxes.
Stop after:

> **p. 15** "You have more than 630 muscles!"

 Ask and have the students use "Turn to Your Partner" to discuss:

Q *What new information did you learn about bones or muscles in the
part I just read?*

Have a couple of students share their thinking with the class.

Reread pages 17, 19, and 20, including the information in the text
boxes. Stop after:

> **p. 20** "Your eye muscles move about 100,000 times each day."

 Ask and have the students use "Turn to Your Partner" to discuss:

Q *What surprising information did you learn about muscles in the
part I just read?*

Have a couple of students share their thinking with the class.

Remind the students that authors often include interesting facts
and information in text boxes. Encourage the students to read the
text boxes in expository texts.

3 ▶ Briefly Explore Other Text Features and Discuss Information from the Reading

Show the students pages 22–23 of *Bend and Stretch,* and explain
that these pages contain other text features sometimes found at the
end of expository nonfiction books.

Point out and read the headings "Bones and Muscles," "Find Your Joints!" and "Tools of the Trade." Explain that these sections give extra information about bones and muscles. Tell the students that sometimes sections like these are called "Fun Facts." Add *fun facts* to the "Expository Text Features" chart.

 Read pages 22–23 aloud. Ask and have the students use "Turn to Your Partner" to discuss:

Q *What new information did you learn in the sections I just read?*

Show page 24 and point out that like *Snails,* this book has a glossary and an index. Review that the index can help the reader find out more about a specific topic in a book. Draw the students' attention to the "To Learn More" section. Explain that this is a list of other books and a website to find out more about bones and muscles. This section is for readers who still have questions or want to find more information on the topic. Add *to learn more* to the chart.

Save the "Expository Text Features" chart for Week 3.

4 ▶ Discuss Taking Responsibility

Remind students that they have been thinking about how they are responsible for their behavior during partner and whole-class discussions. Briefly discuss the following questions:

Q *How did you act in a responsible way today?*

Q *What, if anything, made it difficult to be responsible today? What can you do [differently/the same way] during our next discussion?*

INDIVIDUALIZED DAILY READING

5 ▶ Read Independently/Document IDR Conferences

Have the students read independently for up to 20 minutes. Use the "IDR Conference Notes" record sheet to conduct and document individual conferences.

FACILITATION TIP

Continue to focus on **responding neutrally** with interest during class discussions by refraining from overtly praising or criticizing the students' responses. Instead, build the students' intrinsic motivation by responding with genuine curiosity and interest, for example:

• *Say more about that.*

• *Explain your thinking further.*

• *You have a point of view that's [similar to/different from] what [Jerome] just said. How is it [similar/different]?*

• *Do you agree or disagree with [Maya]? Why?*

• *What question do you have for [Maya] about her thinking?*

Continue to encourage the students to practice monitoring their reading.

 At the end of independent reading, have partners discuss their reading with one another.

EXTENSION

Learn More About Bones and Muscles

Create a chart with questions the students have about bones and muscles. Have the students use the additional resources listed on page 24 in *Bend and Stretch* to find out more about bones and muscles. As a class, discuss answers to the students' questions and other interesting information they learn during their search.

Day 3

Materials

- *Bend and Stretch*
- "Expository Text Features" chart
- Expository texts at appropriate levels for independent reading
- *Assessment Resource Book*

Guided Strategy Practice

In this lesson, the students:

- *Explore text features*
- Identify what they learn from a text
- Read independently for up to 20 minutes
- Take responsibility for their behavior

1 ▶ Review Expository Text

Ask partners to sit together. Remind the students that this week they have continued to explore expository texts. Refer to the "Expository Text Features" chart and remind the students that they identified features of expository text. Ask:

Q *What have you learned about expository text this week?*

2 ▶ Read and Discuss the Information on the Back of the Book and the Table of Contents

Make sure the students have a variety of expository texts at appropriate reading levels available to them. Explain that today they will read and explore text features in their own nonfiction books. Remind them that readers will often read the back cover of an expository text and the table of contents to find out what the book is about.

Explain that each student will read the information on the back cover of her book as well as the table of contents. Then partners will talk about the topics of their books and what information they think they will learn by reading them.

ELL Note

Help your English Language Learners select appropriate books. If necessary, help them with challenging vocabulary.

Have partners share the topics of their nonfiction books and what information they think they will find in them. Ask questions such as:

Q *What is the topic of your book?*

Q *How did the summary on the back of the book and the table of contents help you know what your book is about?*

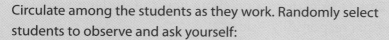
CLASS COMPREHENSION ASSESSMENT

Circulate among the students as they work. Randomly select students to observe and ask yourself:

Q *Do the students recognize text features?*

Q *Are they able to make sense of the features?*

Record your observations on page 23 of the *Assessment Resource Book*.

3 ▶ Reading the Index for Information

Explain that the students will read the index to find specific information in their books. Ask each student to select an entry in the index, identify the pages where he will find that information, and then read those pages.

After students have read for several minutes, have partners share the word or topic they selected, what information they read, and anything they noticed about using the index.

As a class, briefly discuss the following questions:

Q *What word or topic did you look up?*

Q *What information did you find out about [New York City]?*

Q *What did you notice about using the index of your book?*

Remind the students that readers use expository text features to help them find and understand information. Tell them that they should notice, use, and read text features during their independent reading.

Explain that in the coming weeks, the students will read and think more about other types of expository text.

Save the "Expository Text Features" chart for Week 3.

▶4 Reflect on Working Together Responsibly

Facilitate a brief discussion about how the students worked together responsibly. Ask:

Q *What did you do to work responsibly with your partner today?*

Q *What did you like about how you worked together today? What problems did you have? How did you try to solve them?*

INDIVIDUALIZED DAILY READING

▶5 Read Independently and Discuss Text Features

Have the students read expository texts at their appropriate reading levels for up to 20 minutes. Ask the students to pay particular attention to the text features and to be ready to share those features in pairs at the end of IDR.

 At the end of independent reading, have partners discuss what they learned and any text features they noticed. As a class, discuss the different text features in the students' books. Ask questions such as:

Q *What is your book about?*

Q *What text features did you notice?*

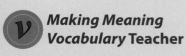

***Making Meaning**
Vocabulary Teacher*

Next week you will revisit
Bend and Stretch to teach
Vocabulary Week 21.

Week 3

Overview

UNIT 8: EXPLORING TEXT FEATURES
Expository Nonfiction

Articles

"Ice Cream Mania!"

This article tells how ice cream is made.

"Giant Panda, Red Panda"

This article introduces the giant panda and the red panda and tells what people around the world are doing to protect them.

Functional Texts

"Classic Smoothie"

This functional text is a set of step-by-step instructions for making a fruit smoothie.

"The City Zoo: Hours, Feeding Times, and Activity Times"

This functional text is a sample of a daily schedule for a zoo.

ALTERNATIVE RESOURCES

Science News for Kids, www.sciencenewsforkids.org

Highlights Kids, www.highlightskids.com

Comprehension Focus

- Students *explore text features* in articles and functional texts.

- Students identify what they learn from articles and functional texts.

- Students read independently.

Social Development Focus

- Students take responsibility for their learning and behavior.

- Students reflect on how their behavior affects others.

DO AHEAD

- Collect a few newspapers and magazines to show the students examples of articles on Day 1.

- (Optional) Collect a variety of functional texts for the students to examine and read on Day 3.

- Make copies of the Unit 8 Parent Letter (BLM8) to send home with the students on the last day of the unit.

Making Meaning Vocabulary Teacher

If you are teaching Developmental Studies Center's *Making Meaning Vocabulary* program, teach Vocabulary Week 21 this week. For more information, see the *Making Meaning Vocabulary Teacher's Manual.*

Day 1

Materials

- "Ice Cream Mania!" (see pages 298–299)
- Newspapers and magazine articles, collected ahead
- *Student Response Book* pages 10–11
- "Reading Comprehension Strategies" chart
- "Expository Text Features" chart from Week 2 and a marker

Reading Comprehension Strategies

- *making connections*

Read-aloud/Strategy Practice

In this lesson, the students:

- *Explore text features*
- Identify what they learn from an article
- Read independently for up to 20 minutes
- Take responsibility for their behavior

▶1 Get Ready to Work Together

Have partners sit together. Remind the students that this year they have been working on taking responsibility for their behavior and their learning by listening to one another, sharing their partners' ideas, looking at the person who is talking, and contributing ideas that are different from others' ideas. Encourage the students to think about how they are taking responsibility for their behavior as they practice these skills.

▶2 Review Recognizing Text Features and Introduce "Ice Cream Mania!"

Remind the students that during the last two weeks they explored a kind of nonfiction called expository nonfiction. They heard expository nonfiction books and used the text features to help them understand the books. Refer to the "Reading Comprehension Strategies" chart and review that *recognizing text features* is a comprehension strategy readers use to help them make sense of expository text.

Explain that this week, the students will use text features to help them understand articles. Explain that articles are short pieces of nonfiction writing that appear in newspapers and magazines and on websites. As examples, show the students articles from the newspapers and magazines you collected.

Ask and briefly discuss:

Q *When have you read or seen someone read a newspaper or magazine?*

Explain that the article you will read aloud today was written by a company that publishes news magazines for young readers. Have the students turn to *Student Response Book* pages 10–11 and explain that this is a copy of the article. Read the title "Ice Cream Mania!" aloud. Explain that *mania* means *excitement*.

Explain that you will read the article aloud and will stop during the reading so partners can talk about the article.

3 Read Aloud

Tell the students that the first part of the article explains why ice cream is one of the world's favorite foods and how ice cream is made. Explain that you will read the first two sections of the article aloud, and ask them to follow along in their *Student Response Books*. Read the text of the article as described on the next page, stopping as needed to clarify vocabulary.

Suggested Vocabulary

process: series of steps (p. 299)
bacteria: very tiny living things that live all around us (p. 299)
churned: stirred (p. 299)
muscle power: strength (p. 299)
contain: include; are made with (p. 299)

ELL Vocabulary

English Language Learners may benefit from discussing additional vocabulary, including:

favorite: best-liked (p. 298)
flavors: kinds of tastes (p. 298)
celebrations: parties (p. 298)
freezer: very cold storage place for foods (p. 299)

Read the opening paragraph and the "How Ice Cream Is Made" section, stopping after:

p. 299 "It takes a lot of muscle power."

 First in pairs, and then as a class, discuss:

Q *What have you found out about ice cream so far?*

Have a few volunteers share their thinking.

Have the students follow along in their *Student Response Books* as you continue reading to the end of the article.

▶ 4 Discuss the Article

 Have the students use "Turn to Your Partner" to discuss:

Q *What did you find out about ice cream from this article?*

Q *What is one thing you found out about ice cream that surprised you?*

Have a few volunteers share their thinking.

▶ 5 Discuss Text Features

Call the students' attention to the photo on *Student Response Book* page 11 and explain that in expository texts, photographs often have captions, or words that tell what the photos show. Read the caption under the photograph on page 299 aloud and explain that nonfiction books and articles often have photos with captions and other text features to help readers understand the topic.

Review the features on the "Expository Text Features" chart and add *captions* to the chart.

Call the students' attention to the graph on *Student Response Book* page 11. Explain that graphs are a way to organize information and allow readers to compare one thing to another. Explain that this graph is called a bar graph. Read the title of the graph and the caption. Point out that it shows five popular flavors of ice cream, and each bar on the graph represents the number of gallons of each flavor that was eaten in the U.S. in 2006. Give pairs a few moments to look at the graph together and have them discuss:

Q *Out of the flavors listed, what flavor of ice cream is the most popular? How do you know?*

Q *Out of the flavors listed, what flavor of ice cream is the least popular? How do you know?*

Q *Which flavor of ice cream do you like best?*

Have a few volunteers share their thinking.

Remind the students that graphs are a text feature often found in articles and other kinds of expository nonfiction. Add *graphs* to the "Expository Text Features" chart.

Explain that tomorrow the students will hear another article and look at more text features.

6 **Reflect on Taking Responsibility**

Ask and briefly discuss as a class:

Q *How did you take responsibility for your behavior today? Why is that important to do?*

INDIVIDUALIZED DAILY READING

7 **Document IDR Conferences/Review Reading Comprehension Strategies**

Review the strategies on the "Reading Comprehension Strategies" chart. Ask the students to notice which strategies they use during IDR today. Have the students read independently for up to 30 minutes.

Use the "IDR Conference Notes" record sheet to conduct and document individual conferences.

Reading Comprehension Strategies

- making connections

At the end of IDR, have several students share with the class a reading comprehension strategy they used and when they used it. Ask the students to explain how the strategy helped them make sense of the text they were reading.

EXTENSION

Make a Graph of Favorite Fruits

Explain that the class will make a graph showing their favorite fruits.

Ask the students to think about an apple, an orange, and a banana. Ask them to think about which of these fruits they like best. Without discussing their choice, ask each student to write their choice on a self-stick note. Ask the students who chose an apple to bring their self-stick notes to the board and help them put their self-stick notes in a column to form a "bar" for a bar graph. Follow the same procedure for the other fruit choices. Then along the bottom, label each bar with the corresponding fruit. Have the students analyze and discuss the data to determine which of the three fruits is most popular among the students in the class.

Ice Cream Mania!

Ice cream is one of the world's favorite foods. Why? There are three big reasons.

1. There are many different flavors of ice cream.
2. Ice cream can be eaten in many different ways. You can have it in a cone, a dish, an ice cream cake, and even a sandwich.
3. Ice cream tastes good! After a healthy meal that includes plenty of veggies, ice cream is a real treat. It is often on the menu at birthday celebrations and other special times.

How Ice Cream Is Made

Ice cream is a simple food. The main ingredients are milk, sugar, and water. It also has other ingredients to make it smooth and creamy.

But making ice cream in a factory is not a simple process. Here's how it is done:

1. The ingredients are mixed together.
2. The mixture is heated to kill bacteria and churned to make it smooth.
3. The mixture is moved into a cold storage tank. It stays there until it is firm.
4. Colors and flavors are added.
5. The ice cream is placed in a freezer. Inside the freezer it is whipped up to force air into the ice cream to make it soft.
6. For some flavors, nuts or candy are then added.
7. Finally, the ice cream is packaged.

e cream is packaged containers.

Most people who eat ice cream buy it from a supermarket. Others make their own ice cream at home. With an electric ice cream maker, the mixture is quickly churned and frozen. Ice cream can also be made the old-fashioned way, using a bowl, a whisk or an electric beater, and a freezer. This takes about four hours and a lot of churning. It takes a lot of muscle power.

Who Ate All the Ice Cream?

Americans eat more ice cream than any other people in the world. In fact, Americans eat about 1.6 billion gallons of ice cream each year.

New Zealanders are the second biggest ice cream eaters. People in Denmark come in third.

The experts say that ice cream is a "sometimes" food. This means that it's better to eat ice cream sometimes rather than all the time. You'll enjoy it more, too!

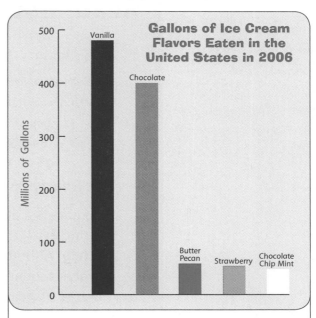

In 2006, almost 500 million gallons of vanilla ice cream was eaten in the United States. The bar graph above shows some other favorite flavors.

Sorbet, Soy, or Rice?

Ice cream isn't the only frozen dessert people love to eat. Another kind is sorbet, which is made from fruit and sugar. Soy ice cream is made from soymilk. Rice ice cream (or rice cream) is made from rice milk. Rice milk is made from brown rice and sugar.

None of these desserts contain milk. This means that people who can't have milk can still have a frozen dessert. Sorbet, soy, and rice ice creams don't taste quite the same as ice cream. But they're just as delicious.

So what's your favorite frozen dessert?

Day 2

Materials

- "Giant Panda, Red Panda" (see pages 306–307)
- *Student Response Book* pages 12–13
- "Expository Text Features" chart and a marker

 Note

Your English Language Learners will benefit from previewing the article prior to today's lesson.

Read-aloud/Strategy Lesson

In this lesson, the students:

- *Explore text features*
- Identify what they learn from an article
- Read independently for up to 20 minutes
- Take responsibility for their behavior

1 ▸ Get Ready to Work Together

Have partners sit together. Remind the students that they are noticing when they take responsibility for their behavior and their learning. Without mentioning students' names, offer a few examples of when students in the class took responsibility for themselves. Ask the students to continue to notice when they are being responsible.

2 ▸ Preview "Giant Panda, Red Panda" Using Text Features

Review that yesterday the students read and discussed the article "Ice Cream Mania!" and thought about what they learned from the text features in the article. Today they will read and discuss another article and look at other text features readers can use to help them make sense of nonfiction.

Explain that the article the students will hear today is about two types of pandas, the giant panda and the red panda. Have them turn to *Student Response Book* pages 12–13 and explain that this is a copy of the article. Draw their attention to the article's title and section headings and point out that they are in bold print so readers can find them easily. Tell the students that a title and section headings are text features that help readers know what information might be in an article.

Have the students follow along in their *Student Response Books* as you read the title and the section headings aloud; then ask and briefly discuss:

Q *After reading the title and section headings, what do you think you might learn from this article?*

Have a few volunteers share their thinking.

Students might say:

"It might tell how giant pandas and red pandas are the same."

"It might tell why giant pandas and red pandas are in danger."

"It might tell how people are trying to help the pandas."

Add *title* and *section headings* to the "Expository Text Features" chart.

Draw the students' attention to the map in the article and explain that giant pandas and red pandas live in China, a country in eastern Asia. Point out that maps give readers more information about important places mentioned in expository nonfiction.

Add *maps* to the "Expository Text Features" chart.

▶ **Read "Giant Panda, Red Panda" Aloud**

Read the article aloud, having the students follow along in their *Student Response Books,* and stopping as described on the next page.

Suggested Vocabulary

dusk: the time of day when the sun has just gone down; evening (p. 306)

endangered species: types of animals in danger of becoming extinct, or dying off (p. 306)

conservation groups: people who work together to take care of forests and animals (p. 307)

breed them: have them give birth to baby pandas (p. 307)

extinction: dying out (p. 307)

Teacher Note

If the students have difficulty answering the question, offer some suggestions like those in the "Students might say" note.

> Expository Text Features
> - table of contents

> **ELL Vocabulary**
>
> English Language Learners may benefit from discussing additional vocabulary, including:
>
> **hind legs:** back legs (p. 306)
> **blends in with:** looks like (p. 306)
> **grasp:** hold (p. 306)

Read "Furry Friends," stopping after:

> **p. 306** "Red pandas eat fruits, berries, and mushrooms as well."

 First in pairs, and then as a class, discuss:

Q *What have you found out about giant pandas and red pandas so far?*

Have a few volunteers share their thinking.

Read "Pandas in Danger" stopping after:

> **p. 307** "Today, pandas are endangered."

 First in pairs, and then as a class, discuss:

Q *What did you learn about giant pandas and red pandas in the part I just read?*

Have a few volunteers share their thinking.

Have the students follow along in their *Student Response Books* as you continue reading to the end of the article.

4 ▶ **Discuss the Article**

Ask and briefly discuss:

Q *What did you learn about giant pandas and red pandas from this article?*

Q *What is one thing you learned about giant pandas or red pandas that surprised you?*

FACILITATION TIP

Reflect on your experience over the past three weeks with **responding neutrally** with interest during class discussions. Does this practice feel natural to you? Are you integrating it into class discussions throughout the school day? What effect is it having on the students? We encourage you to continue to try this practice and reflect on the students' responses as you facilitate class discussions in the future.

Note

You may want to read this information to your English Language Learners.

Have the students work in pairs to look at the pictures and read the captions in the article. After they have had time to look at the pictures and read the captions, ask:

Q *What new information did you learn from reading the captions?*

Have a few volunteers share their thinking.

5 ▶ **Read the "Can We Save Them?" Text Box**

Direct the students' attention to the text box on *Student Response Book* page 13. Remind the students that text boxes such as this one often give readers more information by telling a story or listing more facts about the topic. Have the students follow along as you read the sidebar aloud.

Have the students use "Turn to Your Partner" to discuss:

Q *What new information did you learn from reading the text boxes?*

Have a few volunteers share their thinking.

Explain that tomorrow the students will look at a different kind of expository nonfiction and talk about it in pairs and as a class.

INDIVIDUALIZED DAILY READING

6 ▶ **Discuss Text Features/Document IDR Conferences**

Have the students read expository texts at their appropriate reading levels independently for up to 20 minutes. Ask the students to pay particular attention to the text features and to be ready to share those features in pairs at the end of IDR.

Use the "IDR Conference Notes" record sheet to conduct and document individual conferences.

At the end of independent reading, have partners discuss what they learned and any text features they noticed. As a class, discuss the different text features in students' books. Ask questions such as:

Q *What is your book about?*

Q *What text features did you notice?*

Pandas eat bamboo.

The red panda hides in trees during the day. It looks for food at dusk.

Giant Panda, Red Panda

The San Diego Zoo has a conservation plan for giant pandas. They are trying to stop endangered species from dying out.

Furry Friends

Did you know that there are two kinds of pandas—giant pandas and red pandas? Giant pandas have soft, heavy bodies and black-and-white fur. Their paws are as big as boxing gloves. Giant pandas can stand on their hind legs, like bears can. Red pandas are much smaller than giant pandas. They spend the day resting in trees. Their fur blends in with the leaves. They have striped tails and pale faces and look a little like raccoons.

Both kinds of pandas eat bamboo. They grasp the stalks in their strong paws. Red pandas eat fruits, berries, and mushrooms as well.

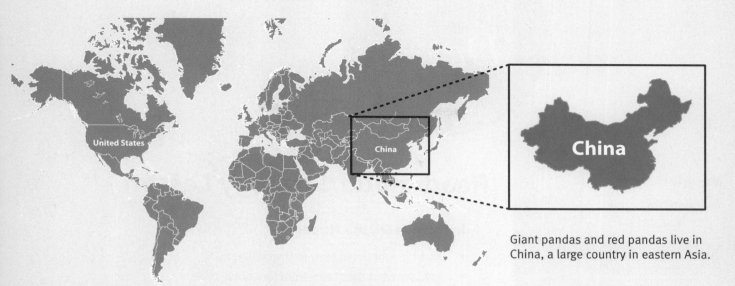

Giant pandas and red pandas live in China, a large country in eastern Asia.

Pandas in Danger

Not many pandas live in the wild today. Scientists say that there are fewer than 2,000 giant pandas in the wild and fewer than 2,500 red pandas.

Once, thousands and thousands of pandas lived in China. They were safe in the cool, rainy forests. But for many years, people have hunted pandas. They wanted panda fur to make clothing. The red panda has been hunted for its bushy tail. People used the tail to make furry hats.

Pandas have also lost much of the forest where they live. The trees have been cut down to build new cities and farms. People and pollution have scared pandas away. When pandas don't have a safe place to live, it is hard for them to breed. Today, pandas are endangered.

Chances of Survival

People must help the pandas, or they will soon be gone forever. Conservation groups are working hard to save pandas from hunters. In the 1990s, new laws about hunting were made in Asia. Not many pandas are hunted today. Animal experts are looking for ways to breed them in zoos and in the wild, too.

People have also made safe places for pandas to live in the wild. The Chinese government has set aside land in the mountains of western China. The giant panda and red panda live there, as well as other endangered animals such as the snow leopard. These beautiful animals are not safe from extinction. They have become endangered as a result of people's actions. They need our help if they are to survive.

Can We Save Them?

Red and giant pandas will have the best chances of survival if people do the following things:

- Protect the places where pandas live by not clearing forests
- Support the work that conservation groups do to protect pandas
- Do not buy products that are made from panda fur

Day 3

Read-aloud/Strategy Lesson

Materials

- "Classic Smoothie" (see page 313)
- "The City Zoo" (see page 314)
- *Student Response Book* pages 14–15
- "Expository Text Features" chart and a marker
- *Assessment Resource Book*
- Unit 8 Parent Letter (BLM8)

In this lesson, the students:

- Identify functional texts in the classroom
- Identify what they learn from functional texts
- Read independently for up to 20 minutes
- Take responsibility for their behavior and learning

1 ▶ Review Articles and Introduce Functional Texts

Have partners sit together. Review that this week the students have read and discussed the articles "Ice Cream Mania!" and "Giant Panda, Red Panda" and thought about how expository text features help readers understand articles. Explain that today the students will explore another kind of expository nonfiction, called "functional" texts.

Teacher Note ▶

Other examples of functional texts are tickets, bills, labels, receipts, calendars, and food wrappers.

Explain that functional texts help readers do things in everyday life. Some examples of functional texts are street signs, menus, maps, recipes, instructions, and schedules.

Point out one or two functional texts in the classroom and explain how they are helpful. For example, you might point at the lunch menu and explain that it is helpful because it lets the reader know what will be served for lunch every day.

 Have the students use "Turn to Your Partner" to discuss:

Q *What other functional texts do you see in our classroom?*

Have several volunteers point out the functional texts they noticed. As they share, briefly discuss how the functional text is helpful.

Students might say:

"I see the class meeting rules. Having the rules posted reminds us to act on them."

"The name tags on our desks help us learn everyone's name."

"The calendar tells us the month and days of the week."

Explain that the students will explore two functional texts today.

2 Introduce and Read Aloud "Classic Smoothie"

Have the students turn to *Student Response Book* page 14. Read the title "Classic Smoothie" aloud and explain that these are directions for making a fruit smoothie. Explain that a set of directions for making something is a type of functional text.

Ask the students to follow along as you read the introductory paragraph and the "You will need" section aloud. Ask and briefly discuss:

Q *What did you find out about making a fruit smoothie in the part I just read?*

Direct the students' attention to the section titled "Here's how to make it" on *Student Response Book* page 14, and then read the section aloud.

Give pairs a few moments to look over the directions together. First in pairs, and then as a class, have the students discuss:

Q *What makes these directions easy to follow?*

Have a few volunteers share their thinking.

Students might say:

"The steps are numbered so you know what to do first."

"There is a 'You will need' section that tells you everything you need to make the smoothie."

"The picture shows what you are making."

Point out that the numbered steps and pictures are features that make this functional text easy for readers to use. Add *numbered steps* to the "Expository Text Features" chart.

◀ **Teacher Note**

If the students have difficulty naming functional texts, offer some suggestions like those in the "Students might say" note. Other examples of functional texts include: charts, such as homework charts, attendance charts, and reading logs; names tags; the daily schedule; maps; and the directions on the fire extinguisher.

◀ **Teacher Note**

If the students have difficulty answering the question, offer some suggestions like those in the "Students might say" note.

Introduce and Read Aloud "The City Zoo"

Explain that the students will look at another kind of functional text. Have them turn to *Student Response Book* page 15. Read the title "The City Zoo" aloud and explain that this functional text provides the reader with information about the city zoo. Point out the section headings "Feeding Times" and "Activity and Show Times" and read them aloud. Remind the students that section headings tell the reader what information can be found in each section.

Call the students' attention to the "Activity and Show Times" chart and explain that charts are another way to organize information. Charts make it easier for the reader to find information they need. Point out the column headings "Time" and "Activity" and read them aloud. Explain that column headings tell the reader what type of information can be found in each column.

 Ask the students to follow along as you read the "Activity and Show Times" chart aloud. First in pairs, and then as a class, discuss:

Q *What information does this chart give you?*

Q *What makes this chart easy to use?*

CLASS COMPREHENSION ASSESSMENT

As you listen to the students, ask yourself:

Q *Are the students able to identify helpful information found in a functional text?*

Q *Are the students taking responsibility for their behavior and learning?*

Record your observations on page 24 of the *Assessment Resource Book*.

Have several volunteers share.

Students might say:

"The chart tells you when each activity begins."

"You can tell the name of each show and how long it is by looking at the chart."

"The times are in order from earliest to latest."

"Putting each activity is in its own box makes it easy to read the chart."

Explain that because the city zoo schedule and the instructions for making a fruit smoothie give different information, they are organized in different ways to help the reader make sense of them. Review that the schedule has information organized in a chart, whereas the instructions for making a smoothie have numbered steps. Tell the students that noticing how functional texts are organized helps readers understand and use them more easily.

Teacher Note

This is the last week of Unit 8. You will reassign partners for Unit 9.

INDIVIDUALIZED DAILY READING

4 ▶ Discuss Text Features

Have the students read expository texts at their appropriate reading levels for up to 20 minutes. Ask the students to pay particular attention to the text features and to be ready to share those features in pairs at the end of IDR.

 At the end of independent reading, have the students discuss in pairs what they learned and any text features they noticed. As a class, discuss the different text features in the students' books. Ask questions such as:

Q *What is your book about?*

Q *What text features did you notice?*

INDIVIDUAL COMPREHENSION ASSESSMENT

Before continuing with Unit 9, take this opportunity to assess individual students' progress in recognizing text features in expository text to help them make sense of their reading. Please refer to pages 42–43 in the *Assessment Resource Book* for instructions.

EXTENSION

Take a School Walk and Create a Functional Text Chart

Take the class on a walk around the school to look for functional texts. Explain that during the walk you will stop a few times so the students can look around and talk about the functional texts they see. Remind the students how you expect them to behave on the walk.

As you walk around the school, point out a few examples of functional texts that you see. For example, you might point to a poster for a school event or the computer lab schedule.

When you return to the classroom, have partners sit together. Have students use "Turn to Your Partner" to discuss the functional texts they saw on the walk. As volunteers share with the class, record functional texts they mention on a chart titled "Functional Texts at Our School." Help the students think about the purposes of functional texts by asking follow-up questions such as:

Q *What information does [the lunch menu] give you?*

Q *How does the [In Case of Emergency poster] help us?*

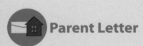

Parent Letter

Send home with each student the Parent Letter for this unit (see "Do Ahead," page 291). Periodically, have a few students share with the class what they are reading at home.

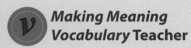

Making Meaning Vocabulary Teacher

Next week you will revisit "Ice Cream Mania!" and "Classic Smoothie" to teach Vocabulary Week 22.

Classic Smoothie

A fruit smoothie is a special treat. It is easy to make, too. You will need to prepare the fruit and put it into the freezer at least 2 hours before you make the smoothie.

You will need:

- Blender
- Knife
- 1 plate
- Drinking glasses
- Straws (optional)
- 1 cup orange juice
- 1 cup fresh strawberries
- 2 fresh bananas

Here's how to make it:

1. At least 2 hours before you want to make the smoothie, wash the strawberries, take out the stem end, and cut the strawberries into quarters. Put them on a plate in the freezer.

2. Peel and slice the bananas and put them on a plate in the freezer.

3. When you are ready to make the smoothie, pour the orange juice into a blender.

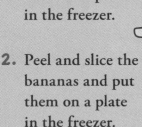

4. Add the strawberries and bananas.

5. Blend until smooth.

6. Pour into glasses, add straws, and enjoy!

The City Zoo

Hours, Feeding Times, and Activity Times

Welcome to The City Zoo. We are open every day from 9:30 AM – 5:30 PM.

Feeding Times

Time	Animals
11:00 AM	Monkeys
12:00 PM	Zebras
1:00 PM	Giant Pandas
2:00 PM	Tigers
3:00 PM	Lions
4:00 PM	Polar Bears
5:00 PM	Chimpanzees

Come to The City Zoo and see the new tiger cubs.

The sea lions play in the Aquatic Arena at 12:00 PM.

Activity and Show Times

Time	Activity
11:00 AM	Spooky Spiders Talk (20 minutes)
12:00 PM	Sea Lion Display (10 minutes)
1:00 PM	Meet the Giraffes (30 minutes)
2:00 PM	World of Birds Talk (15 minutes)
3:00 PM	Tiger Tour (30 minutes, except Mondays)
4:00 PM	Alligator Show at Jurassic Swamp (10 minutes)

Unit 9

Determining Important Ideas

EXPOSITORY NONFICTION AND FICTION

During this unit, the students explore important ideas in expository nonfiction and fiction texts and use inference informally to think about what is important in text. During IDR, the students continue to practice self-monitoring and think about what is important in their independent reading. Socially, they relate the value of fairness to their partner work as they develop the group skill of sharing their partner time. They reflect on this sharing in a class meeting. They also practice giving reasons to support their thinking.

Week 1 **"Wild Rides"** by Lev Grossman
"Summer of the Shark" from *TIME For Kids*
"A Nose for the Arts" from *TIME For Kids*

Week 2 *Me First* by Helen Lester

Week 3 *Big Al* by Andrew Clements
Erandi's Braids by Antonio Hernández Madrigal

Week 1

Overview

UNIT 9: DETERMINING IMPORTANT IDEAS
Expository Nonfiction and Fiction

"Wild Rides"
by Lev Grossman (timeforkids.com, May 10, 2002)

"Summer of the Shark"
from *TIME For Kids* (timeforkids.com, October 14, 2001)

"A Nose for the Arts"
from *TIME For Kids* (timeforkids.com, December 14, 2001)

ALTERNATIVE RESOURCES

ASPCA Animaland, www.aspca.org/kids,

Time For Kids, www.timeforkids.com

Comprehension Focus

• Students *explore important ideas* in texts.

• Students *use inference* informally to think about what is important in text.

• Students read independently.

Social Development Focus

• Students relate the value of fairness to their partner work.

• Students develop the group skills of giving reasons to support their thinking and sharing their partner time in a fair way.

DO AHEAD

• Prior to Day 1, decide how you will randomly assign partners to work together during the unit.

• Collect a variety of newspapers, articles, and magazines at various reading levels for the students to read during IDR. (See "About Important Ideas" on page 318.)

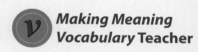

Making Meaning Vocabulary Teacher

If you are teaching Developmental Studies Center's *Making Meaning Vocabulary* program, teach Vocabulary Week 22 this week. For more information, see the *Making Meaning Vocabulary Teacher's Manual.*

Day 1

Materials

- "Wild Rides" (see page 323)
- A variety of newspapers and magazines for independent reading, collected ahead

Being a Writer™ **Teacher**

You can either have the students work with their *Being a Writer* partner or assign them a different partner for the *Making Meaning* lessons.

Teacher Note

During this week's lesson, observe the students as they interact with one another and take note of responsible behaviors you see. You will share your observations with the students throughout the week.

Read-aloud/Strategy Lesson

In this lesson, the students:

- Begin working with new partners
- Hear and discuss an article
- *Explore important ideas* in an article
- Read independently for up to 20 minutes
- Share their partner time in a fair way

About Important Ideas

The focus in this unit is on *determining important ideas*, a powerful strategy for helping readers understand and retain what they read. In the *Making Meaning* program, the focus is on helping the students explore the important ideas in a story or article, rather than identify a single "main idea." The students explore the important ideas and support their opinions with evidence from the text. At times, the students have to infer to determine the important ideas.

In Week 1, the students hear magazine articles read aloud. In Weeks 2 and 3, the students explore important ideas in narrative text.

▶ 1 Pair Students and Get Ready to Work Together

Assign partners and have them sit together. Review that over the past weeks the students have practiced several social skills—taking turns talking and listening, giving reasons for their thinking, and contributing ideas that are different from other people's ideas. Explain that in the next few weeks, they will continue to focus on giving reasons for their thinking and sharing their partner time in a fair way.

Ask:

Q *What are some things you can do today to make sure your new partner feels comfortable sharing?*

Have a few students share their thinking.

Explain that *thinking about what is important* is a strategy that readers use to make sense of text. Explain that when authors write articles and stories, there are things they really want people to learn and remember. Those are the important ideas.

Tell the students that in this unit, they will hear magazine articles and stories and use the comprehension strategies they know to explore the important ideas in what they hear and read.

 ## Review Nonfiction

Review that in the last few weeks, the students heard nonfiction books and articles about people, plants, and animals. They talked about what they learned and what they wondered. Explain that today they will listen to an article from a magazine called *TIME For Kids,* and they will think about the topic of the article and the important information in it. Remind the students that nonfiction magazine and newspaper articles give information or the writer's opinion about a particular topic. (You may want to show examples of nonfiction articles in magazines such as *Ranger Rick, TIME For Kids, Scholastic News,* and *Weekly Reader.*)

 ## Introduce "Wild Rides"

Read the title of the article "Wild Rides" and the author's name. Ask:

Q *What do you think the article "Wild Rides" might be about?*

Students might say:

"I think it might be about riding wild horses."

"It might be about taking a wild ride on a skateboard because some people go over bumps on a skateboard."

"It could be a car race because racers drive very fast."

Explain that you will read the article twice. During the first reading, the students will discuss what the article is about. During the second reading, they will talk about what they think is important in it.

ELL Note

Read the article to your English Language Learners prior to today's read-aloud. Stop frequently to make sure the students understand the article.

ELL Note

English Language Learners
may benefit from talking about
what a roller coaster is before
the reading. If possible, bring in
pictures of roller coasters, and
discuss where you might find a
roller coaster and why people
enjoy riding them.

4 ▶ **Read "Wild Rides" Aloud**

Read "Wild Rides" aloud slowly and clearly, stopping as described
below.

> **Suggested Vocabulary**
>
> **engineers:** people who design and build machines, cars, bridges, roads,
> or other structures (p. 323)
>
> **model:** small or miniature version of the real thing (p. 323)
>
> **verdict:** decision or opinion (p. 323)

Read and stop after:

> **p. 323** "This year's new rides are the wildest ever!"

Ask:

Q *What does the title "Wild Rides" mean?*

Have two or three students share their thinking with the class. Then
read the heading "Picking Up Speed" and read the next paragraph.
Stop after:

> **p. 323** "How did they get that fast? Computers."

Ask:

Q *What are some things you have learned so far about roller
coasters?*

Have two or three students share their thinking with the class.
Reread the last sentence before the stop and continue reading
through the next paragraph. Stop after:

> **p. 323** "'There are limits that you don't go over, because you can
> break a bone,' says Schilke. Yikes!"

Ask:

Q *What else did you learn about roller coasters in the part I just read?*

Have the students use "Turn to Your Partner" to discuss what they have learned. Then have two or three students share their thinking with the class. Reread the last sentence before the stop and continue reading to the end of the article.

 ## 5 ▸ Reread the Article and Discuss Important Ideas

Ask:

Q *If someone asked you what this article is about, what would you tell them?*

Have two or three students share their thinking with the class. Explain that you will reread the article, and the students will discuss what is important to know in different parts of the article.

◀ **Teacher Note**

If the students have difficulty identifying the important ideas, you may need to model the strategy.

Read and stop again after:

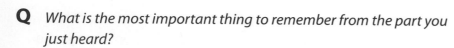 **p. 323** "This year's new rides are the wildest ever!"

Ask:

Q *What is the most important thing to remember from the part you just heard?*

 Have the students use "Think, Pair, Share" to discuss the question. Then have two or three students share their thinking with the class.

Read the section heading "Picking Up Speed" and continue through the next two paragraphs. Stop again after:

 **p. 323** "'There are limits that you don't go over, because you can break a bone,' says Schilke. Yikes!"

Ask:

Q *Why are computers important for building roller coasters?*

 Have the students use "Think, Pair, Share" to discuss the question. Then have two or three students share their thinking with the class.

Read the last sentence before the stop and continue reading to the end of the article.

FACILITATION TIP

During this unit, we invite you to continue practicing **responding neutrally** with interest during class discussions. This week continue to respond neutrally by refraining from overtly praising or criticizing the students' responses. Try responding neutrally by nodding, asking them to say more about their thinking, or asking other students to respond.

 ## Discuss Thinking About Important Ideas

Review that in today's lesson, the students listened to an article and thought about what they learned and what was important. Explain that when authors write articles and stories, there are things they really want people to learn and remember. Those are the important ideas.

 ## Reflect on Working Together

Facilitate a brief discussion about how the students did making their new partners feel comfortable sharing.

INDIVIDUALIZED DAILY READING

 ## Read Independently/Document IDR Conferences

Have the students read nonfiction articles independently for up to 20 minutes.

Use the "IDR Conference Notes" record sheet to conduct and document individual conferences. Continue to encourage the students to self-monitor as they read independently.

 At the end of independent reading, have partners share their reading with one another. As the students share, circulate and listen, observe the students' behaviors and responses, and make notes.

EXTENSION

Read Titles and Articles

Collect a variety of articles at various reading levels. Have partners sit together, and distribute an article to each pair. Have partners read the title, predict what the article might be about, read the article, and discuss it. Have each pair share their title and article with another pair, small group, or the class.

Article

Wild Rides

by Lev Grossman

from *TIME For Kids*, News Scoop Edition
(timeforkids.com, May 10, 2002)

If you've ever been on a roller coaster, you know what it's like: You go up, you go down (boy do you go down!), maybe you go upside down. Then before you know it, it's over. But as ride designers learn new tricks, coasters are getting faster, bigger, and wilder. This year's new rides are the wildest ever!

Picking Up Speed

The first true roller coaster in America was built at Coney Island in New York City in 1884. It rolled along at 6 miles per hour. Now, coasters can reach speeds of 100 miles per hour! How did they get that fast? Computers.

Before engineers build a new roller coaster, they make a computer model that shows how it will run. This helps them make it as safe—and scary—as possible. Allan Schilke is one of the best-known ride designers in the world. He created the ride called X. Computers help him figure out how fast the riders can safely go. "There are limits that you don't go over, because you can break a bone," says Schilke. Yikes!

Most riders have no clue about how coasters are created. They're just along for the ride. Joey Stilphen, 13, of Bay Village, Ohio, tried out the Wicked Twister at Cedar Point last week. His verdict: "It's awesome!"

Day 2

Materials

- "Summer of the Shark"
  (see page 328)

Read-aloud/Strategy Lesson

In this lesson, the students:

- *Explore important ideas* in an article
- Read independently for up to 20 minutes
- Give reasons to support their thinking
- Share their partner time in a fair way

▶1 Get Ready to Work Together

Have partners sit together. Remind the students that in the last lesson they listened to a magazine article and talked about the important ideas in it. Explain that today you will read another magazine article aloud, and they will discuss the important ideas in pairs and with the class. Explain that at the end of the lesson you will ask them to report how they did using their partner time fairly.

▶2 Introduce "Summer of the Shark"

Explain that today you will read another *TIME For Kids* article, called "Summer of the Shark." Ask:

Q *What do you think this article might be about?*

Have two or three students share their thinking with the class.

Explain that you will read the article twice. During the first reading, the students will discuss what they are learning. During the second reading, they will talk about the important ideas in the article.

Read "Summer of the Shark" Aloud

Before reading the article, define the vocabulary word *odds,* and give an example. (For example, you might say, "The odds or chances of your meeting an elephant on your way home are very small. The odds of your meeting someone you know on your way home are much greater.")

 Note

If possible, show your English Language Learners pictures of sharks and seals to enhance their understanding of the article.

Suggested Vocabulary

worldwide: around the world (p. 328)

odds: chances or likelihood of something happening (p. 328)

slim: small (p. 328)

ELL Vocabulary

English Language Learners may benefit from discussing additional vocabulary, including:

shark: large and often fierce fish that feeds on meat and has very sharp teeth (p. 328)

seal: sea mammal that lives in the coastal waters and has thick fur and flippers (p. 328)

shark attacks: sharks' attempts to bite people (p. 328)

splash: throw water around (p. 328)

lightning: flash of light in the sky, usually during a storm (p. 328)

Read the first paragraph aloud twice. Continue reading and stop after:

p. 328 "That's when sharks hunt."

Ask:

Q *What have you learned about sharks so far?*

 Have the students use "Turn to Your Partner" to discuss what they have learned.

Without sharing as a class, reread the last sentence and continue reading to the end of the article.

Have the students use "Turn to Your Partner" to discuss what they have learned. Have two or three students share their thinking with the class. Be ready to reread sentences to help the students recall what they heard.

◀ **Teacher Note**

If the students have difficulty discussing what they have learned in pairs, you may want to have a few students share with the class.

Reread and Discuss Important Ideas

Explain that you will reread "Summer of the Shark." Then they will discuss the important ideas in the article.

Reread "Summer of the Shark" aloud slowly and clearly. Facilitate a whole-class discussion of the article, using the following questions. Remind the students to give reasons for their thinking.

Q *What is this article about?*

Q *What are the important ideas about sharks in this article? Why do you think so?*

 Have the students use "Think, Pair, Share" to discuss the questions before talking as a class.

> **Students might say:**
>
> "I think one important idea is that sharks really don't like to bite people. They only do it by mistake. The story says they might think a foot is a fish."
>
> "I think another important idea is that people get in the way of sharks when sharks are hunting for food and confuse them. I think that because the article says people splash around in the ocean when sharks hunt."
>
> "Sharks hunt in the morning and in the early evening. If you are a skin diver, this is important to know so you don't go diving at those times."

Explain that in the next lesson partners will work together to read and discuss another article.

 Reflect on Working Together

Facilitate a brief discussion about how the students did giving reasons to support their thinking and sharing their partner time fairly.

Explain that in the next lesson you will read another article, entitled "A Nose for the Arts."

Teacher Note ▶

If the students have difficulty identifying important ideas in the article, reread a section and model thinking aloud about the important idea. You might reread the first paragraph and say, "I think the really important idea in this part is that sharks don't really like to bite people. It says they prefer to eat seals."

INDIVIDUALIZED DAILY READING

 Read Independently/Document IDR Conferences

Encourage the students to think about what is important in their reading today. Have them read nonfiction independently for up to 20 minutes.

Use the "IDR Conference Notes" record sheet to conduct and document individual conferences. Continue to encourage the students to self-monitor as they read independently.

At the end of independent reading, have the students discuss their reading with the class. Facilitate the discussion with questions such as:

Q *What have you learned so far?*

Q *What information is important? Why do you think that?*

Summer of the Shark

from *TIME For Kids*, News Scoop Edition
(timeforkids.com, October 14, 2001)

Sharks don't really like to bite people. A great white shark prefers to eat a seal. A bull shark loves fish and even another shark! Then why was this summer full of scary news about shark attacks? Scientists say that is one good question.

Last year sharks bit 84 people worldwide. This year there have been 52 attacks so far. Most were in Florida.

One reason for the high numbers is that more people are in the ocean than ever before. Many splash around in the morning and early evening. That's when sharks hunt.

Sharks that attack humans are probably confused. They might mistake a human foot for a fish. "Sharks are not out to get humans," says scientist Dr. Robert Lea. "It is just humans sharing a spot in the ocean with sharks at the wrong time."

Don't panic. The odds of being attacked by a shark are slim. You are 30 times more likely to be hit by lightning!

Day 3

Read-aloud/Strategy Lesson

In this lesson, the students:

- *Identify important ideas* in an article
- Read independently for up to 20 minutes
- Give reasons to support their thinking

1 ▶ Review the Week

Have partners sit together. Review that in the previous lesson the students listened to an article about sharks and explored the important ideas in it. Explain that today they will hear another article and practice thinking about what they are learning and what is important.

2 ▶ Introduce "A Nose for the Arts"

Explain that today you will read another *TIME For Kids* article, called "A Nose for the Arts." Make sure the students understand the words *arts* and *artist*. Tell the students that the article is about two artists, named Boon Yang and Bird.

Explain that you will read the article twice. During the first reading, the students will discuss what they are learning. During the second reading, they will talk about the important ideas in the article.

3 ▶ Read "A Nose for the Arts" Aloud

Read "A Nose for the Arts" aloud, stopping as described on the next page.

Materials

- "A Nose for the Arts" (see page 334)
- *Assessment Resource Book*
- *Student Response Book,* IDR Journal section

 Note

English Language Learners may benefit from having you act out "making long up-and-down streaks" and "brush…across a canvas" before beginning the read-aloud. They may also benefit from previewing the article prior to the lesson.

Suggested Vocabulary

streaks: long, thin marks or stripes (p. 334)

brush: make strokes or marks with a paintbrush (p. 334)

canvas: surface for painting made from a strong cloth stretched over a wooden frame (p. 334)

orchestra: large group of musicians who play their instruments together (p. 334)

conservation center: place where an animal or a natural environment is protected (p. 334)

ELL Vocabulary

English Language Learners may benefit from discussing additional vocabulary, including:

trunk: the long nose of an elephant, used for drinking, carrying and holding things, and feeding itself (refer to a picture) (p. 334)

elephants: (show a picture) (p. 334)

museums: places where interesting objects of art, history, or science are displayed (p. 334)

CD: short for compact disc, a disc that stores music that can be played on a compact disc player (p. 334)

Read the first paragraph aloud. Stop after:

p. 334 "Bird and Boon Yang hold a paintbrush with a trunk!"

Ask:

Q *What is surprising about the artists Boon Yang and Bird?*

Have two or three students share their thinking with the class. Reread the last sentence before the stop and read the next two paragraphs. Stop after:

p. 334 "The money raised by selling CDs and paintings goes to an elephant-conservation center in Thailand."

Ask:

Q *What have you learned so far in this article?*

Teacher Note ▶

If the students haven't realized that Boon Yang and Bird are elephants, reread the paragraph and ask them to listen carefully for information about the artists.

Have the students use "Turn to Your Partner" to discuss what they have learned. Without sharing as a class, read the subtitle "Can Art Save Elephants?" and continue reading to the end of the article.

Ask:

Q *What did you learn in the last part you heard?*

 Have the students use "Turn to Your Partner" to discuss what they have learned. Have two or three students share their thinking with the class.

 4 ▶ Reread and Discuss Important Ideas

Tell the students that you will reread the article and this time you would like them to think about what the important ideas in the article are. Before rereading, ask:

Q *If a friend asked you what "A Nose for the Arts" is about, what would you tell her?*

Have two or three students share their thinking with the class. Begin rereading and continue through the third paragraph. Stop after:

> **p. 334** "The money raised by selling CDs and paintings goes to an elephant-conservation center in Thailand."

Ask:

Q *What are one or two things the author really wants you to remember from this part?*

 Have the students use "Think, Pair, Share" to discuss the question. Have two or three students share their thinking with the class. Read the subtitle "Can Art Save Elephants?" and continue reading to the end of the article. Ask:

Q *What do you think is really important to remember from the part I just read?*

 Have the students use "Think, Pair, Share" to discuss what they have learned.

CLASS COMPREHENSION ASSESSMENT

Circulate as partners share and ask yourself:

Q *Are the students able to identify what is important to remember or know?*

Record your observations on page 25 of the *Assessment Resource Book*.

5 ▶ Reflect on Working Together

Facilitate a brief discussion about how partners worked together. Ask:

Q *How did you do today sharing your partner time in a fair way?*

Explain that next week the students will have a chance to talk in pairs and with the class about the important ideas in a fiction story.

INDIVIDUALIZED DAILY READING

 ELL Note

You may want to supply your English Language Learners with nonfiction texts in their primary languages.

6 ▶ Write About an Important Idea in Their IDR Journals

Make sure that each student has a nonfiction book or article to read independently. Tell the students that today they will each write about an important idea from their reading in their IDR Journals.

Have the students read independently for up to 20 minutes.

As the students read, circulate among them. Observe their reading behavior and engagement with the text. Ask individual students questions such as:

Q *What is your reading about?*

Q *What are you learning?*

Q *What is an important idea in this [article/book]?*

At the end of independent reading, have the students write about an important idea from today's reading in their IDR Journals.

EXTENSION

Think About the Titles Authors Choose

Point out that sometimes authors use clever titles like "A Nose for the Arts" to attract people's attention and make them curious about an article. At other times, they use titles that tell exactly what the article will be about, like "Summer of the Shark." Ask:

Q *Do you think "A Nose for the Arts" is a good title for the article you heard today? Why or why not?*

Q *What do you think of the title "Wild Rides"? Explain your thinking.*

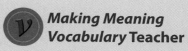

Making Meaning
***Vocabulary* Teacher**

Next week you will revisit this week's articles to teach Vocabulary Week 23.

Article

A Nose for the Arts

from *TIME For Kids,* News Scoop Edition
(timeforkids.com, December 14, 2002)

Boon Yang likes to paint quickly, making long up-and-down streaks in bright colors. Bird prefers to brush deep blue and green across a canvas. People have compared their work to paintings by famous modern artists. But there's a big difference: Bird and Boon Yang hold a paintbrush with a trunk!

Boon Yang and Bird are two of about 100 elephants in Thailand and other Asian lands who have become successful artists. Their paintings have sold for as much as $2,200! Some even hang in museums.

Painting isn't the only kind of artwork done by Asian elephants. Some are making music too. A Thai elephant orchestra has recorded a CD. The money raised by selling CDs and paintings goes to an elephant-conservation center in Thailand.

Can Art Save Elephants?

Elephants in Thailand are in trouble. For years, they worked carrying heavy logs from rain forests. But the animals lost their jobs in 1989, when Thailand decided to protect the forests and stop logging. Some elephants wound up begging for food!

Artists Vitaly Komar and Alex Melamid wanted to help. They set up elephant art schools and brought attention to Thai elephants. Melamid says he's thrilled with the success of the project: "We've shown that anything is possible."

Week 2

Overview

UNIT 9: DETERMINING IMPORTANT IDEAS

Expository Nonfiction and Fiction

Me First

by Helen Lester, illustrated by Lynn Munsinger
(Houghton Mifflin, 1992)

Pinkerton the pig always manages to be first until he rushes for a sandwich and gets a surprise.

ALTERNATIVE BOOKS

The Magic Fish by Freya Littledale

The Empty Pot by Demi

Comprehension Focus

• Students *explore important ideas* in a story.

• Students *use inference* informally to think about what is important in a story.

• Students read independently.

Social Development Focus

• Students relate the value of fairness to their partner work.

• Students develop the group skills of giving reasons to support their thinking and sharing their partner time in a fair way.

• Students have a class meeting to discuss sharing their partner time fairly.

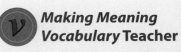

**Making Meaning
Vocabulary Teacher**

If you are teaching Developmental Studies Center's *Making Meaning Vocabulary* program, teach Vocabulary Week 23 this week. For more information, see the *Making Meaning Vocabulary Teacher's Manual.*

Day 1

Materials

- Space for the class to sit in a circle
- "Class Meeting Ground Rules" chart
- "Thinking About My Reading" chart

Class Meeting Ground Rules

- *one person talks at a time*
- *listen to one another*

Class Meeting

In this lesson, the students:

- Review the ground rules and procedure for a class meeting
- Read independently for up to 20 minutes
- Analyze the ways they have been interacting
- Discuss sharing partner time in a fair way

▶1 Gather for a Class Meeting

Tell the students that they are going to have a class meeting today to check in on how they are doing sharing their partner time in a fair way. If necessary, review the procedure and your expectations for how the students will move into a circle for the class meeting.

Have the students move into a circle with partners sitting together. Briefly review the ground rules and remind the students to give reasons to support their own thinking.

▶2 Conduct the Class Meeting

Ask the students to think about how they have worked with their partner and classmates over the past few weeks. Ask the following questions one at a time, giving the students time to think about each question. Then have the students discuss these questions, first in pairs, and then as a class.

Q *I've noticed that sometimes when I call you back from partner work, both partners have not had a chance to share. Why does that happen?*

Q *What are some things you can do to make sure you share your partner time in a fair way?*

Q *Why is it important to make sure that both partners have time to share?*

Encourage the students to try some of their suggestions in the coming days, and plan to check in with them to see how they are doing.

3 ▶ Adjourn the Class Meeting

Close the meeting by having the students briefly reflect on how they did following the ground rules. Adjourn the meeting and have the students return to their desks.

INDIVIDUALIZED DAILY READING

4 ▶ Practice Self-monitoring

Draw the students' attention to the "Thinking About My Reading" chart and explain that they will practice self-monitoring today during IDR.

Have the students read independently for up to 20 minutes.

Stop them at 10-minute intervals and have them monitor their comprehension by thinking about the questions on the "Thinking About My Reading" chart.

As the students read, circulate among them and ask individual students to read a selection aloud and tell you what it is about. Use the questions on the chart to help struggling students be aware of monitoring their own comprehension.

At the end of independent reading, have the students talk about using the questions on the chart to help them monitor their own comprehension.

Thinking About My Reading

- *What is happening in my story right now?*

Day 2

Materials

- *Me First*

Read-aloud

In this lesson, the students:

- Hear and discuss a story
- *Visualize* part of a story
- Read independently for up to 20 minutes
- Give reasons to support their thinking
- Share their partner time in a fair way

1 ▶ Get Ready to Work Together

Have partners sit together. Tell the students that today they will hear and talk about a story. In the next lesson, they will hear the story again and talk about the important ideas in it.

Remind the students that in the last class meeting, they talked about ways to be fair during partner work. They will talk about how they did sharing their partner time at the end of today's lesson.

2 ▶ Introduce *Me First*

Show the cover of *Me First* and read the title and names of the author and illustrator aloud. Explain that this is a story about a pig named Pinkerton. Ask:

Q *What do you think this story might be about?*

Have two or three students share their thinking with the class. Ask for a show of hands in answer to the question:

Q *How many of you have ever wanted to be first?*

Determining Important Ideas
Expository Nonfiction and Fiction

3 ▶ Read *Me First* Aloud

Read *Me First* aloud, showing the illustrations as you read, and stopping as described below.

Suggested Vocabulary

plump: round or chubby (p. 3)
snouts: noses (p. 3)
trough-a-teria: (invented word) cafeteria (p. 5)
faint: not clear (p. 10)
in the distance: far away (p. 10)
pricked up: raised (p. 11)
trot: run slowly (p. 11)
smear: thin layer (p. 12)
at a full gallop: running fast (p. 14)
concerning: about (p. 29)

ELL Vocabulary

English Language Learners may benefit from discussing additional vocabulary, including:

right smack in front: right in front (p. 4)
picnic basket: basket used to carry food for a meal outdoors (p. 9; refer to the illustration)
mayo: short for mayonnaise (p. 12)
jiggled: shook (p. 16)
taking no notice: paying no attention (p. 18)
a few bends: a few turns on a road or path (p. 18)
tuck me in: put me in bed (p. 23)
scooted: ran along (p. 32)

Have the students close their eyes and ask them to visualize as you read pages 3–4 without showing the illustrations. Stop after:

p. 4   "'Me first!' he cried at story time, settling on his round bottom with his big head right smack in front of the book."

Ask:

Q *What picture of Pinkerton do you have in your mind?*

Have two or three students share their thinking with the class.

ELL Note

English Language Learners may benefit from previewing the text and illustrations prior to the lesson and discussing the difference between a *sandwich* and a *sandwitch* prior to the read-aloud. Explain the play on words and what it means to "…care for a sandwich" (one would like a sandwich to eat) and to actually "…care for a sandwitch" (to look after a witch from the sand).

Reread from the beginning of the book, showing the illustrations.

Stop after:

> **p. 17**　"'I am a Sandwitch, and I live in the sand, and you said you
> would care for a Sandwitch, so here I am. Care for me.'"

 Have the students use "Turn to Your Partner" to discuss the following
question. Remind them to use the partner time in a fair way. Ask:

Q　*What has happened so far in the story? What do you think will
happen next?*

Without sharing as a class, reread the last sentence on page 17 and
continue reading to the end of the story.

4 ▶ Discuss the Story as a Class

Facilitate a whole-class discussion, using the following questions. Be
ready to reread passages aloud and show illustrations again to help
the students recall what they heard. Remind them to give reasons
for their thinking.

Q　*What happens in the story?*

Q　*Would you want to be friends with Pinkerton? Why or why not?*

5 ▶ Reflect on Sharing During Partner Time

Facilitate a brief discussion about how the students did using their
partner time fairly. Share any observations you may have made.

Explain that in the next lesson the students will think about the
important ideas in *Me First*.

INDIVIDUALIZED DAILY READING

 Read Independently/Document IDR Conferences

Have the students read independently for up to 20 minutes.

Use the "IDR Conference Notes" record sheet to conduct and document individual conferences. Continue to encourage the students to self-monitor as they read independently.

 At the end of independent reading, have the students discuss their reading in pairs.

Day 3

Materials

- *Me First*
- *Assessment Resource Book*
- *Student Response Book,* IDR Journal section

Strategy Lesson

In this lesson, the students:

- *Use inference* informally to explore important ideas in a story
- Read independently for up to 20 minutes
- Give reasons to support their thinking

▶1 Review Exploring Important Ideas

Have partners sit together. Explain that today the students will hear *Me First* read aloud again so that they can think about the important ideas in the story and the lesson they can learn from Pinkerton. Point out that authors sometimes use characters in a story to help readers think about important ideas or lessons about life.

▶2 Reread *Me First*

Show the cover of *Me First* and reread the story aloud without stopping.

▶3 Discuss the Important Ideas

Facilitate a whole-class discussion about the story. If necessary, remind the students to give reasons for their thinking as they talk about their ideas. First in pairs, and then as a class, discuss:

Q *What is Pinkerton like at the beginning of the story?*

Q *What is he like at the end of the story?*

Q *What is an important lesson that Pinkerton learns? Why is this an important idea for everyone to remember?*

Students might say:

"Pinkerton learned that being first isn't always the best thing. I think this because in the story he tried to be first to get a sandwich and he ended up taking care of a sandwitch."

"I think that it is important for everyone to remember that you don't always have to be first. I think this because you need to take turns and be fair."

CLASS COMPREHENSION ASSESSMENT

Circulate as partners share. Ask yourself:

Q *Are the students able to identify the important lesson Pinkerton learns?*

Q *Are they able to use the text to support their thinking?*

Record your observations on page 26 of the *Assessment Resource Book.*

Remind the students that stories often have messages or important lessons. Readers understand the message or lesson through what the characters say and do. Good readers think about important ideas and messages to help them make sense of a story. Explain that they will have more opportunities to think about important ideas as they hear and read stories.

INDIVIDUALIZED DAILY READING

4 **Document IDR Conferences/Have the Students Write in Their IDR Journals**

Have the students read independently for up to 20 minutes.

Use the "IDR Conference Notes" record sheet to conduct and document individual conferences. Continue to encourage the students to self-monitor as they read independently.

At the end of independent reading, have the students write about their reading in their IDR Journals.

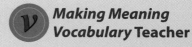

***Making Meaning Vocabulary* Teacher**

Next week you will revisit *Me First* to teach Vocabulary Week 24.

Week 3

Overview

UNIT 9: DETERMINING IMPORTANT IDEAS

Expository Nonfiction and Fiction

Big Al
by Andrew Clements, illustrated by Yoshi
(Aladdin, 1997)

A big, ugly fish has trouble making friends because of his appearance, until the day his scary appearance saves them all from a fish net.

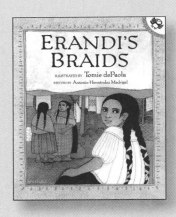

*Erandi's Braids**
by Antonio Hernández Madrigal, illustrated by Tomie dePaola
(Puffin, 2001)

Erandi hopes for a new dress for her birthday. But when her mother finds holes in the family's fishing net, Erandi wonders how they will get the money for the things they need.

*This book was also used in Unit 4, Week 2.

ALTERNATIVE BOOKS

Liang and the Magic Paintbrush by Demi
Leo the Late Bloomer by Robert Kraus

Comprehension Focus

• Students *explore important ideas* in a story.

• Students *use inference* informally to think about what is important in a story.

• Students read independently.

Social Development Focus

• Students relate the value of fairness to their partner work.

• Students develop the group skill of giving reasons to support their thinking.

DO AHEAD

• Make copies of the Unit 9 Parent Letter (BLM9) to send home with the students on the last day of the unit.

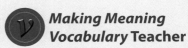

Making Meaning Vocabulary Teacher

If you are teaching Developmental Studies Center's *Making Meaning Vocabulary* program, teach Vocabulary Week 24 this week. For more information, see the *Making Meaning Vocabulary Teacher's Manual.*

Materials

- *Big Al*
- "Reading Comprehension Strategies" chart and a marker

Reading Comprehension
Strategies

- making connections

Read-aloud

In this lesson, the students:

- Hear and discuss a story
- Read independently for up to 20 minutes
- Give reasons to support their thinking
- Share their partner time in a fair way

1 ▶ Add to the "Reading Comprehension Strategies" Chart

Have partners sit together. Review that in the previous lesson they listened to a story and discussed the important ideas or lessons in it. In *Me First,* Pinkerton learned the important lesson that being first isn't always the best thing.

Refer to the "Reading Comprehension Strategies" chart. Write *determining important ideas* on the chart. Remind the students that stories contain important things authors want readers to learn and remember. Sometimes the author doesn't tell the reader directly what the important idea or message is, and the reader has to use clues in the story to figure it out.

Explain that you will read another story today, and the students will continue to think about important ideas. Remind them to think about using their partner time fairly. Let them know that you will check in with them at the end of the lesson to see how they did.

2 ▶ Introduce *Big Al*

Show the cover of *Big Al* and read the title and names of the author and illustrator aloud. Explain that this is a story about a fish named Al. Ask the students to think about what happens to Al in the story.

Read *Big Al* Aloud

Read *Big Al* aloud, showing the illustrations and stopping as described below.

 Note

English Language Learners may benefit from previewing the text and the illustrations prior to the lesson.

Suggested Vocabulary

seaweed: kind of plant that grows in the sea (p. 9)

disguise: clothing or covering that hides who you are (p. 9)

darted: moved suddenly and quickly (p. 15)

plowed: kept going (p. 15)

bulged: swelled (p. 18)

ELL Vocabulary

English Language Learners may benefit from discussing additional vocabulary, including:

steered clear: stayed away (p. 11)

in an instant: immediately (p. 16)

tangled: twisted together in a confused mass (p. 20)

captured: caught or trapped (p. 21)

fierce-looking: looking violent and dangerous (p. 25)

Read pages 2–15 aloud, and stop after:

> **p. 15** "Before he could even say 'Excuse me,' they were gone, and he was all alone again, sadder than ever."

 Ask, and have the students use "Turn to Your Partner" to discuss:

Q *What do you know about Big Al so far?*

Q *What do you think will happen next?*

Have two or three students share their thinking with the class.

Reread the last sentence on page 15. Then continue reading to the end of the story.

4 ▶ Discuss the Story as a Class

Facilitate a whole-class discussion about the story. Be ready to reread passages aloud and show illustrations again to help the students recall what they heard. Remind them to give reasons for their thinking. Discuss questions such as:

Q *What is the problem in this story?*

Q *Why do you think Big Al has trouble making friends?*

Q *What are some things Big Al does to try to be friends with the little fish?*

Q *How is Big Al's problem solved at the end of the story?*

5 ▶ Reflect on the Partner Work

Facilitate a brief discussion about how the students did sharing their partner time in a fair way. Share any observations you may have made.

Explain that in the next lesson the students will have a chance to think about the important ideas in *Big Al*.

INDIVIDUALIZED DAILY READING

6 ▶ Think About and Discuss Important Ideas

Remind the students that they have been thinking about important ideas or messages in stories. Explain that today you want them to think about some important messages or ideas in the stories they are reading.

Have the students read independently for up to 20 minutes.

As the students read, circulate among them. Ask individual students questions such as:

Q *What is your book about?*

Q *What do you think the author wants us to think about or learn from this story?*

At the end of independent reading, have a few volunteers share what their books are about.

Day 2

Materials

- *Big Al*

Teacher Note

During today's lesson, observe the students as they interact with one another and take note of responsible behaviors you see. You will share your observations with the students later in the lesson.

Strategy Lesson

In this lesson, the students:

- *Use inference* informally to explore important ideas
- Read independently for up to 20 minutes
- Give reasons to support their thinking
- Share their partner time in a fair way

▶ 1 Review *Big Al*

Have partners sit together. Review that authors sometimes use characters' actions to give readers some important ideas to think about. Yesterday, they listened to *Big Al* and thought about what happens in the story. Today, they will hear *Big Al* again and discuss the important ideas in the story. Ask:

Q *What do you know about Big Al?*

Q *What do you know about the small fish?*

Have a few students share their thinking with the class.

▶ 2 Reread and Discuss *Big Al*

Show the cover of *Big Al* and explain that you will reread the story, stopping several times so that they can talk more about it. Remind the students to think about using their partner time fairly.

Reread the story aloud, without showing the illustrations, and stopping as indicated. You might want to show the illustration on the page where you stop before starting the discussion.

Stop after:

p. 12 "When the clouds of sand cleared away, all the other fish were gone."

Ask:

Q *What has happened in the story so far?*

Have a few students share their thinking with the class. Reread the last sentence on page 12 and continue. Stop after:

> **p. 15** "Before he could even say 'Excuse me,' they were gone, and he was all alone again, sadder than ever."

Ask:

Q *What are some words besides "sad" you could use to describe how Big Al feels in this part of the story?*

Have the students use "Turn to Your Partner" to discuss the question. Then have two or three students share their thinking with the class. Reread the last sentence and continue. Stop after:

> **p. 21** "How great to be free, but what a shame that the big fellow had been captured."

Ask:

Q *How do the little fish feel in the part of the story I just read?*

Have the students use "Turn to Your Partner" to discuss the question. Then have two or three students share their thinking with the class. Reread the last sentence on page 21 and continue. Stop after:

> **p. 23** "Those fishermen took one look at him, and threw him right back into the ocean."

Ask:

Q *Why did the fishermen throw Big Al back in the water?*

Have the students use "Turn to Your Partner" to discuss the question. Then have two or three students share their thinking with the class. Reread the last sentence on page 23 and continue reading to the end of the story.

Discuss the Important Ideas

Facilitate a whole-class discussion about the important ideas in the story. Remind the students to give reasons for their thinking. Discuss questions such as:

Q *What important lesson can we learn from Big Al and the small fish?*

Q *What do you think the author of this story is telling people about friendship?*

> **Students might say:**
>
> "I think the author is saying don't be afraid to be someone's friend just because they look scary. They might be nice like Big Al."
>
> "I agree with [Nelda] and I think an important idea in this story is to help other people. The reason I think this is that Big Al tore the net to get the fish free."
>
> "Don't judge someone by the outside, but by the inside. I think that because the little fish hurt Big Al's feelings."

 Reflect on Using Partner Time Fairly

Briefly discuss how partners did using the partner time fairly. Share your own observations and encourage the students to continue to think about working with each other in a fair way.

INDIVIDUALIZED DAILY READING

 Read Independently/Document IDR Conferences

Ask the students to think about what their reading is about and an important idea in it. Have them read independently for up to 20 minutes.

Use the "IDR Conference Notes" record sheet to conduct and document individual conferences. Encourage the students to think about the important ideas in their reading.

 At the end of independent reading, have each student read a part of his book that he thinks is important to his partner.

Determining Important Ideas
Expository Nonfiction and Fiction

Day 3

Guided Strategy Practice

In this lesson, the students:

- *Use inference* informally to explore important ideas
- Read independently for up to 20 minutes
- Give reasons to support their thinking

▶1 Get Ready to Work Together

Have partners sit together. Remind the students that in the last few weeks they have been focusing on sharing their partner time in a fair way. Ask:

Q *Why is it important for both partners to have time to share their thinking?*

Q *What are some things you have done to make sure both partners have time to talk?*

▶2 Revisit *Erandi's Braids* and Introduce the Excerpt

Explain that today the students will revisit a story that they heard at the beginning of the year. Show the cover of *Erandi's Braids* and read the title and author's and illustrator's names aloud. Ask:

Q *What do you remember about this story?*

Explain that you will read part of the story today, and they will talk about the important ideas in it.

Have the students open their *Student Response Book* to pages 16–17, and point out that this is an excerpt from *Erandi's Braids*. This is the part of the story when the girl has just had her braids cut off at the barber shop.

Materials

- *Erandi's Braids* from Unit 4, Week 2
- *Student Response Book* pages 16–18
- *Assessment Resource Book*
- "Reading Comprehension Strategies" chart
- *Student Response Book,* IDR Journal section
- Unit 9 Parent Letter (BLM9)

◀ **Teacher Note**

In this lesson, the students work with an excerpt from a familiar text to explore important ideas. If necessary, show the illustrations and summarize to help the students recall the story.

Read the Excerpt Aloud

Ask the students to follow along in their *Student Response Books* as you read pages 26–29 of *Erandi's Braids* aloud. Explain that after they hear the excerpt, the students will talk about the important ideas in it and write their thinking on *Student Response Book* page 18.

Read pages 26–29 aloud, slowly and clearly. Stop after:

> **p. 29** "She gave Erandi a big smile, and Erandi had never felt happier."

 Have the students use "Turn to Your Partner" to discuss:

> **Q** *What important message is the author telling us in this part of the story? Why do you think so?*

Give pairs 5–7 minutes to talk and write about the important ideas in the excerpt.

> **CLASS COMPREHENSION ASSESSMENT**
>
> Circulate among partners. Ask yourself:
>
> **Q** *Are the students able to determine the important ideas in the excerpt?*
>
> Record your observations on page 27 of the *Assessment Resource Book*.

FACILITATION TIP

Reflect on your experience over the past weeks with **responding neutrally** with interest during class discussions. Does this practice feel natural to you? Are you integrating it into class discussions throughout the school day? What effect is it having on the students? We encourage you to continue to try this practice and reflect on students' responses as you facilitate class discussions in the future.

 Discuss the Important Ideas as a Class

Facilitate a whole-class discussion using the following questions. Remind the students to give reasons to support their thinking.

> **Q** *What are some important ideas you and your partner talked about?*

> **Q** *What are some other important ideas in this story? What makes you think that?*

Refer to the "Reading Comprehension Strategies" chart and review that in this unit the students listened to stories and talked about important ideas or messages. Often one important idea in a story is a lesson about giving up something that is important to you to help someone else. Encourage the students to continue to think about important ideas in whatever they read.

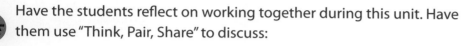

Reading Comprehension Strategies

- making connections

Teacher Note

This is the last week of Unit 9. If you feel your students need more experience exploring important ideas before moving on, you may want to repeat this week's lessons with one of the alternative books listed on the Overview page. You will reassign partners for Unit 10.

5 Reflect on Working Together

Have the students reflect on working together during this unit. Have them use "Think, Pair, Share" to discuss:

Q *How did your partner work go during this unit? What have you learned that will help you work with your next partner?*

Have a few partners share their ideas. Have each student take a minute to thank his partner.

INDIVIDUALIZED DAILY READING

6 Have the Students Write About Important Ideas in Their IDR Journals

Explain that today you want the students to think about an important message or idea in the stories they are reading. At the end of independent reading, each student will write about an important message in the book she is reading.

Have the students read independently for up to 20 minutes.

As the students read, circulate among them. Ask individual students questions such as:

Q *What is your book about?*

Q *What do you think the author wants us to think about or learn from this story?*

At the end of independent reading, have each student write in her IDR Journal about an important idea in her book.

INDIVIDUAL COMPREHENSION ASSESSMENT

Before continuing with Unit 10, take this opportunity to assess individual students' progress in identifying important ideas and messages. Please refer to pages 44–45 in the *Assessment Resource Book* for instructions.

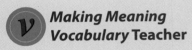

Parent Letter

Send home with each student the Parent Letter for this unit (see "Do Ahead," page 347). Periodically, have a few students share with the class what they are reading at home.

Making Meaning Vocabulary Teacher

Next week you will revisit *Big Al* to teach Vocabulary Week 25.

Unit 10

Revisiting the Reading Life

During this unit, the students reflect on the books they like and want to read. They answer questions to understand stories, and they think about the comprehension strategies they use to understand books. During IDR, the students continue to practice self-monitoring, think about their summer reading, and use the comprehension strategies as they read independently. Socially, they develop the group skills of giving reasons to support their thinking and sharing their partner time in a fair way. They participate in a class meeting to discuss what they liked about their reading community.

Week 1 *little blue and little yellow* by Leo Lionni

Week 1

Overview

UNIT 10: REVISITING THE READING LIFE

little blue and little yellow
by Leo Lionni
(HarperTrophy, 1959)

This is the story of a blue dot and a yellow dot that are best friends and what happens to them when they hug each other.

ALTERNATIVE BOOKS

Dear Juno by Soyung Pak

Cornelius by Leo Lionni

Comprehension Focus

• Students answer questions to understand stories.

• Students reflect on books and stories they like and want to read.

• Students think about the comprehension strategies they use to understand books.

• Students read independently.

Social Development Focus

• Students analyze the effect of their behavior on others and on the group work.

• Students develop the group skills of giving reasons to support their thinking and sharing their partner time in a fair way.

• Students participate in a class meeting to discuss what they liked about their reading community.

DO AHEAD

• Prior to Day 1, decide how you will randomly assign partners to work together during the unit.

• Collect one read-aloud book from each unit in the *Making Meaning* program. Choose fiction and nonfiction that the students enjoyed (see Day 2, Step 1, on page 366).

• Prepare a chart with the title "Kinds of Books We Like" (see Day 2, Step 2, on pages 366–367).

• Make copies of the Unit 10 Parent Letter (BLM10) to send home with the students on the last day of the unit.

Making Meaning Vocabulary Teacher

If you are teaching Developmental Studies Center's *Making Meaning Vocabulary* program, teach Vocabulary Week 25 this week. For more information, see the *Making Meaning Vocabulary Teacher's Manual*.

Read-aloud

In this lesson, the students:

- Begin working with new partners
- Hear and discuss a story
- Think about the reading comprehension strategies they use
- Give reasons to support their thinking
- Read independently for up to 20 minutes

About Revisiting the Reading Life

The purpose of this unit is to help the students reflect on the reading work they have done in the *Making Meaning* program and the strategies they have learned to help them understand what they read. This week they will think about the books they like and reflect on their reading community.

Have all the *Making Meaning* program books and other books you read aloud available for Individualized Daily Reading and the lesson extensions. Select nine or more of these books to use on Day 2.

▶1 Pair Students and Get Ready to Work Together

Randomly assign partners and have them sit together. Tell the students that this week they will think about books they like and their reading community. Today, they will talk about the strategies they learned to help them understand what they read. They will also hear a new story.

▶2 Review the "Reading Comprehension Strategies" Chart

Remind the students that they practiced several strategies this year that helped them understand their reading. Refer to the "Reading Comprehension Strategies" chart and briefly review each strategy.

Materials

- *little blue and little yellow*
- "Reading Comprehension Strategies" chart
- "Thinking About My Reading" chart

***Being a* Writer™ Teacher**

You can either have the students work with their *Being a Writer* partner or assign them a different partner for the *Making Meaning* lessons.

Reading Comprehension Strategies

- making connections

Tell the students that you would like them to think about the comprehension strategies they are using as they listen to today's read-aloud.

 Introduce *little blue and little yellow*

Show the cover of *little blue and little yellow* and read the title and name of the author aloud. Explain that this is a story about a friendship between two dots, a blue one and a yellow one.

Remind the students that as they listen to the story you want them to think about the strategies they are using to help them understand it.

 Read *little blue and little yellow* Aloud

Read *little blue and little yellow* aloud, showing the illustrations and stopping as described below.

Suggested Vocabulary

tunnel: passage built under the ground (p. 23)

ELL Vocabulary

English Language Learners may benefit from discussing additional vocabulary, including:

Hide-and-Seek: game in which players hide while one person ("it") looks for them (p. 8)

Ring-a-Ring-O' Roses: game in which players sing and walk in a circle (p. 9)

chased: ran after (p. 24)

pulled themselves together: stopped crying (p. 32)

Read pages 3–21 aloud, and stop after:

    p. 21   "…until they were green."

 Ask and have the students use "Turn to Your Partner" to discuss:

Q *What has happened in the story so far?*

◀ Teacher Note

As you mention each strategy, you might show the class a book and connect the book to the strategy. (For example, you might say, "When you listened to 'Dry Skin' from *Poppleton* you visualized to get a picture in your mind of what was happening in the story.")

Have a few volunteers briefly share their thinking.

Reread the lines on pages 19–21; then continue reading to the end of the story.

5 ▸ Discuss the Story

 First in pairs, and then as a class, discuss the following questions. Remind the students to give reasons for their thinking.

Q   *What happens to little blue and little yellow?*

Q   *What can we learn about friendship from this story?*

> **Students might say:**
>
> "You can have a friend who is different than you."
>
> "It doesn't matter if you're different from your friend."
>
> "Friends stick together."

Q   *Which comprehension strategy did you use as you listened to the story? When did you use [wondering]?*

6 ▸ Reflect on Working Together

Facilitate a brief discussion about how the students interacted during the read-aloud and discussion.

 Ask partners to tell each other one thing they liked about how they worked together.

After sufficient time, signal for the students attention and have a few students share their partners' ideas.

INDIVIDUALIZED DAILY READING

 ## Practice Self-monitoring

Direct the students' attention to the "Thinking About My Reading" chart and remind them that stopping and thinking about the questions on the chart helps them keep track of how well they are understanding their reading. Read the questions and tell them that they will practice this procedure again today.

Have the students read independently and stop them at 5-minute intervals. At each stop, read the questions on the chart and have them think about each question.

As the students read, circulate among them and ask individual students to tell you what their books are about. Encourage them to think about the charted questions.

At the end of independent reading, have the students share their reading with the class.

EXTENSIONS

Revisit Read-alouds

Give pairs time to read, retell, and talk about books you have read aloud this year. Make time each day for pairs to share a book briefly, together or with another pair.

Share Personal Favorites

Have the students share a favorite book from home or school in pairs or with the class. Have each student talk about why she likes the book, tell about her favorite part, or show an illustration.

Thinking About My Reading

- What is happening in my story right now?

Day 2

Reflect on Reading Lives

In this lesson, the students:

- Discuss the kinds of stories they like to read
- Read independently for up to 20 minutes
- Share partner time in a fair way

1 Review Familiar Books

Have partners sit together. Tell them that today they will think about the kinds of stories they like and want to read this summer.

Direct their attention to the read-aloud books you selected from the year. Explain that these are some of the books they heard or read this year. Remind them that some of these books are fiction (about imaginary people and events) and some are nonfiction (about real people, events, or things). If necessary, give a brief summary of each of the books you selected.

2 Discuss Favorite Kinds of Books

 Have the students use "Think, Pair, Share" to talk about the selected books and the kinds of books they like. Remind them to focus on sharing their partner time in a fair way. Ask:

Q *Which of these books did you enjoy the most? Why did you like that book?*

Q *What kinds of books do you like to read? Why do you like to read these books?*

Materials

- Read-aloud books from this year, selected ahead
- "Kinds of Books We Like" chart, prepared ahead, and a marker
- *Student Response Book* page 19

Teacher Note

If the students have difficulty categorizing the kinds of books they like, point out some they heard or read this year, for example, animal stories *(McDuff Moves In, The Tale of Peter Rabbit)*, true stories *(Beatrix Potter)*, books about science *(Plants that Eat Animals)*, funny stories *(Alexander and the Terrible, Horrible, No Good, Very Bad Day)*, and stories that teach a lesson *(Me First)*.

366 | Making Meaning®

Students might say:

"I like true stories because you learn about real people like astronauts."

"I like funny stories like 'Captain Underpants' because they make me laugh."

"I like the Magic School Bus stories because I like reading about science."

As the students share their ideas, record them on the "Kinds of Books We Like" chart.

 ## Write About Summer Reading

Ask the students to open to *Student Response Book* page 19, "Thoughts About My Reading Life." Read the title and explain that the students will write about the kinds of books and stories they want to read this summer and where they think they will do their summer reading. Later they will share their thoughts with their classmates.

Read the first question on *Student Response Book* page 19 and have each student individually write his answer to the question. Follow the same procedure for the second question.

As the students work, circulate among them. Probe the students' thinking with questions such as:

Q *What kinds of stories do you like to read or listen to? Why do you like that kind of story?*

Q *Do you like books about real things? What kinds of things do you want to learn about?*

Q *I plan to [sit outside in my backyard] to do my summer reading. Where can you picture yourself reading this summer?*

 ## Share Thoughts About Summer Reading

 Explain that partners will talk about what they wrote on *Student Response Book* page 19. Give pairs time to talk; then facilitate a brief whole-class discussion by asking questions such as those on the next page.

Q *What kinds of books and stories do you want to read this summer? Why?*

Q *Where do you think you might want to read a book this summer?*

Q *Who wants to read [the same/different] kinds of books as [Aiden] wants to read?*

5 ▶ **Discuss Partner Work**

Briefly discuss how partners did sharing the partner time in a fair way. Explain that in the next lesson the students will talk about what they liked about their reading community this year.

INDIVIDUALIZED DAILY READING

6 ▶ **Revisit the Students' Reading Lives**

Have the students read independently for up to 20 minutes.

As the students read, circulate among them and talk to individuals about their reading lives. To guide your discussion, use what they have written on *Student Response Book* page 19 or questions such as:

Q *What is one of your favorite books to read? Why do you like that book?*

Q *What kinds of books do you like to read? Do you prefer fiction or nonfiction books? Why?*

Q *What do you want to read this summer? What would you like to read next year?*

Q *What do you like about reading?*

At the end of independent reading, give the students a few minutes to share what they read either with a partner or as a class.

EXTENSIONS

Revisit Read-alouds

Give pairs time to read, retell, and talk about books you have read aloud this year. Make time each day for pairs to briefly share a book together or with another pair.

Visit the Community Library

If possible, arrange a visit to the community library. Check with the librarian about the procedure for obtaining a library card. Familiarize the students with the library and encourage them to go to the library to borrow books to read during their summer break.

Day 3

Reflection and Class Meeting

Materials

- *Student Response Book* pages 19–20
- "Class Meeting Ground Rules" chart
- *Assessment Resource Book*
- *Student Response Book,* IDR Journal section
- Unit 10 Parent Letter (BLM10)

In this lesson, the students:

- Reflect on and write about how they worked together in a community
- Share ideas
- Have a class meeting to discuss their reading community
- Read independently for up to 20 minutes

1 ▶ Get Ready to Think About the Reading Community

Have partners sit together. Remind them that yesterday they talked about books they liked and thought about their summer reading. Today they will think about how they worked together this year as a reading community. Explain that they will talk and write about what they liked about their reading community. Later, they will share their ideas in a class meeting.

FACILITATION TIP

Reflect on your experience over the past year using the facilitation tips included in the *Making Meaning* program. Did using the facilitation techniques feel natural to you? Have you integrated them into your class discussions throughout the school day? What effect did using the facilitation techniques have on your students? We encourage you to continue to use the facilitation techniques and reflect on students' responses as you facilitate class discussions in the future.

2 ▶ Discuss How the Students Worked Together in Their Reading Community

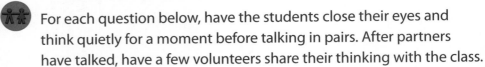

For each question below, have the students close their eyes and think quietly for a moment before talking in pairs. After partners have talked, have a few volunteers share their thinking with the class.

Q *How do you think we did this year in our classroom community? What makes you think that?*

Q *How has being a part of this community made you feel?*

Q *What did you like about working with a partner?*

Draw and Write About the Reading Community

Ask the students to turn to *Student Response Book* page 20, "What I Liked About Our Reading Community." Explain that they will draw a picture and write about what they liked about their community. They will share their pictures and writing later at a class meeting.

Have the students complete the *Student Response Book* page.

 ### Gather for a Class Meeting

When most students have finished drawing and writing, have them bring their *Student Response Books* and come to the circle, with partners sitting together. Make sure the students can see one another.

Briefly review the "Class Meeting Ground Rules" chart.

 ### Conduct the Class Meeting

Explain that the purpose of the class meeting is to share what the students drew and wrote about what they liked about their reading community. Have partners share their *Student Response Book* pages with each other. Remind them to share the partner time in a fair way.

After partners have talked, have a few volunteers share their drawing and writing with the class. Facilitate a discussion by asking:

Q *Did you or your partner write something similar to what [Joslyn] wrote? Share it with us.*

Q *Who drew and wrote an idea that is different from [Joslyn's]? Share it with us.*

Q *What question do you want to ask [Joslyn] about what [she] shared?*

 ### Reflect on the Class Meeting

Briefly discuss how the students did following the rules during the class meeting; then have the students return to their desks or tables.

Teacher Note

As the students work, circulate among them. If the students have difficulty thinking of ideas, probe their thinking with questions such as:

Q *What did you like about working with a partner?*

Q *What was helpful when you were listening to books?*

Q *In what ways were other students kind and caring during independent reading time?*

Teacher Note

You may want to hold the class meeting later in the day or on the following day.

Class Meeting Ground Rules

- one person talks at a time
- listen to one another

INDIVIDUALIZED DAILY READING

7 ## Revisit the Students' Reading Lives/Have the Students Write in Their IDR Journals

Have the students read independently for up to 20 minutes.

As the students read, circulate among them and talk to individual students about their reading lives. To guide your discussion, use what they have written on *Student Response Book* page 19 or questions such as:

Q *What is one of your favorite books to read? Why do you like that book?*

Q *What kinds of books do you like to read? Do you prefer fiction or nonfiction books?*

Q *What do you want to read this summer? What would you like to read next year?*

Q *What do you like about reading?*

At the end of independent reading, have the students write in their IDR Journals about what they like about the books they read.

SOCIAL SKILLS ASSESSMENT

Take this opportunity to reflect on your students' social development over the year. Review the "Social Skills Assessment" record sheet on pages 2–3 of the *Assessment Resource Book* and note student growth. Use this information to help you plan for next year. Ask yourself questions such as:

Q *What was challenging for my students this year in terms of their social development?*

Q *How might I help next year's students grow socially?*

Q *What skills should I emphasize with the students next year to help them build a safe and caring reading community?*

EXTENSION

End-of-year "Book-sharing Party"

Have students share a favorite book from home or school in pairs or with the class. Have each student talk about why he likes the book, talk about her favorite part, or show an illustration. Have the students display their books and give the students an opportunity to walk around and look at the books. At the end of the sharing time, briefly discuss which books the students might like to read over the summer. If possible, provide refreshments for the students to enjoy.

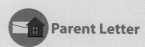

Parent Letter

Send home with each student the Parent Letter for this unit (see "Do Ahead," page 361).

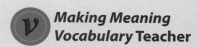

Making Meaning Vocabulary Teacher

Next week you will revisit *little blue and little yellow* to teach Vocabulary Week 26. *Vocabulary Teacher's Manual*.

Appendices

Grade 2

	Lesson	Title	Author	Form	Genre/Type
Unit 1	▶ Week 1	*McDuff Moves In*	Rosemary Wells	picture book	fiction
		Poppleton: "The Library"	Cynthia Rylant	picture book	fiction
	▶ Week 2	*Sheila Rae, the Brave*	Kevin Henkes	picture book	fiction
	▶ Week 3	*Eat My Dust! Henry Ford's First Race*	Monica Kulling	picture book	narrative nonfiction
Unit 2	▶ Week 1	*Jamaica Tag-Along*	Juanita Havill	picture book	realistic fiction
	▶ Week 2	*Alexander and the Terrible, Horrible, No Good, Very Bad Day*	Judith Viorst	picture book	realistic fiction
Unit 3	▶ Week 1	*A Tree Is Nice*	Janice May Udry	picture book	narrative nonfiction
		Fathers, Mothers, Sisters, Brothers: A Collection of Family Poems: "My Baby Brother"	Mary Ann Hoberman	poetry collection	poetry
	▶ Week 2	*Poppleton and Friends*: "Dry Skin"	Cynthia Rylant	picture book	fiction
	▶ Week 3	*The Paperboy*	Dav Pilkey	picture book	realistic fiction
Unit 4	▶ Week 1	*What Mary Jo Shared*	Janice May Udry	picture book	realistic fiction
	▶ Week 2	*Erandi's Braids*	Antonio Hernández Madrigal	picture book	realistic fiction
	▶ Week 3	*Chester's Way*	Kevin Henkes	picture book	fiction
Unit 5	▶ Week 1	*The Incredible Painting of Felix Clousseau*	Jon Agee	picture book	fiction
		The Ghost-Eye Tree	Bill Martin Jr. and John Archambault	picture book	realistic fiction
	▶ Week 2	*Galimoto*	Karen Lynn Williams	picture book	realistic fiction
	▶ Week 3	*The Paper Crane*	Molly Bang	picture book	fiction
Unit 6	▶ Week 1	*The Tale of Peter Rabbit*	Beatrix Potter	picture book	fiction
		Beatrix Potter	Alexandra Wallner	picture book	narrative nonfiction
	▶ Week 2	*The Art Lesson*	Tomie dePaola	picture book	narrative nonfiction
		"'Draw, Draw, Draw:' A Short Biography of Tomie dePaola"		essay	narrative nonfiction
Unit 7	▶ Week 1	*It Could Still Be a Worm*	Allan Fowler	picture book	expository nonfiction
		Plants that Eat Animals	Allan Fowler	picture book	expository nonfiction
	▶ Week 2	*Fishes (A True Book)*	Melissa Stewart	picture book	expository nonfiction
	▶ Week 3	*POP! A Book About Bubbles*	Kimberly Brubaker Bradley	picture book	expository nonfiction
Unit 8	▶ Week 1	*Snails*	Monica Hughes	picture book	expository nonfiction
	▶ Week 2	*Bend and Stretch*	Pamela Hill Nettleton	picture book	expository nonfiction
	▶ Week 3	"Ice Cream Mania!"		article	expository nonfiction
		"Giant Panda, Red Panda"		article	expository nonfiction
		"Classic Smoothie"		functional text	expository nonfiction
		"The City Zoo"		functional text	expository nonfiction
Unit 9	▶ Week 1	"Wild Rides"	Lev Grossman	article	expository nonfiction
		"Summer of the Shark"		article	expository nonfiction
		"A Nose for the Arts"		article	expository nonfiction
	▶ Week 2	*Me First*	Helen Lester	picture book	fiction
	▶ Week 3	*Big Al*	Andrew Clements	picture book	fiction
		Erandi's Braids	Antonio Hernández Madrigal	picture book	fiction
Unit 10	▶ Week 1	*little blue and little yellow*	Leo Lionni	picture book	fiction

Grade K

Brave Bear	Kathy Mallat
Building Beavers	Kathleen Martin-James
Cat's Colors	Jane Cabrera
"Charlie Needs a Cloak"	Tomie dePaola
Cookie's Week	Cindy Ward
A Day with a Doctor	Jan Kottke
A Day with a Mail Carrier	Jan Kottke
Flower Garden	Eve Bunting
Friends at School	Rochelle Bunnett
Getting Around By Plane	Cassie Mayer
Henry's Wrong Turn	Harriet M. Ziefert
I Want to Be a Vet	Dan Liebman
I Was So Mad	Mercer Mayer
If You Give a Mouse a Cookie	Laura Joffe Numeroff
Knowing about Noses	Allan Fowler
A Letter to Amy	Ezra Jack Keats
Maisy's Pool	Lucy Cousins
Moon	Melanie Mitchell
My Friends	Taro Gomi
Noisy Nora	Rosemary Wells
On the Go	Ann Morris
A Porcupine Named Fluffy	Helen Lester
Pumpkin Pumpkin	Jeanne Titherington
A Tiger Cub Grows Up	Joan Hewett
Tools	Ann Morris
When Sophie Gets Angry— Really, Really Angry…	Molly Bang
Whistle for Willie	Ezra Jack Keats

Grade 1

Caps for Sale	Esphyr Slobodkina
Chrysanthemum	Kevin Henkes
Curious George Goes to an Ice Cream Shop	Margret Rey and Alan J. Shalleck (editors)
A Day in the Life of a Garbage Collector	Nate LeBoutillier
Did You See What I Saw? Poems about School	Kay Winters
Dinosaur Babies	Lucille Recht Penner
Down the Road	Alice Schertle
An Elephant Grows Up	Anastasia Suen
An Extraordinary Egg	Leo Lionni
George Washington and the General's Dog	Frank Murphy
A Good Night's Sleep	Allan Fowler
A Harbor Seal Pup Grows Up	Joan Hewett
Hearing	Sharon Gordon
In the Tall, Tall Grass	Denise Fleming
It's Mine!	Leo Lionni
Julius	Angela Johnson
A Kangaroo Joey Grows Up	Joan Hewett
A Look at Teeth	Allan Fowler
Matthew and Tilly	Rebecca C. Jones
McDuff and the Baby	Rosemary Wells
Peter's Chair	Ezra Jack Keats
Quick as a Cricket	Audrey Wood
Raptors!	Lisa McCourt
Sheep Out to Eat	Nancy Shaw
The Snowy Day	Ezra Jack Keats
Throw Your Tooth on the Roof	Selby B. Beeler
When I Was Little	Jamie Lee Curtis
Where Do I Live?	Neil Chesanow

Grade 3

Alexander, Who's Not (Do you hear me? I mean it!) *Going to Move*	Judith Viorst
Aunt Flossie's Hats (and Crab Cakes Later)	Elizabeth Fitzgerald Howard
Boundless Grace	Mary Hoffman
Brave Harriet	Marissa Moss
Brave Irene	William Steig
Cherries and Cherry Pits	Vera B. Williams
City Green	DyAnne DiSalvo-Ryan
A Day's Work	Eve Bunting
Fables	Arnold Lobel
Flashy Fantastic Rain Forest Frogs	Dorothy Hinshaw Patent
The Girl Who Loved Wild Horses	Paul Goble
Have You Seen Bugs?	Joanne Oppenheim
Julius, the Baby of the World	Kevin Henkes
Keepers	Jeri Hanel Watts
Knots on a Counting Rope	Bill Martin Jr. and John Archambault
Lifetimes	David L. Rice
Mailing May	Michael O. Tunnell
The Man Who Walked Between the Towers	Mordicai Gerstein
Miss Nelson Is Missing!	Harry Allard and James Marshall
Morning Meals Around the World	Maryellen Gregoire
Officer Buckle and Gloria	Peggy Rathmann
The Paper Bag Princess	Robert Munsch
Reptiles	Melissa Stewart
The Spooky Tail of Prewitt Peacock	Bill Peet
What is a Bat?	Bobbie Kalman and Heather Levigne
Wilma Unlimited	Kathleen Krull

Grade 4

Amelia's Road	Linda Jacobs Altman
Animal Senses	Pamela Hickman
A Bad Case of Stripes	David Shannon
Basket Moon	Mary Lyn Ray
The Bat Boy & His Violin	Gavin Curtis
Chicken Sunday	Patricia Polacco
Coming to America	Betsy Maestro
Digging Up Tyrannosaurus Rex	John R. Horner and Don Lessem
Farm Workers Unite: The Great Grape Boycott	
Flight	Robert Burleigh
Hurricane	David Wiesner
In My Own Backyard	Judi Kurjian
Italian Americans	Carolyn P. Yoder
My Man Blue	Nikki Grimes
The Old Woman Who Named Things	Cynthia Rylant
Peppe the Lamplighter	Elisa Bartone
A Picture Book of Amelia Earhart	David A. Adler
A Picture Book of Harriet Tubman	David A. Adler
A Picture Book of Rosa Parks	David A. Adler
The Princess and the Pizza	Mary Jane and Herm Auch
Slinky Scaly Slithery Snakes	Dorothy Hinshaw Patent
Song and Dance Man	Karen Ackerman
Teammates	Peter Golenbock
Thunder Cake	Patricia Polacco

Grade 5

Big Cats	Seymour Simon
Chinese Americans	Tristan Boyer Binns
Earthquakes	Seymour Simon
Everybody Cooks Rice	Norah Dooley
Harry Houdini: Master of Magic	Robert Kraske
Heroes	Paul Dowswell
Hey World, Here I Am!	Jean Little
Letting Swift River Go	Jane Yolen
Life in the Rain Forests	Lucy Baker
The Lotus Seed	Sherry Garland
Richard Wright and the Library Card	William Miller
A River Ran Wild	Lynne Cherry
Something to Remember Me By	Susan V. Bosak
Star of Fear, Star of Hope	Jo Hoestlandt
The Summer My Father Was Ten	Pat Brisson
Survival and Loss: Native American Boarding Schools	
Uncle Jed's Barbershop	Margaree King Mitchell
The Van Gogh Cafe	Cynthia Rylant
Wildfires	Seymour Simon

Grade 6

America Street: A Multicultural Anthology of Stories	Anne Mazer, ed.
And Still the Turtle Watched	Sheila MacGill-Callahan
Asian Indian Americans	Carolyn P. Yoder
Baseball Saved Us	Ken Mochizuki
Chato's Kitchen	Gary Soto
Dear Benjamin Banneker	Andrea Davis Pinkney
Encounter	Jane Yolen
Every Living Thing	Cynthia Rylant
Life in the Oceans	Lucy Baker
New Kids in Town: Oral Histories of Immigrant Teens	Janet Bode
Out of This World: Science-Fiction Stories	Edward Blishen, ed.
Rosie the Riveter: Women in a Time of War	
The Strangest of Strange Unsolved Mysteries, Volume 2	Phyllis Raybin Emert
Train to Somewhere	Eve Bunting
Voices from the Fields	S. Beth Atkin
Volcano: The Eruption and Healing of Mount St. Helens	Patricia Lauber
Whales	Seymour Simon
Why Mosquitoes Buzz in People's Ears	Verna Aardema

Grade 7

Ancient Ones: The World of the Old-Growth Douglas Fir	Barbara Bash
Children of the Wild West	Russell Freedman
Death of the Iron Horse	Paul Goble
The Dream Keeper and Other Poems	Langston Hughes
Finding Our Way	René Saldaña, Jr.
the flag of childhood: poems from the middle east	Naomi Shahib Nye, ed.
The Friendship	Mildred D. Taylor
It's Our World, Too!	Phillip Hoose
The Land I Lost	Huynh Quang Nhuong
Life in the Woodlands	Roseanne Hooper
New and Selected Poems	Gary Soto
Only Passing Through: The Story of Sojourner Truth	Anne Rockwell
Roberto Clemente: Pride of the Pittsburgh Pirates	Jonah Winter
Shattered: Stories of Children and War	Jennifer Armstrong, ed.
Sports Stories	Alan Durant, ed.
Step Lightly: Poems for the Journey	Nancy Willard, ed.
The Village That Vanished	Ann Grifalconi
What If...? Amazing Stories	Monica Hughes, ed.
Wolves	Seymour Simon
The Wretched Stone	Chris Van Allsburg

Grade 8

the composition	Antonio Skármeta
The Giver	Lois Lowry
Immigrant Kids	Russell Freedman
In the Land of the Lawn Weenies	David Lubar
Life in the Polar Lands	Monica Byles
Nellie Bly: A Name to Be Reckoned With	Stephen Krensky
The People Could Fly	Virginia Hamilton
Satchel Paige	Lesa Cline-Ransome
Sharks	Seymour Simon
She Dared: True Stories of Heroines, Scoundrels, and Renegades	Ed Butts
When I Was Your Age: Original Stories About Growing Up, Volume One	Amy Ehrlich, ed.

Bibliography

Anderson, Richard C., Elfrieda H. Hiebert, Judith A. Scott, and Ian A. G. Wilkinson. *Becoming a Nation of Readers: The Report of the Commission on Reading*. Washington, DC: The National Institute of Education, 1985.

Anderson, Richard C., and P. David Pearson. "A Schema-Theoretic View of Basic Process in Reading Comprehension." In *Handbook of Reading Research*, P. David Pearson (ed.). New York: Longman, 1984.

Armbruster, Bonnie B., Fred Lehr, and Jean Osborn. *Put Reading First: The Research Building Blocks for Teaching Children to Read*. Jessup, MD: National Institute for Literacy, 2001.

Asher, James. "The Strategy of Total Physical Response: An Application to Learning Russian." *International Review of Applied Linguistics* 3 (1965): 291–300.

———. "Children's First Language as a Model for Second Language Learning." *Modern Language Journal* 56 (1972): 133–139.

Beck, Isabel L., and Margaret G. McKeown. "Text Talk: Capturing the Benefits of Read-Aloud Experiences for Young Children." *The Reading Teacher* 55:1 (2001): 10–19.

Beck, Isabel L., Margaret G. McKeown, and Linda Kucan. *Bringing Words to Life: Robust Vocabulary Instruction*. New York: Guilford Press (2002).

Block, C. C., and M. Pressley. *Comprehension Instruction: Research-Based Best Practices*. New York: Guilford Press, 2001.

Calkins, Lucy M. *The Art of Teaching Reading*. New York: Addison-Wesley Longman, 2001.

Contestable, Julie W., Shaila Regan, Susie Alldredge, Carol Westrich, and Laurel Robertson. *Number Power: A Cooperative Approach to Mathematics and Social Development Grades K–6*. Oakland, CA: Developmental Studies Center, 1999.

Cummins, James. "The Role of Primary Language Development in Promoting Educational Success for Language Minority Students." In *Schooling and Language Minority Students: A Theoretical Framework*. Los Angeles, CA: California State University, Evaluation, Dissemination, and Assessment Center, 1981.

Cunningham, Anne E., and Keith E. Stanovich. "What Reading Does for the Mind." *American Educator* Spring/Summer (1998): 8–15.

Developmental Studies Center. *Blueprints for a Collaborative Classroom*. Oakland, CA: Developmental Studies Center, 1997.

———. *Ways We Want Our Class to Be*. Oakland, CA: Developmental Studies Center, 1996.

DeVries, Rheta, and Betty Zan. *Moral Classrooms, Moral Children*. New York: Teachers' College Press, 1994.

Dewey, J. *Democracy and Education*. New York: Macmillan, 1916.

Farstrup, Alan E., and S. Jay Samuels. *What Research Has to Say About Reading Instruction*. 3rd Ed. Newark, DE: International Reading Association, 2002.

Fielding, Linda G., and P. David Pearson. "Reading Comprehension: What Works." *Educational Leadership* 51:5 (1994): 1–11.

Fountas, Irene C. and Gay Su Pinnell. *Leveled Books, K–8: Matching Texts to Readers for Effective Teaching*. Portsmouth, NH: Heinemann, 2006.

———. *Leveled Books for Readers Grade 3–6*. Portsmouth, NH: Heinemann, 2002.

———. *Matching Books to Readers: Using Leveled Books in Guided Reading, K–3*. Portsmouth, NH: Heinemann, 1999.

Gambrell, Linda B., Lesley Mandel Morrow, Susan B. Neuman, and Michael Pressley, eds. *Best Practices in Literacy Instruction*. New York: Guilford Press, 1999.

Hakuta, Kenji, Yoko Goto Butler, and Daria Witt. *How Long Does It Take English Learners to Attain Proficiency?* Santa Barbara, CA: University of California, Linguistic Minority Research Institute, 2000.

Harvey, Stephanie. *Nonfiction Matters: Reading, Writing, and Research in Grades 3–8*. York, ME: Stenhouse Publishers, 1998.

Harvey, Stephanie, and Anne Goudvis. *Strategies That Work: Teaching Comprehension to Enhance Understanding*. York, ME: Stenhouse Publishers, 2000.

Harvey, Stephanie, Sheila McAuliffe, Laura Benson, Wendy Cameron, Sue Kempton, Pat Lusche, Debbie Miller, Joan Schroeder, and Julie Weaver. "Teacher-Researchers Study the Process of Synthesizing in Six Primary Classrooms." *Language Arts* 73 (1996): 564–574.

Herrell, Adrienne L. and Michael L. Jordan. *Fifty Strategies for Teaching English Language Learners*. Upper Saddle River, NJ: Merrill, 2000.

International Reading Association. "What Is Evidence-Based Reading Instruction? A Position Statement of the International Reading Association." Newark, DE: International Reading Association, 2002.

Johnson, David W., Roger T. Johnson, and Edythe Johnson Holubec. *The New Circles of Learning: Cooperation in the Classroom*. Alexandria, VA: Association for Supervision and Curriculum Development, 1994.

Kagan, Spencer. *Cooperative Learning*. San Juan Capistrano, CA: Resources of Teachers, 1992.

Kamil, Michael L., Peter B. Mosenthal, P. David Pearson, and Rebecca Barr, eds. *Handbook of Reading Research, Volume III*. Mahwah, NJ: Lawrence Erlbaum Associates, 2000.

Keene, Ellin O., and Susan Zimmermann. *Mosaic of Thought: Teaching Comprehension in a Reader's Workshop*. Portsmouth, NH: Heinemann, 1997.

Kohlberg, Lawrence. *The Psychology of Moral Development*. New York: Harper and Row, 1984.

Kohn, Alfie. *Beyond Discipline: From Compliance to Community*. Association for Supervision and Curriculum Development, 1996.

———. *Punished by Rewards: The Trouble with Gold Stars, Incentive Plans, A's, Praise, and Other Bribes*. New York: Houghton Mifflin Company, 1999.

Krashen, Stephen D. *Principles and Practice in Second Language Acquisition*. New York: Prentice-Hall, 1982.

Moss, Barbara. "Making a Case and a Place for Effective Content Area Literacy Instruction in the Elementary Grades." *The Reading Teacher* 59:1 (2005): 46–55.

NEA Task Force on Reading. *Report of the NEA Task Force on Reading 2000*.

Neufeld, Paul. "Comprehension Instruction in Content Area Classes." *The Reading Teacher* 59:4 (2005): 302–312.

Nucci, Larry P., ed. *Moral Development and Character Education: A Dialogue*. Berkeley, CA: McCutchan Publishing Corporation, 1989.

Optiz, Michael F., ed. *Literacy Instruction for Culturally and Linguistically Diverse Students*. Newark, DE: International Reading Association, 1998.

Pearson, P. David, J. A. Dole, G. G. Duffy, and L. R. Roehler. "Developing Expertise in Reading Comprehension: What Should Be Taught and How Should It Be Taught?" In *What Research Has to Say to the Teacher of Reading*, J. Farstup and S. J. Samuels (eds.). Newark, DE: International Reading Association, 1992.

Piaget, Jean. *The Child's Conception of the World*. Trans. Joan and Andrew Tomlinson. Lanham, MD: Littlefield Adams, 1969.

———. *The Moral Judgment of the Child*. Trans. Marjorie Gabain. New York: The Free Press, 1965.

Pressley, Michael. *Effective Beginning Reading Instruction: The Rest of the Story from Research*. National Education Association, 2002.

———. *Reading Instruction That Works*. New York: Guilford Press, 1998.

Pressley, Michael, Janice Almasi, Ted Schuder, Janet Bergman, Sheri Hite, Pamela B. El-Dinary, and Rachel Brown. "Transactional Instruction of Comprehension Strategies: The Montgomery County, Maryland, SAIL Program." *Reading and Writing Quarterly: Overcoming Learning Difficulties* 10 (1994): 5–19.

Routman, Regie. *Reading Essentials: The Specifics You Need to Teach Reading Well*. Portsmouth, NH: Heinemann, 2003.

Serafini, Frank. *The Reading Workshop: Creating Space for Readers*. Portsmouth, NH: Heinemann, 2001.

Soalt, Jennifer. "Bringing Together Fictional and Informational Texts to Improve Comprehension." *The Reading Teacher* 58:7 (2005): 680–683.

Taylor, Barbara M., Michael Pressley, and P. David Pearson. *Research-Supported Characteristics of Teachers and Schools That Promote Reading Achievement*. National Education Association, 2002.

Trelease, Jim. *The Read-Aloud Handbook*. New York: Penguin Books, 1995.

Weaver, Brenda M. *Leveling Books K–6: Matching Readers to Text*. Newark, DE: International Reading Association, 2000.

Williams, Joan A. "Classroom Conversations: Opportunities to Learn for ESL Students in Mainstream Classrooms." *The Reading Teacher* 54:8 (2001): 750–757.

Blackline
Masters

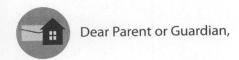

Dear Parent or Guardian,

This year I am excited to introduce the *Making Meaning*® program to your child. *Making Meaning* is a new reading program designed to help children build their reading comprehension and social skills. The children hear books read aloud and discuss the stories with partners and as a class. This year your child will learn several comprehension strategies such as making inferences about characters, determining important ideas, and wondering. The program is helping our class become a community of readers by making everyone feel welcome and safe. In addition, each child in our class reads books that are at his or her reading level for up to 30 minutes every day. This part of the *Making Meaning* program is called Individualized Daily Reading (IDR).

At the end of each unit in the *Making Meaning* program, you will receive a letter telling you about the most recent reading comprehension strategy and social skill your child has learned. Each letter will also include ways to support your child's home reading life.

Our class just finished the first unit of the program, which focuses on the children's reading lives. The children talked about what they like to read, heard stories read aloud, and discussed those stories. The children also learned to make connections between the stories and their own experiences. The program calls this reading comprehension strategy *making connections*. When children make connections between the stories they hear and their own lives, they are able to understand the stories better.

During the first unit, the children also practiced the social skill of listening carefully to others. Listening well to others is a skill that helps students learn and become active members of the reading community.

Here are some ways to build your child's reading life at home:

- Make weekly trips to the local library to borrow books.

- Set aside a time to read together every day.

- Stop every so often while reading aloud to discuss what you both are wondering about the story.

- Model good listening by paying attention to your child when the two of you discuss the story.

Reading and discussing books is one of the most important gifts you can give your child. I hope reading together every day can be an enjoyable time for you and your family.

Sincerely,

Apreciado padre de familia o guardián:

Este año estoy muy entusiasmado en presentarle a su niño el programa *"Making Meaning.®"* Este es un nuevo programa de lectura diseñado para ayudar a los niños a que adquieran destrezas en comprensión de lectura y se desarrollen socialmente. Los niños escuchan los libros leídos en voz alta y luego hablan con un compañero y con la clase en grupo acerca de la historia que escucharon. Este año su niño va a aprender varias estrategias de comprensión como el volver a contar la historia, visualizar y el hacer preguntas. El programa está ayudando a que nuestra clase se convierta en una comunidad de lectores al hacer que todos se sientan bienvenidos y seguros. Además durante 30 minutos al día, los niños en la clase leen libros adecuados para el nivel de cada uno de ellos. Esta parte del programa *"Making Meaning"* se llama lectura diaria individualizada.

Al final de cada unidad del programa *"Making Meaning"* usted va a recibir una carta dejándole saber la destreza social y la estrategia de comprensión de lectura que su niño acaba de aprender. Cada carta va a incluir maneras en las que usted puede apoyar la lectura de su niño en la casa.

Nuestra clase acaba de finalizar la primera unidad del programa, la cual se enfoca en la vida de los niños como lectores. Los niños hablaron acerca de lo que les gusta leer, escucharon historias que se les leyeron en voz alta y discutieron esas historias. Los niños también aprendieron a hacer conexiones entre las historias y sus vidas. El programa llama esta estrategia de comprensión *hacer conexiones*. Los niños pueden entender las historias mejor cuando hacen conexiones entre las historias que escuchan y sus propias vidas.

Durante la primera unidad los niños también practicaron la destreza social de escuchar con atención a otros. El escuchar con atención a otros es una destreza que ayuda a que los estudiantes aprendan y que activamente formen parte de la comunidad de lectores.

A continuación se encuentran algunas maneras de desarrollar la lectura de su niño en casa:

· Vaya a la biblioteca una vez por semana a sacar libros.

· Tome tiempo todos los días para leer juntos.

· Cuando esté leyendo en voz alta, pare de vez en cuando para que ambos puedan hablar acerca de lo que están pensando y preguntándose sobre la historia que están leyendo.

· Sea modelo para su niño y escúchelo con atención cuando ambos estén hablando acerca de la historia.

El leer un libro y charlar acerca de la historia es uno de los mejores regalos que usted le puede dar a su hijo. Yo espero que usted y su familia disfruten del tiempo que pasen leyendo a diario.

Sinceramente,

Dear Parent or Guardian,

Our class just finished the second unit of the *Making Meaning®* program. The children love the stories we are reading! During this unit, the students continued to practice the comprehension strategy *making connections* by hearing and discussing stories and finding connections between the stories and their own lives. They also answered questions to help them understand the stories they heard.

During this unit, the children also practiced the social skill of talking and listening to one another. Listening well and talking to others are skills that help students learn and become active members of the reading community. One powerful way to build your child's ability to listen and talk is to pay attention to your child when the two of you talk about stories.

You can help your child make personal connections to stories. Before reading, ask your child to listen and think about what in the story is like his or her own life. While reading, stop every so often to ask questions such as:

- How do you think this person or animal feels?

- Have you ever felt that way? Tell me about it.

Another way to help your child think about a story more deeply is to ask questions while reading aloud, such as:

- What has happened in the story so far?

- What do you think will happen next?

Have fun reading, talking, and listening to each other!

Sincerely,

Apreciado padre de familia o guardián:

Nuestra clase acaba de finalizar la segunda unidad del programa "*Making Meaning.®*" ¡A los niños les encantan mucho las historias que estamos leyendo! Durante esta unidad los niños siguieron practicando la estrategia de comprensión de *hacer conexiones* al escuchar y hablar acerca de las historias y al encontrar conexiones entre las historias y sus propias vidas. También, ellos contestaron preguntas que les ayudaron a entender mejor la historia que habían escuchado.

Durante esta unidad los niños también practicaron la destreza social de hablar entre ellos y de escucharse unos a otros. El escuchar con atención y el hablar con otros son destrezas que ayudan a los estudiantes a aprender y a que activamente formen parte de la comunidad de lectores. Al ponerle atención a su niño cuando los dos hablan acerca de las historias es una manera poderosa de desarollar la habilidad de escuchar y de hablar de su niño.

Usted puede ayudar a que su niño haga conexiones personales con las historias. Antes de empezar a leer, pídale a su niño que escuche y piense que parte de la historia es parecida a su vida. Mientras lee, pare de vez en cuando para hacer preguntas como éstas:

- ¿Cómo crees que esta persona o animal se siente?

- ¿Alguna vez te has sentido así? Hablemos de eso.

Otra manera de ayudar a que su niño se piense más profundamente en la historia es hacer preguntas mientras se está leyendo en voz alta, como:

- Hasta ahora, ¿qué es lo que ha pasado en la historia?

- ¿Qué crees que va a pasar?

Diviértanse al leer, al hablar y al escucharse el uno al otro.

Sinceramente,

Dear Parent or Guardian,

Our class just finished the third unit of the *Making Meaning®* program. The children love the stories and poems we are reading! During this unit, the students visualized to make sense of the stories we read. *Visualizing* means making mental images while reading. Readers might imagine sights, sounds, smells, tastes, sensations, and feelings. Visualizing helps readers understand, remember, and enjoy reading.

The children also continued to practice the social skill of talking and listening to one another. Listening well and talking to others are skills that help students learn and become active members of the reading community. One powerful way to build your child's ability to listen and talk to others is to pay attention to your child when the two of you talk about stories.

You can help your child visualize by stopping every so often while reading aloud and asking questions such as:

- What do you see in your mind as I read to you?

- What words did you hear in the story that helped you create that picture in your mind?

In addition to stopping and discussing the story with your child, you might:

- Ask your child to close his or her eyes as you read and get a mental picture of the story.

- Give your child the opportunity to draw what he or she visualized, and then talk about the drawing.

Have fun reading, visualizing, talking, and listening to each other!

Sincerely,

Apreciado padre de familia o guardián:

Nuestra clase acaba de finalizar la tercera unidad del programa "*Making Meaning.®*" ¡A los niños les gustan mucho las historias y poemas que estamos leyendo! Durante esta unidad los estudiantes visualizaron para poder entender las historias que leímos. *El visualizar* quiere decir que hacemos imágenes mentales mientras leemos. Los lectores pueden imaginarse sonidos, imágenes, olores, sabores, sensaciones y sentimientos. El visualizar ayuda a los lectores a entender, recordar y a disfrutar de la lectura.

Los niños también practicaron la destreza social de hablar entre ellos y de escucharse unos a otros. El escuchar con atención y el hablar con otros, son destrezas que ayudan a los estudiantes a aprender y a que activamente formen parte de la comunidad de lectores. Una manera poderosa de ayudar a que su niño desarrolle la habilidad de hablar y de escuchar es poniéndole atención a su niño cuando los dos hablan acerca de las historias que han leído.

Cuando están leyendo en voz alta, usted puede ayudarle a su niño a visualizar parando de vez en cuando y haciendo preguntas como:

- ¿Qué es lo que te viene a la mente cuando leo esto?

- ¿Qué palabras escuchaste en la historia que te ayudaron a crear esa imagen en la mente?

Además de parar y de hablar acerca de la historia con su niño, usted puede:

- Pedirle a su niño que cierre los ojos mientras usted lee para que así pueda obtener una imagen mental de la historia.

- Darle a su niño la oportunidad de dibujar lo que ha visualizado y después pueden hablar acerca del dibujo.

Diviértanse al leer, al visualizar, al hablar y al escucharse el uno al otro.

Sinceramente,

Dear Parent or Guardian,

Our class just finished the fourth unit of the *Making Meaning*® program. During this unit, the students heard and discussed stories, or "narrative texts." Narrative texts include chapter books, picture books, and short stories in a wide range of genres (mystery, adventure, science fiction, historical fiction, realistic fiction, fable, folktale, myth, legend, biography, and memoir).

The students learned that most stories are about characters, the problems they face, how the characters deal with those problems, and how they change as a result. They also made inferences to help them understand characters in the stories they heard. Readers *make inferences* when they use clues the author gives to infer things that aren't stated directly in the story. For example, if a character is stomping his feet and shouting, the reader might infer that the character is angry.

You can help your child make inferences by stopping every so often while you read aloud to ask questions such as:

- What clues has the author given us so far about the main character?

- What do those clues tell you about the character?

After reading, you can help your child understand the story more deeply by discussing questions such as:

- What happens in the story?

- What problem does the main character face in the story? How does that problem get solved?

- How does the main character feel at the beginning of the story? At the end?

Most importantly, enjoy your time reading together!

Sincerely,

Apreciado padre de familia o guardián:

Nuestra clase acaba de terminar la cuarta unidad del programa "*Making Meaning.*®" Durante esta unidad los estudiantes escucharon y hablaron acerca de historias o "textos de narración". Los textos narrativos incluyen libros con ilustraciones, libros con capítulos y cuentos, en una amplio gama de géneros (misterio, aventura, ciencia ficción, ficción histórica, ficción realista, fábula, folclor, mito, leyendas, biografías y autobiografías).

Los estudiantes aprendieron que la mayoría de las historias son acerca de personajes, los problemas que enfrentan, como lidian con esos problemas, y como han cambiado como resultado de todo esto. Los estudiantes también hicieron deducciones lo cual les ayudo a entender a los personajes de las historias que escucharon. Los lectores *hacen deducciones* cuando utilizan las pistas que el autor da para dar a deducir algunas cosas que no están presentadas directamente en la historia. Por ejemplo, si un personaje está pataleando y gritando, el lector puede deducir que el personaje está enojado.

Cuando esté leyendo en voz alta con su niño, usted le puede ayudar a que haga deducciones si para la lectura de vez en cuando y le hace preguntas tales como:

- Hasta ahora, ¿qué pistas nos ha dado el autor acerca del personaje principal?

- ¿Qué nos dejan saber estas pistas acerca del personaje principal?

Después de haber leído la historia, usted le puede ayudar a su niño a entender lo que leyeron más a fondo al hacerle las siguientes preguntas:

- ¿Qué pasa en la historia?

- ¿Cuál es el problema que enfrenta el personaje principal de la historia? ¿Cómo lo resuelve?

- ¿Cómo se siente el personaje principal de la historia al principio, y luego al final?

Lo más importante es que disfruten del tiempo que pasan leyendo juntos.

Sinceramente,

Dear Parent or Guardian,

Our class just finished the fifth unit of the *Making Meaning*® program. During this unit, the students continued to make predictions about stories, referring to the story to support their thinking. They also asked questions about the fiction stories we read aloud. *Wondering and asking questions* about fiction stories helps readers understand story characters and plot and helps them remember what they read. Socially, the students continued to develop the ability to share ideas with one another.

Before reading a story aloud to your child, look at the cover of the book together. Read the title and talk about what your child might be wondering about the story. You can support your child's understanding by stopping every so often while reading aloud to ask and discuss questions such as:

- What has happened so far in the story?

- What do you wonder about the story right now?

- What do you think might happen next?

You can also help your child understand stories more deeply by talking about the stories after you read. As you work together, I hope you and your child delight in reading!

Sincerely,

Apreciado padre de familia o guardián:

Nuestra clase acaba de finalizar la quinta unidad del programa "*Making Meaning.®*" Durante esta unidad los estudiantes continuaron haciendo predicciones acerca de la historia y se refirieron a ella para sostener las ideas que tuvieron. También hicieron preguntas acerca de las historias de ficción que leímos en voz alta. *El hacer preguntas* acerca de las historias de ficción le ayuda al lector a entender los personajes, la trama y también les ayuda a recordar lo que leyeron. Socialmente, los estudiantes desarrollaron aún más la habilidad de compartir entre si.

Antes de empezar a leerle a su niño una historia en voz alta, muéstrele la cubierta del libro, léale el título del libro y hablen acerca de las preguntas que se le vienen a la mente debido al libro. Usted puede ayudarle a su niño a entender la historia, al parar la lectura de vez en cuando para hablar y hacer preguntas como las siguientes:

- ¿Qué ha pasado en la historia hasta ahora?

- En este momento, ¿qué preguntas tienes acerca de la historia?

- ¿Qué crees que puede suceder después de esto?

El hablar acerca de las historias después de haberlas leído juntos puede ayudarle al niño a entender lo que leyeron más a fondo. A medida que trabajan juntos, yo espero que tanto usted como su niño se deleiten en la lectura.

Sinceramente,

 Dear Parent or Guardian,

Our class just finished the sixth unit of the *Making Meaning®* program. During this unit, the students explored differences between fiction and nonfiction texts and used the strategies of *wondering*, *visualizing*, and *making connections* to their own lives to help them make sense of nonfiction. Nonfiction texts give readers true information about a topic and include not only books, but also other kinds of informational texts, such as magazine articles, recipes, baseball cards, menus, and game directions.

You can support your child's reading life at home by:

· Stopping every so often while reading aloud to talk about what questions you both have about the reading.

· Talking about the differences between fiction and nonfiction that you notice in your reading. For example, you might say, "I notice that nonfiction often has photographs instead of drawings."

Before reading nonfiction together, you might ask your child:

· What do you already know about this topic?

· What do you think we will find out about this topic?

· What do you wonder about this topic?

During and after reading fiction or nonfiction it can be helpful to ask:

· What did you learn that surprised you?

· What do you still wonder about this topic?

I hope you and your child enjoy learning together about topics of interest to both of you. Happy reading!

Sincerely,

Apreciado padre de familia o guardián:

Nuestra clase acaba de finalizar la sexta unidad del programa "*Making Meaning.®*" Durante esta unidad los estudiantes exploraron las diferencias entre los textos de ficción y no ficción y utilizaron las estrategias de *visualizar*, *hacer preguntas*, y *hacer conexiones* con sus propias vidas para que les ayudaran a entender el género de no ficción. Los textos del género de no ficción le brindan al lector información de hechos verídicos acerca de un tema e incluye libros y otras clases de textos informativos tales como: artículos de revistas, recetas, tarjetas para coleccionar, menús y direcciones de un juego.

En casa usted puede apoyar la lectura de su niño haciendo lo siguiente:

- Cuando estén leyendo juntos, usted puede parar de vez en cuando para hablar acerca de las preguntas que ustedes puedan tener acerca de lo que están leyendo.

- Hablar de las diferencias entre ficción y no ficción que ustedes notan en su lectura. Por ejemplo, usted puede decir "yo noto que los textos de no ficción generalmente tienen fotos en vez de tener dibujos".

Antes de empezar a leer textos de no ficción juntos, usted le puede preguntar a su niño:

- ¿Qué sabes acerca del tema?

- ¿Qué crees que vamos a descubrir acerca de este tema?

- ¿Qué preguntas tienes acerca del tema?

Durante y después de la lectura que hacen juntos, puede ser útil el hacer las siguientes preguntas:

- ¿Qué aprendiste que te sorprendió?

- ¿Cuáles son las preguntas que aún tienes acerca del tema?

Espero que se diviertan aprendiendo juntos acerca de temas de mutuo interés. ¡Feliz lectura!

Sinceramente,

Dear Parent or Guardian,

Our class just finished the seventh unit of the *Making Meaning*® program. During this unit, the students continued to hear and discuss nonfiction texts. They talked about what they learned from the nonfiction texts, and wondered about the topics they heard about during the read-alouds. *Wondering* about a topic before, during, and after reading helps readers actively engage with the text and make sense of what they are reading.

You can support your child's reading life at home by collecting nonfiction texts that interest your child, and talking about what your child is learning from the nonfiction that you read aloud or that your child reads independently.

Before reading a nonfiction text to your child, it is helpful to ask questions such as:

- What do you think you know about [seals]?

- What do you wonder about [seals]?

Consider stopping every so often during the reading to ask what your child is learning and what he or she is still wondering about.

After reading you might ask questions such as:

- What did you learn about [seals] from this book?

- What did you learn that surprised you?

- What are you still wondering about [seals]?

I hope you and your child continue to enjoy reading together. Happy reading!

Sincerely,

Apreciado padre de familia o guardián:

Nuestra clase acaba de finalizar la séptima unidad del programa *"Making Meaning.®"* Durante esta unidad los estudiantes siguieron escuchando y hablando acerca de textos de no ficción. Ellos hablaron acerca de lo que aprendieron de los textos y artículos de no ficción y formularon preguntas referentes a los temas que escucharon durante las sesiónes de lectura en voz alta. *El hacer preguntas acerca de un tópico, antes, durante y después de la lectura, ayuda a que los lectores se involucren activamente con el texto y que entiendan lo que están leyendo.*

Usted puede dar apoyo a la lectura que su niño hace en la casa al coleccionar textos y libros de no ficción que sean de interés para su niño. También puede dar ese apoyo al hablar con su niño acerca de lo que aprende al leer y al escuchar cuando usted le lee en voz alta del género de no ficción.

Es de gran ayuda, si antes de leerle textos de no ficción a su niño le hace preguntas como:

- ¿Qué sabes acerca de (las focas)?

- ¿Qué preguntas tienes acerca de (las focas)?

Considere parar la lectura en voz alta para preguntarle a su niño que está aprendiendo y si aún tiene alguna duda.

Después de haber leído hágale a su niño preguntas tales como:

- ¿En este libro qué fue lo que aprendiste acerca de (las focas)?

- ¿Qué aprendiste que te sorprendió?

- ¿Qué preguntas tienes todavía acerca de (las focas)?

Espero que continúen disfrutando de la lectura que comparten juntos. ¡Feliz lectura!

Sinceramente,

Dear Parent or Guardian,

Our class just finished the eighth unit of the *Making Meaning®* program. During this unit, the students read expository nonfiction books and articles about specific topics. They also examined functional texts, such as instructions and schedules. The students *explored text features* often found in nonfiction, such as tables of contents, indexes, headings, photographs, maps, and diagrams.

You can support your child's reading life at home by collecting nonfiction texts that interest your child, talking about what you both learn from the nonfiction you read, and noticing and talking about functional texts you encounter throughout the day, such as food labels, calendars, or traffic signs.

Before reading a nonfiction book or article it can be helpful to have your child read the title and section or chapter headings. Then ask:

- What do you think we might learn about [sharks]?

After reading nonfiction it can be helpful to ask your child questions such as:

- What did you find out about [sharks]?

- What extra information did this [photograph] give you about [sharks]?

After reading a functional text, you might ask your child:

- What information does this tell you?

- How is the information helpful?

I hope you and your child enjoy learning together about topics of interest to both of you. Happy reading!

Sincerely,

Apreciado padre de familia o guardián:

Nuestra clase acaba de finalizar la octava unidad del programa "*Making Meaning.®*" Durante esta unidad los estudiantes leyeron artículos y libros de temas específicos en el género de relato expositivo. También examinaron textos funcionales como horarios e instrucciones. Los estudiantes exploraron algunos de los aspectos que a menudo se encuentran en no ficción como listas de contenido, índices, encabezamientos, mapas y diagramas.

Usted puede apoyar a la lectura que su niño hace en la casa al:

• Coleccionar textos y libros de no ficción que sean de interés para su niño.

• Al hablar con su niño acerca de lo que ambos están aprendiendo de los libros y textos de no ficción que leen juntos.

• Al darse cuenta y al hablar acerca de textos funcionales que ustedes encuentran durante el día, como los rótulos de las comidas, calendarios o señales de tráfico.

A su niño le puede ayudar si usted hace que lea los títulos y encabezamientos de secciones o capítulos antes de que empiece a leer un libro o artículo de no ficción. Hágale preguntas como:

• ¿Qué crees que podamos aprender de (los tiburones)?

Después de leer un texto de no ficción puede ser útil el preguntar:

• ¿Qué aprendiste acerca de (los tiburones)?

• ¿Qué información extra te dio (esta fotografía) acerca de (los tiburones)?

Después de leer un texto funcional usted puede hacer las siguientes preguntas:

• ¿Qué información te dan aquí?

• ¿Cómo te ayuda esta información?

Espero que usted y su niño disfruten el aprender juntos acerca de tópicos que son de interés para ustedes. ¡Feliz lectura!

Sinceramente,

Dear Parent or Guardian,

Our class just finished the ninth unit of the *Making Meaning®* program. During this unit, the students focused on *determining important ideas* in nonfiction and fiction. They explored all of the important ideas in the stories and articles they read rather than trying to identify one "main idea." Socially, the students practiced sharing their partner time fairly and giving reasons to support their thinking.

You can continue to support your child's reading at home by taking time to discuss the text before, during, and after your reading together.

Before reading, ask your child questions such as:

- (nonfiction) What do you think this [book] might be about? What do you know about this topic? What do you wonder about this topic?

- (fiction) What do you think this story might be about? What are you wondering about this story?

During reading, stop every so often and ask:

- (nonfiction) What have you learned so far? What are you wondering?

- (fiction) What is happening in the story? What do you think might happen next?

After reading, ask questions such as:

- (fiction or nonfiction) If someone asked you what this [book] is about, what would you tell them?

- (fiction or nonfiction) What are some important ideas in this [story]? Why do you think that?

Most importantly, have fun reading and talking about the stories you read together. Happy reading!

Sincerely,

Apreciado padre de familia o guardián:

Nuestra clase acaba de terminar la novena unidad del programa "*Making Meaning.®*" Durante esta unidad los estudiantes se enfocaron en poder *determinar las ideas importantes* del género de no ficción y ficción. Ellos exploraron las ideas importantes de una historia o artículo en vez de identificar solamente una "idea principal." En el área de desarrollo de destrezas sociales, los estudiantes practicaron compartir el tiempo con sus compañeros en forma igual y dar las razones por las cuales piensan de esa manera.

Usted puede dar apoyo a la lectura que su niño hace en la casa al tomar el tiempo para hablar acerca del texto antes, durante y después de ponerse a leer juntos.

Antes de la lectura, hágale a su niño preguntas como éstas:

- (Para no ficción) ¿De qué crees que se trate este (libro)? ¿Qué sabes de ese tema? ¿Tienes preguntas acerca de ese tema?

- (Para ficción) ¿De qué crees que se trate esta historia? ¿Qué preguntas tienes acerca de esta historia?

Durante la lectura, pare periódicamente y pregúntele a su niño:

- (Para no ficción) Hasta ahora, ¿qué has aprendido? ¿Qué preguntas tienes?

- (Para ficción) ¿Qué está pasando en la historia? ¿Qué crees que va a pasar a continuación?

Después de la lectura, hágale a su niño preguntas como éstas:

- (Para ficción y no ficción) ¿Si alguien viniera a preguntarte, ¿de qué se trata este (libro)? ¿Qué le dirías? ¿Cuáles son algunas de las ideas importantes de la historia? ¿Por qué piensas así?

- (Para ficción y no ficción) ¿Qué crees que el autor quiere que pensemos al leer esta historia? ¿Qué crees que el autor quiere que aprendamos al leer esta historia? ¿Por qué piensas así?

Lo más importante es que continúen divirtiéndose al leer juntos y al hablar acerca de las historias que leen. ¡Feliz lectura!

Sinceramente,

Dear Parent or Guardian,

We have come to the end of our school year and the end of the *Making Meaning*® grade 2 reading comprehension program. The children have shown great enthusiasm for the variety of texts we read aloud and the conversations we had about reading. They eagerly explored a number of reading comprehension strategies, including: making connections, visualizing, wondering, making inferences, exploring text features, and determining important ideas. The use of these comprehension strategies strengthened the children's reading comprehension skills and should continue to be a source of support for them for years to come.

In the last unit of the *Making Meaning* program, the students thought about the books and stories they liked this year and considered the strategies that helped them understand the stories.

While reading with your child this summer, you might reflect on the reading comprehension strategies your child used this year. This will help your child continue to use the reading comprehension strategies.

Remember that the more your child reads, the more successful he or she will be as a reader. During the summer, read aloud to your child and encourage your child to read independently every day.

I hope you have a great summer filled with books, fun, and enjoyment.

Sincerely,

Apreciado padre de familia o guardián;

Hemos llegado al final del año escolar y al final del programa de comprensión de lectura para el segundo año de *"Making Meaning.®"* Los niños han mostrado mucho entusiasmo por la variedad de textos que leímos en voz alta y por las conversaciones que tuvimos acerca de la lectura. Ellos exploraron afanosamente un número de estrategias de comprensión de lectura, incluyendo: hacer conexiones, visualizar, el hacer preguntas, hacer deducciones, el explorar los aspectos del texto, y determinar ideas importantes. El uso de estas estrategias de comprensión fortalece las destrezas de comprensión de lectura que los niños tienen y esto ha de continuar siendo una fuente de apoyo para ellos por muchos años más.

En la última unidad del programa *"Making Meaning®"* los estudiantes se pusieron a pensar sobre los libros y las historias que les gustaron durante el año y consideraron las estrategias que les ayudaron a entender esas historias.

Este verano mientras lee con su niño, puede ponerse a reflexionar en la estrategia de comprensión de lectura que su niño utilizó este año. Esto le ayudará a su niño a continuar utilizando las estrategias de comprensión de lectura que aprendió y será de mucho apoyo cuando su niño entre al tercer grado.

Recuerde que mientras más lea su niño, más éxito va a tener como lector. Durante el verano, léale en voz alta y aliéntelo a que lea individualmente a diario.

Espero que gocen un gran verano lleno de libros y diversiones.

Sinceramente,

Reading Log

Date	Title of Book	Author of Book	Comment

© Developmental Studies Center

Making Meaning® | **BLM11**

My Baby Brother
by Mary Ann Hoberman

My baby brother's beautiful,
So perfect and so tiny.
His skin is soft and velvet brown;
His eyes are dark and shiny.

His hair is black and curled up tight;
His two new teeth are sharp and white.
I like it when he chews his toes;
And when he laughs, his dimple shows.

Contents

Excerpt from *Snails* by Monica Hughes. Reprinted by permission of Pearson Education.

Teacher's Facilitation Bookmark

After photocopying this page, cut along the heavy dotted line and fold along the light dotted line. Laminate if you wish.

Making Meaning®
SECOND EDITION
Strategies That Build Comprehension and Community

Prompts
to get students talking to one another

"[Miguel] is going to talk now. Let's all turn and look at him, and get ready to comment on what he says."

"What would you like to add to what [Ann] said?"

"Do you agree or disagree with what [Jeremy] said? Why?"

"What question can we ask [LaToya]?"

Making Meaning®
SECOND EDITION
Strategies That Build Comprehension and Community

Tips
for facilitating discussion

Use wait-time. Give the students 5–10 seconds to think before calling on anyone to respond.

Keep the discussion moving. It is not necessary to call on every student who raises his hand.

Use "Turn to Your Partner" when you notice only a few students contributing to a discussion, or when many students want to contribute at the same time.

Avoid repeating or paraphrasing. Encourage the students to listen carefully to one another (not just to you) by not repeating or paraphrasing what you hear them say. If the students can't hear the person speaking, encourage them to ask the speaker to repeat what she said.

Encourage use of prompts. Have the students use "I agree with [Rosa] because…," "I disagree with [Kim] because…," and "In addition to what [Allan] said, I think…."

© Developmental Studies Center

Resource Sheet for IDR Conferences

General questions you can ask to probe student thinking:

▸ *Why did you choose this book?*

▸ *Why do you like/dislike this book?*

▸ *What kinds of books do you want to read?*

Genre-specific questions you can ask:

Fiction

▸ *What is this story about?*

▸ *What has happened so far?*

▸ *What do you know about the character(s)?*

▸ *What part have you found interesting or surprising? Why?*

▸ *What are you wondering about?*

▸ *What do you visualize (see/hear/feel) as you read these words?*

▸ *What do you think will happen next?*

Nonfiction/Expository

▸ *What is this [book/article] about?*

▸ (Read the information on the back cover.) *What have you found out about that so far?*

▸ (Look at the table of contents.) *What do you think you will find out about* _____ *in this book?*

▸ *What have you learned from reading this article?*

▸ *What's something interesting you've read so far?*

▸ *What are you wondering about?*

▸ *What do you expect to learn about as you continue to read?*

▸ *What information does this [diagram/table/graph/other text feature] give you?*

Poetry

▸ *What is this poem about?*

▸ *What do you visualize (see/hear/feel) as you read these words?*

▸ *What do you think the poet means by* _____ *?*

IDR Conference Notes

Student: _____ **Date:** _____

Book title: _____

EVIDENCE:

1 **Ask: What is your book about so far?**

Is the student able to describe the book? | YES |

2 **Have the student read a passage silently, then read it aloud for you.**

Does the student:

| | YES |

Attend to meaning?

Pause/reread if having difficulty?

Read most words accurately?

Try to make sense of unfamiliar language?

Read fluently?

3 **Ask: What is the part you just read about?**

Does the student recall what's important in the passage? | YES |

If the student has difficulty, have him/her reread the passage and repeat Step ▶3.
If the student doesn't understand after the second reading, go to Step ▷4. Otherwise, go to Step ▶4.

4▷ **If the student doesn't understand after the second reading, ask yourself:**

Is the difficulty caused by:

Lack of background knowledge?

Unfamiliar vocabulary?

Too-difficult text (lack of fluency)?

Not using an appropriate comprehension strategy?

4▶ **Ask: What do you think will happen, or what do you think you will learn, as you keep reading?**

5▶ **Ask yourself: Is the student using comprehension strategies to make sense of text?**

5▷ **Intervene using one or more of the following:**

- Define unfamiliar words.
- Provide necessary background knowledge.
- Suggest an appropriate strategy on the "Reading Comprehension Strategies" chart and have the student reread again, starting at an earlier place in the text.
- Ask clarifying questions about the text.
- Help the student find a more appropriately leveled book.

Next steps:

BLM16 | Making Meaning®

Making Meaning® SECOND EDITION Reorder Information

Kindergarten

Complete Classroom Package   MM2-CPK

Contents: Teacher's Manual, Orientation Handbook and DVDs, and 27 trade books

Available separately:

Classroom materials without trade books	MM2-TPK
Teacher's Manual	MM2-TMK
Trade book set (27 books)	MM2-TBSK

Grade 1

Complete Classroom Package   MM2-CP1

Contents: Teacher's Manual, Orientation Handbook and DVDs, Assessment Resource Book, and 28 trade books

Available separately:

Classroom materials without trade books	MM2-TP1
Teacher's Manual	MM2-TM1
Assessment Resource Book	MM2-AB1
Trade book set (28 books)	MM2-TBS1

Grade 2

Complete Classroom Package   MM2-CP2

Contents: Teacher's Manual, Orientation Handbook and DVDs, class set (25 Student Response Books, Assessment Resource Book), and 29 trade books

Available separately:

Classroom materials without trade books	MM2-TP2
Teacher's Manual	MM2-TM2
Replacement class set	MM2-RCS2
CD-ROM Grade 2 Reproducible Materials*	MM2-CDR2
Trade book set (29 books)	MM2-TBS2

Grade 3

Complete Classroom Package   MM2-CP3

Contents: Teacher's Manual (2 volumes), Orientation Handbook and DVDs, class set (25 Student Response Books, Assessment Resource Book), and 26 trade books

Available separately:

Classroom materials without trade books	MM2-TP3
Teacher's Manual, vol. 1	MM2-TM3-V1
Teacher's Manual, vol. 2	MM2-TM3-V2
Replacement class set	MM2-RCS3
CD-ROM Grade 3 Reproducible Materials*	MM2-CDR3
Trade book set (26 books)	MM2-TBS3

* CD-ROMs available Summer 2009

Grade 4

Complete Classroom Package   MM2-CP4

Contents: Teacher's Manual (2 volumes), Orientation Handbook and DVDs, class set (30 Student Response Books, Assessment Resource Book), and 24 trade books

Available separately:

Classroom materials without trade books	MM2-TP4
Teacher's Manual, vol. 1	MM2-TM4-V1
Teacher's Manual, vol. 2	MM2-TM4-V2
Replacement class set	MM2-RCS4
CD-ROM Grade 4 Reproducible Materials*	MM2-CDR4
Trade book set (24 books)	MM2-TBS4

Grade 5

Complete Classroom Package   MM2-CP5

Contents: Teacher's Manual (2 volumes), Orientation Handbook and DVDs, class set (30 Student Response Books, Assessment Resource Book), and 19 trade books

Available separately:

Classroom materials without trade books	MM2-TP5
Teacher's Manual, vol. 1	MM2-TM5-V1
Teacher's Manual, vol. 2	MM2-TM5-V2
Replacement class set	MM2-RCS5
CD-ROM Grade 5 Reproducible Materials*	MM2-CDR5
Trade book set (19 books)	MM2-TBS5

Grade 6

Complete Classroom Package   MM2-CP6

Contents: Teacher's Manual (2 volumes), Orientation Handbook and DVDs, class set (30 Student Response Books, Assessment Resource Book), and 19 trade books

Available separately:

Classroom materials without trade books	MM2-TP6
Teacher's Manual, vol. 1	MM2-TM6-V1
Teacher's Manual, vol. 2	MM2-TM6-V2
Replacement class set	MM2-RCS5
CD-ROM Grade 6 Reproducible Materials*	MM2-CDR6
Trade book set (19 books)	MM2-TBS6

Ordering Information:

To order call 800.666.7270 * fax 510.842.0348
log on to www.devstu.org * e-mail pubs@devstu.org

Or Mail Your Order to:

Developmental Studies Center * Publications Department
2000 Embarcadero, Suite 305 * Oakland, CA 94606-5300

DEVELOPMENTAL STUDIES CENTER™